MEASURING THE MOMENT

Strategies of Protest in
Eighteenth-Century Afro-English Writing

Keith A. Sandiford

Selinsgrove: Susquehanna University Press
London and Toronto: Associated University Presses

Associated University Presses
440 Forsgate Drive
Cranbury, NJ 08512

Associated University Presses
25 Sicilian Avenue
London WC1A 2QH, England

Associated University Presses
P.O. Box 488, Port Credit
Mississauga, Ontario
Canada L5G 4M2

The paper used in this publication meets the requirements
of the American National Standard for Permanence of Paper
for Printed Library Materials Z39.48-1984.

Library of Congress Cataloging-in-Publication Data

Sandiford, Keith Albert, date
    Measuring the moment.

    Bibliography: p.
    Includes index.
    1. African prose literature (English)—History and
criticism.   2. Protest literature, African (English)—
History and criticism.   3. Africans—Great Britain—
History—18th century.   4. Slavery—Anti-slavery
movements—History—18th century.   5. Slavery and
slaves in literature.   6. Slave-trade in literature.
7. Blacks in literature.   I. Title.
PR9340.S26   1988   828   86-63364
ISBN 0-941664-79-1 (alk. paper)

PRINTED IN THE UNITED STATES OF AMERICA

This book is dedicated to the chief formative influences of my life. To my mother, from whom I learned industry and compassion. To my late father, to whom I owe my sense of humor. To the memory of the late Mrs. Vicie Brathwaite, who helped to shape my boyhood years. And to my alma mater, Combermere School (Barbados), her pupils and teachers, past, present, and future, with whom I share a great tradition.

Contents

Preface

It is now widely acknowledged that the emancipation of the slaves in the British West Indian colonies was achieved by a coalition of powerful political, economic, and humanitarian forces that had been slowly gathering momentum over the three hundred–year period of slavery's existence. It is not so widely acknowledged, however, that the presence in England of three African writers—Ignatius Sancho (1729–80), Ottobah Cugoano (1757–?), and Olaudah Equiano (1745–97), sometimes styled Gustavus Vassa—and the publication of their writings, had a significant impact on the public conscience and on the antislavery movement in that country.

Ten years ago I read the first selections from those three authors, whose lives and writings supply the subject matter of this book. Anthologized in a modest paperbound volume edited by Francis D. Adams and Barry Sanders, those excerpts from Sancho's *Letters* (1782), Cugoano's *Thoughts and Sentiments on the Evil of Slavery* (1787), and Olaudah Equiano's *Interesting Narrative* (1789) opened for me several rooms in the store house of the African past and the Black experience in the Western world. The resultant exploration would later claim three years of serious sustained study and research.

The first major work to issue from that engagement was a doctoral dissertation that I completed at the University of Illinois in 1979, and which, with some revison, supplies the main corpus of this book. Up to that time, the quantum of formal literary scholarship that treated these writings with any critical depth and consequence was still quite small, relatively unknown, and largely unnoticed—three unpublished dissertations, Paul Edwards's critical introductions to the modern reprints of the three works, and, at the most, no more than half a dozen journal articles. Edwards deserves high credit for being the first scholar in modern times to devote so large a part of his intellectual endeavor to promoting the availability of these texts and disseminating knowledge about their African authors' importance and achievement. The first two years of the present decade produced at least four further articles and a book (*Black Personalities in the Era of the Slave Trade,* 1983). Written jointly by Edwards and James Walvin, that book is essentially a document of social history, but its chief value for the literary specialist is the witness it bears that Sancho, Cugoano, and Equiano, as three nonwhite, uncanonized figures, still continue to command more than cursory interest. Only this year, a colleague, just returned from traveling in Africa, brought back the news that a Nigerian scholar, S. E.

Ogude, had published a book, *Genius in Bondage: A Study of the Origins of African Literature* (University of Ife [Nigeria] Press, 1983) on the three authors. Regrettably, Ogude's book may be obtained in this country only with great difficulty, but the appearance of another book, the premises implied in its very title, together with Ogude's primary insistence on the fundamental literariness of the texts argue further the merit of these writings and evidence a quickening impetus in the growth of scholarship about them.

The present inquiry attempts to establish that the contexts and content of Sancho's collected letters, Cugoano's antislavery treatise, and Equiano's autobiographical narrative recommended them to a wider audience than may be supposed and earned them a leading role as agents in the abolitionist campaign. Between 1782 and 1803, the *Letters of Ignatius Sancho* went through five editions. Among the first-edition recipients of Cugoano's *Thoughts and Sentiments* were such luminaries as King George III, the Prince of Wales, and Edmund Burke. On its first appearance in 1789, *The Interesting Narrative of Olaudah Equiano* listed an impressive catalog of notable subscribers. It was later to enjoy wide public notice and reach some fifteen editions by the date of emancipation, 1834. Contemporary reviewers were quick to recognize in these productions the very moral and intellectual qualities that proslavery apologists had consistently denied the African race. More recent critics have reaffirmed these qualities and attempted to assign the works their rightful place in the larger traditions of English and African literatures. Still, the sum total of critical attention has been comparatively small. Therefore, this study seeks to extend the discussion so as to accord the authors and their works a just literary and historical valuation. It argues that the three works document and characterize three distinguishable phases in the evolution of antislavery thought, the underlying rhetorical structures of each text revealing strategies calculated to reshape the audience's preconditioned responses about everything the authors represented and about these texts as text. Sancho's *Letters* exemplifies the early strategy of moral suasion, his protest muted and disguised by an enthusiastic identification with the current fashion of cultivated benevolism. Cugoano's representations in the *Thoughts* are polemical and uncompromising: his argument is an eloquent rebuttal of the major proslavery rationalizations and an effective vindication of the Black's moral and intellectual authenticity. In time, this was to become one of the most persuasive arguments for emancipation. Equiano's *Life* furthers this evolutionary process by uniting religious and humanitarian sentiments with his personal experience of slavery to define the Black struggle in its clearest racial and political terms.

Collectively, these writings represent a uniquely subversive act. They serve to lay to rest the old myths of African inferiority and so to discredit the proslavery publicists. They propose Blacks affirmatively as authentic beings to whom the society owed a moral responsibility. These writings symbolize the earliest emergence of Black self-consciousness in England.

Even as the addition of another critical work on these authors furthers the interpretation of that authority subsumed beneath the literary works produced by eighteenth-century Anglo-African writers, that opportunity also gives rise to the more sobering reflection that it has taken over two centuries before a book-length critique could be published on eighteenth-century Anglo-African writing.

Of course, that the primary texts existed to be written about at all is itself an equally sobering historical paradox. The legal sanctions interdicting a slave's attainment of literacy denied him access to ways of knowing and feeling that the master class considered subversive to the arrangements of slavocratic political economy. Thus, in those salient cases where slaves achieve dominion over written language, the documents transmitted under the traditional category of slave narratives are, effectively, speech acts that simultaneously alienate the master from any customary prerogative over this newly created category of work and exclude his proslavery apologists from this special category of life writing. In mastering the master's language, slave writers usurp certain of the slave master's hegemonic prerogatives: the slaves neutralize their masters as a circumscribing presence and expropriate the authority to write themselves into history. These interactive forces of alienation and exclusion may explain in part why the three subjects of this book were themselves so flagrantly neglected in the major documents of literary history and criticism until the present decade. This book, it is hoped, will place Sancho, Cugoano, and Equiano rightfully among the highly accredited Enlightenment thinkers, political and religious reformers, and leading literary figures who contributed so distinctively to the ultimate success of antislavery.

Acknowledgments

The accomplishment of published scholarship is seldom the work of a single hand. This study would not have been possible without the invaluable assistance of many people. I am deeply indebted to Professor Richard Barksdale, who shared his wisdom and expertise from the very beginning. His enthusiasm for the significance of this project, and his appreciative support over the years of its elaboration I can acknowledge but hardly ever repay. I wish also to thank Professor Keneth Kinnamon, whose interest was unfailing and whose critical judgments added depth to my own insights; and Professor Lynn Altenbernd, who so generously placed his years of experience in teaching and the gifts of his scholarship at my disposal. I am indebted to James Olney and Henry Louis Gates, colleagues both selfless and unstinting, who read the manuscript in its most recent emanations.

Finally, I acknowledge a Summer (1986) Faculty Researh Grant from the Louisiana State University Council on Research. That support made the final months of revision possible.

I wish to thank the following publishers for granting permission to quote from published works:

Wm. Dawson & Sons, Limited, for permission to quote from Ignatius Sancho, *Letters of the Late Ignatius Sancho*; Ottobah Cugoano, *Thoughts and Sentiments on the Evil of Slavery*; and Olaudah Equiano, *The Life of Olaudah Equiano*.

University of North Carolina Press, for permission to quote from *The Poems of Phillis Wheatley*, edited by Julian D. Mason, Jr., copyright 1966.

MEASURING
THE MOMENT

1

The Black Presence

Ignatius Sancho, Ottobah Cugoano, and Olaudah Equiano were undoubtedly the three best-known Africans in eighteenth-century England.
But it is important to establish at the outset that they were also members of
a considerable Black community that grew up in England as a direct consequence of that country's participation in the slave trade. The fact that
several thousand Africans made their home in England during this period is
not yet as fully appreciated as it might be, mainly because standard histories
have tended either to minimize or to ignore altogether the significance of the
African presence at this early time in Europe as a whole.

This chapter will delineate the social environment created for Blacks by
the special conditions of slavery and by their own racial identity. For the
literary achievement of Sancho, Cugoano, and Equiano can be properly
understood only in relation to those specific conditions and within the wider
context of the Black community's group experiences. One of the major
propositions of this study is that these three writers were highly conscious of
their social responsibility as literate members of that community. This chapter will show specifically that their sense of racial awareness was deeply
rooted in a longer tradition of literacy and learning begun by earlier African
scholars and personalities who were exposed to European culture and
education. Sancho, Cugoano, and Equiano were distinctive as the first to
transfigure Black awareness into a literary form, celebrating the validity of
their common racial origin and advocating the liberation of their fellow
Africans from the disabilities that circumscribed their lives and actions, both
on the plantations of the West Indies and within the bounds of freedom-
loving Britannia itself. Chapters 3, 4, and 5 will demonstrate that their literary works played a significant part in the widespread awakening of the British national consciousness to the urgency of abolition and emancipation.

Yet, the very image of Blacks and the assumptions that defined their relationships with the white colonial and metropolitan society were in large
measure a legacy of history, with foundations anterior to the period of slavery. To the older myths about the darkness of Africa and the barbarism of
her peoples were added new arguments calculated to promote the expediency of a new economic order. Thus, a complex of attitudes was evolved that
justified the commerce in Black human flesh in the West Indies and in England alike and relegated Blacks to a status of degradation which they were

to endure until legal redress was finally won in the nineteenth century.

The earliest history of African peoples in Britain predates the period of this study. Latin chroniclers of the Roman conquest record the presence of dark-skinned inhabitants among the primitive tribes of the island. In his account of Britain under Agricola's governorship, Tacitus describes a people of "swarthy complexion and curled hair" coexisting alongside the ruddy-haired, large-limbed Caledonians.[1] The Afro-American ethnologist and historian, J. A. Rogers, states that these people were undeniably of African extraction.[2] More recent commentators suggest that the Romans may have had Black soldiers among their legions in Britain.[3] This view is usually based on the following incident from the life of Severus, the Roman emperor:

> On another occasion when he [Severus] was returning to his nearest quarters from an inspection of the wall at Luguvallum in Britain, at a time when he had not only proved victorious, but had concluded a perpetual peace, just as he was wondering what omen would present itself, an Ethiopian soldier, who was famous among buffoons and always a notable jester, met him with a garland of cypress boughs.[4]

Severus is reported to have been enraged and frightened by the soldier's "ominous" skin color and the color of the garland. It seems clear that the emperor was reacting to the traditional equation of black with evil. The term "Ethiopian," used in antiquity as a generic denotation for all Africans, is the most definite evidence here of the African presence in early Britain. Archaeological excavation on the site of a Romano-British cemetery in use at Trentholme, York, between A.D. 140 and the end of the fourth century, provides further, if not entirely conclusive, evidence for the African claim. Several of the human remains have been identified as approximating the physical features of negroid peoples.[5]

In Tudor and Stuart times Africans continue to appear in the literary and official documents under the designation of "moors" and "blackamoors." Descriptions of Elizabethan and Jacobean court entertainments and public ceremonies attest to the participation of authentic African characters—not white faces painted black.[6]

The English entered the slave trade in 1562 as interlopers in a market monopolized by the Portuguese. Thereafter the gentlemen and merchant adventurers of the trade supplied slaves not only to the Spanish colonies of the New World, but also to the households of the rich and titled of England. Queen Elizabeth herself retained a Black page and a Black entertainer at court.[7] Still, the influx of Africans into the realm in the closing years of the sixteenth century, although as yet comparatively small, was considerable enough to incur the royal displeasure.

In a letter to her Privy Council, dated 11 July 1596, Elizabeth adverted to "divers blackamoores brought into this realm of which kinde of people there are already too manie." Seven days later, the queen issued a license to have several newly arrived Blacks deported.[8] Elizabeth's was the first official measure designed to forestall the potential competition such Africans offered to native English subjects as household servants. Her complaint was to be reiterated with greater urgency and alarm by several observers in the middle of the eighteenth century, when the Black population in England reached twenty thousand.

In the seventeenth century, the number of Blacks in England grew in proportion to England's commercial excursions on the slave coast of Guinea. These were at best spasmodic and generally unofficial. But in 1662, Charles II rationalized the haphazard slaving practices of Englishmen on the Guinea coast by granting a monopoly to the Company of Royal Adventurers.[9] By this gesture, and with the financial backing of other members of the royal family, the country committed itself to full partnership in the "curious" institutions of slavery and the slave trade. Hereafter, Blacks came to be defined as merchandise, commodities to be bought and sold, like horses or fine wines—and were traded as such. Inevitably, as the merchants did a brisk trade in human cargo at the port towns of London, Bristol, and Liverpool, citizens of substance came increasingly to staff their households with Black servants. Captains of slaving ships and government officials returning from colonial outposts all followed the fashion of appearing in public attended by Black body servants to signify their rank and opulence.

Sailors smuggled into England Africans stolen on the slave coast and sold them to willing buyers. Again, literary sources and the public press provide the clearest reflection of the growing vogue for Black servants and of the newcomers' impact on English life. Samuel Pepys records having seen a little Turk and a Black boy in the home of a friend and notes that the two were being kept as pages for his host's daughters. Seven years later, we find that Pepys himself occasionally hired "a black moor of Mrs. Betelier's who dresses meat mighty well. . . ."[10] African serving boys were to be found in several households, and ladies of quality appeared in public with their lapdogs on leash and their blackamoors in tow.

Advertisements for the sale of Black servants and for the recovery of runaways were common.[11] The following is typical: "On Monday last, a Negroe Boy, about 14 Years old, of a good Complexion, indifferent Tall, speaks good English, with a Drugget Coat, silk waistcoat, with red and yellow stripes, run away. . . ."[12]

By the year 1700, the English had sent some 200,000 slaves to the colonies. In 1713, the Treaty of Utrecht gave Britain the right to transport slaves to the Spanish colonies. Her participation in the slave trade was now legally and internationally recognized. The way was paved for plantation slavery to flourish into a mature economic system.[13]

As could be expected, this intensification of Britain's role in the trade swelled the numbers of Africans within her own shores. The new century saw a diverse collection of these uprooted people settling in England for different reasons; their influence on England's social and economic life became fully visible and often worrying. In the key ports of the trade, London, Bristol, and Liverpool, slaves were being landed by the hundreds to be sold at auction.[14] Some were stowaways who quickly vanished into enclaves already established by their fellow Africans near the docks and rivers. Others were servants destined for wealthy households. It was in this wave of Black humanity that Sancho, Cugoano, and Equiano came to England.

It is convenient at this point to classify and describe the various conditions of Blacks to be found in England during this time. They may be divided into three main groups: (1) those brought to England by returning planters and colonial officials; (2) those brought by merchants and traders for sale or personal use; and (3) those African youths, usually sons of local chiefs and officials, studying in England, either on the initiative of their fathers or under the sponsorship of English philanthropic organizations.[15]

Servants accounted for the majority of the first group. Until their status became the subject of legal debate later in the century, their masters treated them as chattels, to be retained or disposed of as the masters pleased. They were not usually paid wages but were maintained in food and clothing. In the household, they performed the duties of valets, servingboys, and stable lads. In public they were paraded in colorful liveries, their necks girded by metal collars inscribed with their owners' initials. Both of these insignia identified Blacks as slaves and exemplified their masters' affluence and prestige.

It appears that younger Africans were commonly kept as pets. Some became the playmates and companions of their owners' children; others were the favorite pages of noble ladies. Almost all were saddled with pompous names of oriental and classical origin. Sultan, Socrates, Pompey, and Caesar were not uncommon appellations. The many Black pages retained at Knole by the earls and dukes of Dorset were all styled "John of Morocco."[16] Ignatius Sancho got his own name as a token of his owners' partiality for Don Quixote's famous squire.

The second group was composed of those slaves who were brought to England by merchants and captains of the Guinea trade. On the slave ships, they were manifested as common cargo. Landed in England, they were set up for sale on the steps of popular coffeehouses, in public squares, and even in the custom-house. According to one historical account, "The personal traffic in slaves resident in England had been as public and authorised in London as in any of our West Indian possessions. . . ."[17]

The third group was the smallest, but its members, by virtue of their social rank in Africa, enjoyed privileged treatment and high visibility in England. They were usually the sons of chiefs, sent to England (as well as to other parts of Europe) to be educated in Western languages, diplomacy, and commerce. Perhaps the most distinguished members of this group were Anthony William Amo and Philip Quaque, both natives of the Gold Coast.[18] Together with other European-educated African scholars, they vindicated the moral and intellectual capabilities of Blacks in a century when it was convenient to deny these in the interest of economic expediency. Their academic achievements were celebrated in Europe and will be discussed later in this chapter. It will be shown that the precedence of their literacy and the excellence of their academic achievements cooperated with other factors to lend credibility to Sancho, Cugoano, and Equiano and, ultimately, to facilitate the movement toward emancipation of the slaves.

It ought not be supposed, however, that the fundamental tools of literacy were reserved only for this small and exclusive group. While there was no concerted attempt to educate even lower-class Englishmen until the later part of the century, and education for slaves was stoutly resisted and prohibited by law in the colonies, it suited the peculiar needs of English employers at home to provide their Black servants with limited instruction in the rudiments of English.[19] In 1734, the duke of Marlborough paid some £10 15s. for the books and tuition of two blacks in his service.[20] Both Colonel Bathurst, father of Samuel Johnson's associate, and Johnson himself supported the well-known manservant, Francis Barber, in acquiring a rather sound education.[21] Although Sancho's early education was neglected through the narrow-mindedness of his first guardians—they feared that with learning he might forget his place and prove intractable—the duke of Montagu, his first patron, encouraged his avid interest in books by supplying his needs from his library. Cugoano relates that he was taught to read and write by the gentleman who rescued him from slavery in the West Indies. Equiano received regular instruction from the very beginning of his life as a slave; first he was sent to school by his mistress, Miss Guerin, and later, in his seafaring days, he was frequently provided with books and tutors. Thus, Black slaves and servants in England came to acquire skills that were essential for smooth communication with their masters and for their functional intercourse with the society at large.

The picture of Blacks in eighteenth-century England would be incomplete without some reference to those who were not restricted by bonds of servitude or protected by indulgent patrons. Some free Blacks made their living as musicians, entertainers, actors, apprentices, and sailors in the slave trade.

From all accounts, Black performing artists were extremely popular with English audiences.[22] A Black woman played the part of Polly in *The Beggar's Opera*, according to John Jackson's *History of the English Stage*. Another Black is reported to have appeared on stage as early as 1770 at the Smock Alley Theatre in Dublin.[23]

It appears that many Blacks were taught to play musical instruments out of a curious myth that they were possessed of an extraordinary racial aptitude for music. African drummers and trumpeters became popular figures in military bands and ceremonial parades, penetrating even the elite ranks of the Life Guards, the Grenadiers, and the Cold Stream Guards.

Such Blacks lived largely independent and transient lives; their greater mobility was a powerful magnet to others, who had escaped from service or servitude either in the West Indies or in England itself, and to those who were unable to find employment. For this latter element the specter of poverty and hardship was no less haunting than it was for those derelicts of white society whose abject misery and despair William Hogarth depicted in "Gin Lane" and "Calais Gate."[24] Many undoubtedly took to stealing, gambling, and other illicit activities; some were recommitted to slavery in the West Indies. On the whole, their freedom was precarious, if not illusory.[25]

The English showed warm appreciation for artistically talented Blacks by providing avenues for their gainful employment; they were not so ready, however, to encourage those who were skilled in manual crafts and mechanical trades. The traditional conservatism of the guilds institutionalized this discrimination into an almost impregnable barrier. Still, some youths managed to find apprenticeships as artisans, but it was costly to train them, and sponsors were reluctant to invest in members of a group that was growing restive for freedom and making increasing demands for social equality. The fears of the establishment were formally expressed in an ordinance, passed by the lord mayor and aldermen of the city of London in 1731, prohibiting the admission of Blacks into trade apprenticeships.[26]

Another group of Africans, who were at least part-time residents of London, was made up of those who found employment as sailors on ships plying the slave coast. They were usually taken on by the trading companies and taught English in order to assist the English crews in the management of their human cargoes. When not on the sea, their home ports were London, Bristol, and Liverpool. But the very nature of their life made them a highly transient, though not invisible, group.

"Hundreds" of American ex-slaves were among the Loyalists who returned to England in 1783 with the British forces after the revolutionary war ended.[27] Fired by the prospect of freedom, they had thrown in their lot with the supporters of the king, who in turn promised to compensate them with land and provisions. Now they were suddenly transplanted to a strange country, with different laws and unfamiliar customs. Their adjustment was all the more problematic because the commission appointed to examine their claims proved generally unsympathetic. Only a small number secured compensation. A few found jobs, but the great majority were reduced to vagrancy and destitution. White poverty was already a dire social problem; now this new wave of Black immigrants, together with their previously settled brothers and sisters, aggravated the situation. At the best of times, the English attitude to the poor was one of fear and distrust: they considered them as a class of shiftless, improvident (and therefore disloyal) citizens. The presence of this alien community of Blacks was, accordingly, calculated to exacerbate these traditional tensions and sensitivities to the point of xenophobia.

For some time now in the eighteenth century, the total Black population of England had become the subject of wild and widely varying speculation, especially among individuals espousing what they claimed to be the national interest. In 1764, the *Gentleman's Magazine* estimated the number of Blacks living in London to be 20,000 and growing.[28] One year later, the *Morning Chronicle* raised that number to 30,000. The latter figure was patently unreliable. It was only during the celebrated Somerset trial (1772) that the Lord Chief Justice Mansfield adopted an official estimate of 15,000. Granville Sharp, that tireless champion of the Black cause, himself placed the figure at 20,000 for all England.[29] Even the best contemporary sources are inexact, but in view of Sharp's association with the Black community through political and humanitarian activism, his estimate seems the most acceptable.

In the face of growing hostility from their English hosts, therefore, the Black community was forced to pool its own resources and devise strategies for the group's protection and survival. Contemporary sources all concur in their testimony that the community was a tightly knit, cohesive body, supporting its members in a variety of ways. The literature of Sancho, Cugoano, and Equiano often reflects those writers' sensitivity to their people's plight and shares something of the solidarity that was to become part of the ethos of Black community life in England.

Sancho's effusive sympathy for human suffering moved him to intercede with his privileged connections on behalf of the needy. In Letter 25, he appealed to Mr. B—— to take a fellow Black into service.[30] Evidence from other letters suggests that he made similar appeals regularly, although he kept his representations on a private level.[31] His distaste for overt political action did not, however, diminish in his eyes the several public philanthropic organizations working for the improvement of conditions among the plantation slaves and London's Black poor.

Cugoano planned to use the proceeds from the sale of his book to start a school for Black in London. He was deeply concerned that conditions there were fast driving his brothers into a state of mental torpor and moral decadence. He wrote: "Nothing engages my Desire so much as the Descendants of my Countrymen, so as to have them educated in the Duties and knowledge of that Religion which all good Christian people enjoy . . ." (*Thoughts and Sentiments,* introduction, xiii).[32]

Of the three, Equiano was the most instrumental—because the most personally involved—in the struggle to win freedom and human dignity for the Blacks in England. Unprincipled white masters and their marauding slave hunters were in the habit of recapturing freed Blacks and placing them under constraint in England or shipping them back to slavery in the West Indies.[33] In the spring of 1774, Equiano found a job for another black, John Annis, as a cook on board the ship in which he was then sailing. Two months later, Annis was illegally apprehended by his former master. Equiano intervened personally on his behalf and himself initiated some of the legal proceedings, meanwhile drawing on the more expert assistance of Granville Sharp in an abortive attempt to secure the man's release.[34] "I proved the only friend he had who attempted to regain him his liberty if possible, having known the want of liberty myself," Equiano wrote (*Narrative* 2: 121).[35] It was Equiano also who brought to Sharp's notice the shocking details of the "Zong Case," in which 132 Africans were willfully drowned at sea in 1783. Later he was to serve on the London Committee for the Black Poor, and in 1786 he was appointed Commissary of Stores for the Sierra Leone expedition, organized to resettle destitute London Blacks. Equiano's energetic activism was a prime force in shaping the literary character of his *Narrative*. Its larger significance will be examined at greater length in chapter 5.

Sancho, Cugoano, and Equiano were exceptional in possessing a higher level of literacy than most Blacks in their time. Their special relationships with the privileged classes and with influential humanitarians were decided personal advantages. But for the faceless masses who could claim no such connections, the evidence shows that their greatest security lay in a strong sense of racial identity and in a social cohesiveness forged by the legal uncertainty of their status in a society that was growing progressively resentful of their presence.

Proslavery interests consistently abused and vilified Blacks. They exploited the English people's ordinary distrust of strangers by denouncing the Black community as a refuge for criminal escapees from abroad. They also promoted the idea that Blacks were displacing English workers. The hard facts of poverty and distress shared by Black and white masses alike scarcely supported these fears: "Life was so hard and enjoyments so few, it could scarcely be claimed that immigrant Blacks were taking anything from the whites; there was nothing to take in the first place."[36] Despite some antipathy whipped up by racist foes, Blacks in general seemed to have continued popular both with the masters they served and with the English lower classes among whom they lived. This considerable harmony that prevailed in the latter case was nowhere more evident than in specific demonstrations of solidarity and in the high incidence of interracial marriage.[37]

Fugitive slaves and Black victims of injustice often found aid and comfort among white working-class communities. Bands of sympathetic whites regularly wrested Blacks from the hands of their captors or kept such captors at bay with threats of mass violence.[38] Kenneth Little suggests that without the spirit of friendship at this level and the support of the liberal classes higher up, the Black poor could hardly have survived.[39]

Lower-class white women showed a strong partiality for Black mates. The story is told of a female haymaker who followed Frank Barber all the way from Lincolnshire to London. The romantic appeal Barber held for this and other white female admirers was not lost on his master Johnson: "Frank carried the Empire of Cupid further than most men," Johnson told his friends.[40] Naturally, such liaisons provoked widespread anxiety and exacerbated tensions in the minds of the conservative middle class.[41]

The specter of miscegenation was horrifying to the orthodox English imagination. The fear that sexual commingling would be an inescapable consequence of Black immigration was the foremost ground for objection to the Black presence from the very beginning. Perhaps Elizabeth I, that supreme symbol of English purity, beauty, and virtue, ever watchful of the national interest, intended to forestall "contamination" of the pure English genetic strain by deporting the blackamoors in her 1596 decree.[42] Thereafter critics of the Black presence followed her lead in yoking together fears of overcrowding with insinuations about the supposed deleterious effects of Black-white unions. In the eighteenth century, plantocratic interests often veiled their fear of the greater "evil" of interracial marriage beneath the more credible, if specious, objection that Blacks were displacing too many whites in domestic service. A letter in the *London Chronicle* clearly illustrates the typical conjunction of these two attitudes:

> Was a full enquiry to be made, it would appear that their [the Blacks'] numbers now in this kingdom amount to many thousands, and as they fill the places of so many whites, we are by this means depriving so many [Englishmen] of the means of getting their bread, and thereby decreasing our native population in favour of a race whose mixture with us is disgraceful, and whose uses cannot be so various and essential as those of white people.[43]

That most implacable detractor of the African race, Edward Long, in an alarming opinion typical of his racist reactionism, denounced miscegenation as "a venomous and dangerous ulcer that threatens to disperce [sic] its malignity far and wide until every family catches the infection from it."[44]

However, such strictures did little to discourage Black-white unions. Circumstances made them inevitable. The numerical predominance of African males over females, arising from the peculiar needs of plantation economy, ensured that the former would turn to native English women for companionship. Even individuals as proud of their racial identity as Cugoano

and Equiano married English wives. The products of such unions drew responses ranging from gaping curiosity to irrational fear. The sensation
created by the "Spotted Negro Boy," 'a fanciful child of nature formed
in her most playful mood," was the subject of gossip columns for many a
month. The hapless child was at various times set up for public viewing and
depicted in several art forms.[45]

James Tobin, a planter who lived in Saint Kitts, saw the proliferation
of this "dark and contaminated breed" as an "evil" requiring urgent
redress.[46] And Philip Thicknesse, a former governor of the West Indies who
was captious about many things in his travels, noticed on his return to England, "in almost every village, a little race of mulattoes, mischievous as
monkeys, and infinitely more dangerous."[47]

For all the prejudice and emotion with which these observations are
charged, it is significant that they had little effect in mobilizing anything like
mass hostility against Blacks. Historians analyzing the general public attitude towards the immigrants are in broad agreement that virulent racism
of the kind proclaimed by vested interests like Tobin and Long was not
widespread.[48] The unintended effect of extremist reactions was to bind the
Black community closer together. The same mixed unions that race purists
were opposing became one of the specific recourses Blacks used to streng-
then their foothold in Britain.

Sensitive to at least the antipathy of the English middle and upper classes,
Blacks therefore formed societies to protect their interests and to promote
the welfare of their fellows. The functions of these societies seem curiously
to approximate those of modern social service and counseling agencies. In
particular, they encouraged servants to desert their masters and contract
marriage as soon as possible after their arrival in the country. The notion
prevailed within the Black community that marriage conferred automatic
freedom on slaves. Sir John Fielding, a noted jurist of the period, described
what seemed to have been the regular pattern:

> Many of these gentlemen [merchants and absentee planters] have either
> at a vast expense caused some of their blacks to be instructed in the
> necessary qualifications of a domestic servant, or have purchased them
> after they have been instructed; they then bring them to England as
> cheap servants having no right to wages; they no sooner arrive here
> than they put themselves on a footing with other servants, become in-
> toxicated with liberty, grow refractory, and either by persuasion of
> others or from their own inclinations, begin to expect wages according
> to their own opinion of their merits; and as there are already a great
> number of black men and women who made themselves troublesome
> and dangerous to the families who have brought them over as to get
> themselves discharged, these enter into societies and make it their
> business to corrupt and dissatisfy the mind of every black servant that

comes to England; first by getting them christened or married, which, they inform them, makes them free (tho' it has been adjudged by our most able lawyers, that neither of these circumstances alter the master's property in a slave).[49]

A further index of the high level of organization within the Black community is the solidarity it showed to those of its members who from time to time were caught in the clutches of an uneven justice. During the celebrated Somerset case of 1772, a delegation of Blacks attended the courtroom daily, and when on 22 June 1772 Chief Justice Mansfield delivered his final judgment, they made visible and vocal demonstration of their approval. The report in the *London Chronicle* reads:

> Several [Africans] were in Court to hear the event of the above cause so interesting to their tribe, and after the judgment of the court was known, bowed with profound respect to the Judges, and shaking each other by the hand, congratulated themselves upon the recovery of the rights of human nature, and their happy lot that permitted them to breathe the free air of England. No sight could be more pleasingly affecting to the mind, than the joy which shone at that instant in these poor men's countenances.[50]

In a similar expression of fraternalism, London Blacks came to the aid of two men committed to Bridewell for begging in 1773. Some three hundred visited them and the whole community subscribed to their support while they remained in prison.[51]

There is strong evidence that members of the servant class formed the orgainizing nucleus for such social and political causes. Their leadership and modus operandi have already been referred to in the foregoing citation from Fielding. Philip Thicknesse was piqued by their astuteness: "London abounds with an incredible number of these black men, who have clubs to support those who are out of place," he squirmed.[52] That they were able to respond so successfully and function so effectively is certainly a tribute to their organizing ability and an indication that they had developed their network of clubs and societies to a high order of efficiency.

Through these agencies they developed a social life distinct from that of the dominant culture and marked by a style that has been closely identified with the universal Black experience across the ages. Numerous notices reflect the fact that they celebrated the occasions of communal life in a manner that was uniquely their own and under circumstances calculated to emphasize their cohesiveness and separate racial identity. One of their "fashionable routs," held in 1764, was described thus: "On Wednesday last, no less than fifty-seven of them, men and women, supped, drank, and entertained themselves with dancing and music, consisting of violins, French horns, and other instruments, at a public house on Fleet Street, till four in the morning. No whites were allowed to be present, for all the performers were black."[53] Servants visited each other in their masters' homes, where they held parties and "assemblies." Francis Barber was invited by the servants of the Thrale household to their annual party, and he reciprocated by having his friends over to Johnson's.[54] After the Mansfield decision, the Blacks celebrated the triumph of their cause in a Westminster tavern. Tickets for admission were five shillings each.[55] Although the commentator in the following record seems to praise with faint damns and damn with faint praise, there is no mistaking the characteristic quality of Black festive culture in his description of the christening:

> 1st came the reputed Father, a Guiney Black, a very clever well-drest Fellow, and another Black who was to be the Godfather. 2ndly, the Midwife or rather her deputy, a White Woman, carrying the little sooty Pagan, who was to be metamorphos'd into a Christian. 3rdly, the Mother, who was also a Black, but not of the Guiny Breed, a well shaped well dress'd woman. 4thly, the Two intended Godmothers, attended by 6 or 8 more, all Guiney Blacks, as pretty, genteel Girls, as could be girt with a girdle, and setting aside the Complexion, enough to tempt an old frozen Anchorite to have crack'd a commandment with any of them.[56]

Together with weddings and funerals, such occasions helped to transmit and preserve the communal nature of their past lives in Africa.[57] No doubt these experiences laid the groundwork for that solid sense of community which saw its full maturity in the writings of Cugoano and Equiano.

So far, this discussion has illustrated how the lower orders of Blacks in eighteenth-century England used their artistic talents, the expedient of marriage, and the common bond of racial affinity to legitimize their human validity in English eyes. These were necessary survival measures in a legal environment more inclined to maintain the status quo of a thriving economic system than to extend to these uprooted strangers the basic human rights and freedoms enshrined in English law.

But there was a class of Africans whom the English (and the Europeans at large) accorded unreserved equality at the highest levels of social and intellectual life. This privileged group consisted of African protégés of European nobility, youths sponsored by philanthropic organizations, and individual sons and relations of African officials. Their credentials were those of intellect—proven or promised—and such other personal qualifications as served to extenuate the facts of their race and color. This group of Blacks is important as a contextual factor in this study because the tradition of its members' moral and intellectual qualities helped to facilitate the acceptance of Sancho, Cugoano, and Equiano when they came to propose themselves as serious exemplars of Black intelligence and as credible spokesmen for the ultimate vindication of African selfhood.

A tradition of African literacy and learning was established in Europe at the height of the Spanish Renaissance. While the West might persist, through blindness and deceit, in denying to African peoples any significant achievements in science, arts, or letters, it could hardly controvert the educability of the African, exposed to the influences of its own intellectual systems. The achievement of the sixteenth-century Black, Juan Latino, is eloquent testimony to the intellectual equality of his race.[58]

Juan Latino was born in Guinea in 1516. At the age of twelve, he was brought with his mother to Spain, where they both became the slaves of Dona Elvira Fernandez, daughter of the distinguished general, Gonzalo Fernandez. Latino's duties were to attend a young master, Dona Elvira's son, to school and to carry his books. In due course, his inquiring mind prompted him to read them also. Within a short time, he was admitted to the Cathedral School of Granada, where he studied alongside his master. Later, he proceeded to the University of Granada, where he excelled in Latin. It was to mark this excellence that he changed his original slave name, Juan de Sessa, to Juan Latino. He took his bachelor's degree in 1546. His career from then on was one of distinguished scholarship and teaching in Latin Grammar and Humane Letters. In 1556 he was appointed to the chair of Latin in his alma mater, with the full concurrence of the *claustro* (faculty). It was his good fortune and crowning honor to be invited to give the Latin address for the opening of the academic year in 1565.

Juan Latino's most celebrated work is the *Austrias* (1573), a Latin eulogy to Don Juan, victor of Lepanto, whom he had met and played cards with in 1569. Latino wrote another work, the *Translatione,* under royal commission, to mark Philip II's solemn ingathering of his ancestors' remains from their original resting places to a mausoleum in the monumental Escorial, then only recently completed. The six-hundred-line poem, finished in 1574, was dedicated to the king and extolled his virtue and filial piety.

Latino was widely acclaimed both in and after his own time. His lecture halls were filled with students from every social class. They came with fervid enthusiasm for the fruits of the New Learning that he dispensed with generosity and zeal. Cervantes himself recognized Latino's excellence by naming him alongside other illustrious figures in the invocatory verses of the *Quixote.* Diego Jimenez de Enciso immortalized him in *The Famous Drama of Juan Latino,* a play based on Latino's life. Latino's contribution to the revival of classical learning in Renaissance Spain was a labor of love for humane scholarship: Miguel Gutierrez paid tribute to that devotion by describing him as "a Negro who spoke in the ex-court of the Moors the language of Virgil with the purity of Horace, and expounded profound doctrines in the Royal and Pontifical University created by Charles V, the Emperor."

Juan Latino lived and made his mark during the grandest epoch of Spanish history—from the accession of Charles V until after the defeat of Philip II's armada. There is some uncertainty about the exact date of Latino's death, but it is believed he lived to a ripe old age and died some time between 1594 and 1597.

Although we cannot claim that Sancho, Cugoano, or Equiano knew Latino or that his work influenced theirs, it is important to elucidate Latino's achievement so that eighteenth-century Black writers can be seen in the light of his precedence. It must be more than a coincidence that Latino's works demonstrate that pervasive conflict between Black self-awareness and Western acculturation which is to be found prominently in the three writers of this study. Herein lies a crucial affinity. In it, a kinship of common blood is bound up with a kinship of common experience, notwithstanding a distance of two hundred years that separated the Renaissance man on the one hand from the Enlightenment trio on the other. The persistence of that shared consciousness transcends time and local experiences to create an independent text or a single *oeuvre*. This might well be the subject of another inquiry.

Two other African scholars, more nearly coeval to the subjects of the present inquiry, continued the tradition of black learning in Europe by acquitting themselves with distinction in academic study and scholarship. The first was Anthony William Amo.[59] Like Latino, he was born on the Guinea Coast, at Axim in Ghana. He was brought to Europe in 1707, when he was four years old, and educated under the patronage of the duke of Brunswick-Wolfenbüttel. His outstanding career started at the University of Halle about 1726. In 1729 he made the public defence of his dissertation, "De Jure Maurorum in Europa." In it he argued that, through royal patents granted by the Roman Emperor Justinian, Africans were entitled to legal exemption from enslavement by Christian Europe. From Halle, Amo went on to the University of Wittenberg where he became Master of Philosophy (Kant was yet a boy) in 1734. His dissertation on this occasion was entitled "Dissertatio Inauguralis Philosophica de humanae mentis. . . ,"[60] an inquiry concerning the presence of sensations in the body and their absence in the mind. According to report, some of his conclusions were quite in advance of his time. He could not accept that ideas of perception existed in the mind. He found self-contradictory the proposition that the mind was both active and passive. Amo's philosophical critiques bear closely on the rationalism of Leibnitz, whom he met at the duke of Brunswick's. Also in 1734, he published another work on a related subject: the distinctions between the operations of the mind and the operations of the senses.

In 1738 Amo published his masterpiece, a work on logic, theory of knowledge, and metaphysics. One year later, he took up a teaching post at the University of Jena.

Highly respected in the German academic community, Amo was proficient in the classical languages—Hebrew, Greek, and Latin—as well as in the three main European languages—Dutch, French, and German. The great measure of respect accorded his scholarship was echoed by the president of the University of Wittenberg who declared that Amo's dissertation "underwent no change, because it was well executed."

Evidently, Amo prosecuted his intellectual convictions in the traditional spirit of academic freedom. He could hardly have felt any fear or reservations on account of those disabilities which traditionally limited the actions of his fellow Africans in diaspora. For, in defiance of an official edict made by Frederick of Prussia against the works of Christian von Wolff, he asserted his intellectual independence by lecturing on Wolff's political ideas at the University of Halle.

The chairman of the faculty commended Amo's entire achievement in this encomium: "Having examined the system of the ancients and moderns, he selected all that was best of them." And as an example of that fine eclecticism, Amo chose this maxim of Epictetus as his motto: "He that accommodates himself to necessity is a wise man, and he has an inkling of things divine."

Amo was equally well recognized in public life. In 1733 he was chosen to lead the procession during the visit to Halle of Frederick of Prussia. He was later to be nominated as Counselor to the Court of Berlin.

The second African scholar and writer of this period was Jacobus Eliza Capitein.[61] He was born in Africa—the exact place is unknown—in 1717. At about age seven, he was sold to Arnold Steinhart, a ship's captain, who took him to Holland and gave him to a friend, Jacobus van Goch. First, Capitein applied himself to the study of painting and later to the disciplines of Latin, Greek, Hebrew, and Dutch at the Hague.

In 1737 he entered the Divinity School of the University of Leyden, after completing his classical training in rhetoric, logic, and catechism at the Hague Latin School. On 10 March 1742 he had the signal honor, not unlike Juan Latino at Granada, of delivering a public oration at Leyden. Ironically, it was a dissertation defending slavery. Capitein contended that there was no specific biblical injunction against slavery and that the state did not preclude Christian freedom.[62]

Capitein was ordained to the sacred ministry on 17 May 1742 in Amsterdam. Later that same year, he was appointed to the position of preacher and school teacher at the Dutch trading post of Elmina on the Gold Coast (Ghana). There he taught mulatto children the rudiments of reading and writing. He was one of the earliest native pioneer scholars to commit African vernacular languages to writing. His vernacular translations of the Lord's Prayer, the Twelve Articles of Belief, and the Ten Commandments were published in Holland in 1744. His more extensive and better known scholarly works are *De Vocatione Ethnicorum,* which reached three editions, and a book of sermons in Dutch.

Probably about the same time Amo and Capitein were starting their university careers on the Continent, a free Black from the West Indies was studying Latin, literature, and mathematics at Cambridge University in England. Francis Williams was born in 1702 in Jamaica. There the duke of Montagu (later Sancho's patron) took a fancy to him and decided to have him educated.[63] The duke's motive was "to see whether a black boy taken and trained at an English school and then at a university, could not equal in intellectual attainments a white youth similarly educated." Williams went down from Cambridge with his bachelor's degree and moved immediately into the fashionable circles of Georgian society. He soon tired of that leisured life, however, and returned sometime between 1738 and 1748 to his native Jamaica.[64] The duke, eager to follow through with his experiment, nominated him to sit on the Council of the island. That prospect was, however, denied him on strong objections from the conservative Governor Trelawny.[65]

Unfortunately, the most extensive account of Williams's life was written by a prejudiced witness, Edward Long. Out of Long's fabric of distortion and innuendo, one may extricate a few substantive facts about Williams's personality and achievements. By the time of his return, Williams had attained a standard of education equal to that of most Cambridge graduates of his day. He opened a school in Spanish Town, where he taught reading, writing, Latin, and elements of mathematics to the children of local planters.

Williams mastered the formal features of conventional eighteenth-century verse, even if his productions are markedly imitative. He found the ode congenial to [his] abilities and wrote several occasional poems in this manner to mark successive inaugurations of the island's governors. One of the odes, "Integerrimo et Fortissimo Viro. . . ," was addressed to George Haldane,[66] who became governor in 1758. It is written in the balanced, stately manner of neoclassical poetry. The sentiment is high and the images are drawn from the well of Greek and Roman antiquity. Although the distinctive qualities of poise, order, and optimism associated with the spirit of neoclassical poetry predominate in Williams's verses, these beauties do not conceal the ambivalence and tension he felt about his status as an educated Black in slave society. The diffidence and self-abasement evident in the following lines are more a reflection of inner confusion than of the usual rhetorical convention of modesty:

Yet may you deign to accept this humble song,
Tho' wrapt in gloom and from a faltr'ing tongue;
Tho' dark the stream on which the tribute flows,
Not from the skin, but from the heart it rose.
("Integerrimo et Fortissimo Viro . . . ," trans. Long)[67]

Long considered this poem highly labored, artificial, and derivative but conceded grudgingly that it showed some imagination and skill.[68] He thought that Cambridge ought to have produced greater excellence, but the truth is that Williams was no better and no worse than scores of versifiers who were to be found pleading the virtues of their pedestrian verses around the fashionable coffee house of London. David Hume, another critic of Black intellect, refused to pay Williams even a modest compliment: "Tis likely he is admired for very slender accomplishments, like a parrot who speaks a few words plainly."[69]

Two other commentators of more reasonable persuasion (and one, more eminently qualified than either Long or Hume) were better disposed toward the West Indian's poetry. The Reverend Robert Boucher Nicholls, dean of Middleham, gave the lie to narrow-minded colonists like Long who were in the habit of ranking Blacks physically and intellectually with apes. Nicholls objected: "I have never heard that an orang outang composed an ode. Among the defenders of slavery we do not find one half of the literary merit of Francis Williams."[70]

James Ramsay, whose observations on the African in the West Indies were the antithesis of the slavocrats' malicious calumnies, saw Williams's poems in a vastly different light:

> Though his verses bear no great marks of genius, yet, there have been bred at the same university a hundred white masters of arts, and many doctors, who could not improve them and, therefore, his particular success in the field of science cannot operate against the natural abilities of those of his colour, till it be proved, that every white man bred there outstripped him. But allowance is to be made for his being a solitary assay, and the possibility of a wrong choice having been made of him.[71]

While Long painted Williams as a pompous, self-opinionated "white man acting under a black skin," scornful of other Blacks and conceited in his learning, Ramsay reported that "other gentlemen of Jamaica speak highly of [his] abilities and of the favour they procured for him."[72]

Whatever the truth of these opinions, the importance of Francis Williams as one of the first Blacks from the West Indies to excel academically ought not to be overlooked. His attainments attested, both to the curious patrons of African intelligence and to the unremitting denigrators of the slaves, that the Black was after all an intelligent being, capable of cultivation and improvement. As we will see later, Sancho, Cugoano, and Equiano each personified these assumptions, and each was conscious that to vindicate them was one of the critical imperatives of black literary expression in the eighteenth century.

A considerable portion of Black scholarship has demonstrated that it is well nigh impossible to reconstruct the truth of the Black past without resorting to a certain amount of stridency and exaggeration. This is perhaps pardonable, if not entirely desirable, because the scholar labors always against a formidable historical structure of systematic negation, vicious calumnies, grudging concessions, artful diminishing, and downright denial of everything that was reputable in the African past. He inherits a critical tradition that is by necessity and definition corrective. It is a severe duty whose object must be to retrieve and repair the image of Africa and her peoples, so that their achievements can be irremovably established among the legitimate acts of human civilization.

Were it possible to reverse history, it might be possible not to have to mention Francis Williams in the same breath as another, more gifted Black poet of the last quarter of the century, Phillis Wheatley. For when all is said and done, Williams, despite his enviable qualifications, was only a minor versifier. Miss Wheatley, on the other hand, was a prodigy for her time and social condition.[73]

The little girl who was later to be named Phillis Wheatley landed in Boston on a slave ship, probably in July 1761. She was bought by Susannah Wheatley, wife of John Wheatley, a respectable Boston tailor. She was then little more than seven years old, frail and sparsely clad, but was destined to become the darling of the Wheatley family. Mary, one of the Wheatley girls, took her in hand and supervised her early education. Her initial mental growth was exceptional: from an untutored Senegalese girlhood, she emerged with a competence in reading, writing, grammar, history, geography, and Latin, uncommon even among white Bostonians of her age. Her favorite reading was the Bible, Virgil, Ovid, and Pope's translation of Homer. Her own essays in verse writing followed naturally from these influences and quickly superseded the original purpose for which Mrs. Wheatley had bought her; namely, to be her personal attendant. Phillis was given access to some of the best libraries and introduced into the circle of Boston literati.

In 1771, Phillis was baptized in the Old South Meeting House in Boston. In that year, too, her childhood friend and tutor, Mary Wheatley, left home to be the wife of the Reverend John Lathrop. New England winters impaired Phillis's health, and her doctor recommended a sea voyage for her convalescence.

Phillis sailed for England in May of 1773 aboard the Wheatley ship, *London*, accompanied by Nathaniel Wheatley. Mrs. Wheatley had announced her arrival in advance in a letter she wrote to the countess of Huntingdon on 30 April 1773. The countess was a patroness of the Calvinist Evangelicals, George Whitefield's sect of Methodism.[74] Phillis's earliest biographers all state that she met the countess on this occasion, but evidence subsequently advanced shows that the countess was in Wales at the time.[75] It is not unlikely, however, that the noble lady was instrumental in getting Phillis introduced into the most fashionable circles of London society.

The notables Phillis met in England treated her with great deference and hospitality. Brook Watson, afterwards lord mayor of London, presented her with a copy of the 1770 Glasgow folio edition of *Paradise Lost* and a copy of Smollett's translation (1770) of the *Quixote*. Lord Dartmouth and other English nobility entertained her royally, and she would have been presented to King George III, had Mrs. Wheatley's illness not occasioned her hasty return to Boston.[76]

Phillis Wheatley's visit to England was not only a rare personal triumph, but also a landmark in the history of Black literature. Her volume, *Poems on Various Subjects, Religious and Moral*, published in London in 1773, was not only the first volume of poetry to be published by a Black American, but it was very likely the first published work of any Black writer in England.[77] Yet Phillis's fame had been made in England before 1773. She had composed an elegy on the death of George Whitefield in 1770, with a dedication to the countess of Huntingdon, and at least four poems later included in the 1773 volume had been printed previously.[78]

The 1773 volume, then, established her reputation and counterposed a solid, coherent collection of literary works written by a Black poet to the strictures of biased negrophobes. Eighteen of Boston's most respected citizens vouched for the authenticity of her poems by signing a testimonial letter that was appended to the collection. Among them were Thomas Hutchinson, governor of Massachusetts; the Honorable Andrew Oliver, lieutenant-governor; John Hancock, signatory of the Declaration of Independence; the Reverend Matthew Byles, Tory poet; and Phillis's master, John Wheatley.

Phillis Wheatley wrote almost exclusively in the formal manner of neoclassical poetry. Influenced primarily by Alexander Pope, her verses reflect the strictest attention to those features of felicitous diction, regular rhythmic patterns, and decorous sentiments that are characteristic of Pope and his school. Her allusions are abundant, drawn from biblical and classical lore; the feelings are controlled, and the presiding consciousness is one of moderation, remarking the general rather than the particular in the whole universe of experience:

Creation smiles in various beauty gay,
While day to night, and night succeeds to day:
That Wisdom, which attends Jehovah's ways
Shines most conspicuous in the solar rays:
Without them, destitute of heat and light,
This world would be the reign of endless night.
                          ("Thoughts on the Works of Providence," 1773)

Critical opinion has been as sharply divided over Phillis's claim to poetic merit as over her identity as a Black poet. Her most generous critics were those who marveled at her high aspirations in relation to her tender years, the fact that she was a woman, and that she was an African by origin. All through the eighteenth and nineteenth centuries, her poetry was widely reviewed both in England and America, particularly at the height of the abolitionist movement.[79]

The reviewer in the *London Magazine* for 1773 wrote: "These poems display no astonishing power of genius; but when we consider them as the production of a young untutored African, who wrote them after six [*sic*] months casual study of the English language and of writing, we cannot suppress our admiration of talents so vigorous and lively." Sancho, whom she preceded in publicaton by seven years, praised the truth of nature and the genius he found in her poetry.[80] Peter Peckard did not think her a poet of the first water but still considered her poems of "great and uncommon merit."[81] Thomas Clarkson included some of her verses in his *Slavery and Commerce of the Human Species* and pointed to her achievement as an index of the potentiality of the African mind when given full scope for development.[82] Joseph Snelling, reviewing her *Memoir and Poems* for the *Christian Examiner* in 1834, devoted over three pages to a fair, balanced commentary. He allowed for Phillis's limitations, while at the same time affirming her superiority over poetasters who had been acclaimed for much less. "What proportion of the rhymesters who enrich our newspapers and magazines with their effusions, can write half so well as Phillis Wheatley? She had no assistance. . . . Accordingly we find some ill-constructed and harsh and prosaic lines, but not so many by half as in the verses of most of her contemporary American poets," Snelling wrote.[83]

Critics from Thomas Jefferson to Imamu Baraka (Leroi Jones) have been severe about her faults, although with diverse motivation. Jefferson could not disavow his habitual bigotry towards Blacks to discover anything of merit in her poetry. He wrote: "Religion, indeed, has produced a Phillis Wheatley but it could not produce a poet. The compositions published under her name are below the dignity of criticism."[84] A scurrilous, satirical piece, entitled "Dreadful Riot on Negro Hill. . ." and written anonymously in New York in 1828, attempts to ridicule Phillis's image as a Black poet by identifying her with the dialectal speech of her illiterate brethren.

Adverse critical reaction from black critics has mainly concerned itself with the absence of any strong racial themes or any militant protest against slavery in Phillis's work. Addison Gayle claims that she could have adapted neoclassical forms "to call a new nation into being." "Oblivious of the lot of her fellow blacks," he continues, "she sings not of a separate nation, but of a Christian Eden."[85] Baraka dispraises her imitation and, in an ill-considered judgment, rates her as only mediocre when placed alongside other Black practitioners of formal literature.[86]

To judge Phillis Wheatley by any kind of absolute criterion, applicable either to her own time or to ours, is to disregard the ambiguities with which she, like Sancho, Cugoano, and Equiano, lived and wrote. Too many modern commentators, blinded by a curious habit of reading history backwards, pass sentence on these early writers from the safety of a world vastly different from the world Blacks knew in eighteenth-century England and America. They forget that in those times Blacks exercised literacy only at the sufferance of a few benevolent whites and often under risk of prosecution. They discount the fact that even those whites who supported abolition often drew the line at universal equality. They protest the absence of vehement denunciation of social and political inequalities as though they think that Blacks then owned or controlled the organs of communication. Because they overlook these things, their impatience with what appears superficially as a weak, compliant rhetoric blinds them to the finer levels of subtlety and ambivalence that recent critics are uncovering through harder, more perceptive scrutiny.[87] This study will reveal similar subsurface meanings, particularly in Sancho's letters.

In appraising the social and political consciousness of both Phillis Wheatley and Ignatius Sancho, critics will have to turn more diligently to what might be called a quality of immanence if they are to discover the assertiveness they say they miss. Sancho was quick to recognize that Phillis's power lay in her immanent condemnation of society through emphasis on moral values; for it was through that seemingly harmless manifesto that he too expressed the tensions he felt about the status of Blacks. He must have recognized, in her emphasis on Christianity and other subjects of general morality, affinities and intentions kindred to his own emphasis on benevolence and virtue; for such appeals were the only form of remonstrance white audiences found palatable issuing from Black voices.

To complete this description of the main categories of educated Africans whose demonstrated mental abilities helped to ameliorate English attitudes to Blacks, it remains only to refer to the "student princes."[88] These were the sons of African royalty, chiefly those living in close proximity to European trading forts, who were traditionally sent abroad to learn the "white man's book."[89] Their parents hoped that their exposure to Western civilization would prepare them for wise and enlightened leadership as well as equip them to handle commercial transactions with Europeans more efficiently in their own interest. The Europeans, on their part, found it sound policy actively to encourage African chiefs to send their sons away in the charge of ships' captains or under sponsorship of organizations like the African Committee and the Company of Merchants Trading to Africa. The young boys thus became the means by which governments and their agents cemented their relations with Africa. Sometimes the princes also became hostages and were held in Europe or at European forts in Africa, while their chieftain fathers worked out their disagreements with the foreigner. Kidnapping was not unknown, especially in cases where persuasion failed. Cases have been documented of merchants violating the trust of African chiefs by detaining their sons in England, France, and Spain or even selling the African youths into slavery.[90]

Philip Quaque, son of Birempon Cudjo, a Gold Coast district chief, was one of the most widely noticed of these students.[91] He arrived in England in 1754, when he was thirteen years old, along with two other African youths, Thomas Caboro and William Cudjo. The three boys were sponsored by the Society for the Propagation of the Gospel and entered a school in Islington, where they were instructed by a Mr. Hickman, the headmaster. Their early lessons were in preparation for Christian baptism, and, after satisfying an examining committee of their knowledge of the Creed, the Lord's Prayer, and the Catechism, they were baptized in Islington Parish Church on 17 January 1759.

Shortly thereafter, the students were put in the care of the Reverend John Moore, a member of the society and curate-lecturer of Saint Sepulchre's Church. Philip Quaque's African schoolfellows did not survive their training in England. Thomas Caboro died of consumption in 1758, and William Cudjo of a mental breakdown in 1764.

Philip Quaque probably received the kind of education typical for students of this group who studied in or near London.[92] Religious instruction, Latin, and other classical subjects were almost certainly the main subjects in their curriculum. In March 1765 he was ordained deacon by the Bishop of Exeter in the Chapel Royal of Saint James's Palace, and in May he was elevated to the priesthood by the bishop of London.[93] That same month he was also married to Catherine Blunt, an Englishwoman. In May 1765, Quaque was appointed catechist, missionary, and schoolmaster to the natives of the Gold Coast.

He returned to that region in 1765 and opened a school for mulatto children. "The rougher sort" were admitted later. Both his educational and pastoral activities were beset by intractable problems. Quaque was himself an enigma to the very people he endeavored to serve: he had forgotten his native language and had to speak through an interpreter, and the fact that his wife was a white foreigner further alienated him from the Africans' support. He was ridiculed by certain governors and European officials at the fort, who refused to attend services conducted by a Black man.

Philip Quaque's importance lies more in his contribution to the idea of African educability than in any exceptional learned attainments. While he does not rank with Amo and Capitein because he was not as extensively trained, he was one of the first Africans to be ordained to the priesthood in England and, like Capitein, was a pioneer both in the missionary and educational fields. To Quaque's early work as a teacher may be traced the earliest foundations of modern Ghanian education.

The last royal visitor who will be described here was perhaps the best known and certainly the most highly born and learned of this group. Job Ben Solomon was born in 1701, the son of Solomon Diallo, the Moslem high priest of Boonda, in Gambia.[94] In February 1730, while on an errand to sell two Africans for his father, Job was captured by Mandingoes and sold to the captain of an English ship. Conscious that his new state was incongruous with his princely rank, he asked leave to send word to his father for his release. The message took some fifteen days to reach his hometown, during which time the ship sailed for Maryland where Job was handed over to Mr. Vachell Dunton, the ship's agent there.

In Maryland, Job was sold to Alexander Tolsey. He was put to work first in the tobacco fields and later to tend cattle, but his background as an assistant priest to his father and as a serious student of Islamic learning unfitted him for both of these occupations, and he soon ran away to Kent County on the Delaware. There he was seen by Thomas Bluett (who was later to become his English teacher and biographer), a clergyman with the mission of the Society for the Propagation of the Gospel. Bluett discerned immediately that Job was no ordinary slave, and, after further signs and the interpretations of a Jolof slave, Job was returned to his master.

Two distinctive features identified Job to his white masters as a special person. He had been noticed regularly to withdraw for private prayer, and he could write Arabic. Indeed it was a letter he wrote to his father in Arabic that turned the tide of his fortunes for the better. That letter came to the attention of James Oglethorpe, then a member of Parliament and deputy governor of the Royal African Company.[95] Oglethorpe sent the letter to Oxford for translation and entered into a bond to purchase Job. In March 1733, the young African sailed for England, but owing to a delay, he missed Oglethorpe, who had by this time sailed for Georgia. Arrangements were made to have Job placed in the care of the Royal African Company.

Unlike his princely counterparts, Job did not come to England to receive formal education; instead, he became the source through which an eager audience of English hosts was enlightened concerning the highest potentialities of the African. Thomas Bluett, who had traveled on the ship with him from Maryland, introduced him into a circle of intelligent and cultivated persons at Cheshunt, where the gentry "were mightily pleased with his Company, and concerned for his misfortunes."[96] Job's English was, understandably, halting at first, but he improved with time and practice, his conversations providing a wealth of new knowledge about the flora and fauna, the customs and the peoples, the agriculture, morality, and religion of his native Africa.

The English marveled at Job's remarkable qualities of mind and his demonstrated capability for superior reasoning. He was found to have a prodigious memory and was puzzled that forgetting seemed so common among his new acquaintances: Bluett said "he hardly forgot Anything in his life, and wondered that anybody ever should."[97]

The news of this extraordinary personage reached Sir Hans Sloane, celebrated botanist and antiquary. Sir Hans was then physician to Queen Caroline and introduced Job to George II and other members of the royal family. Job's extensive erudition in those Arabic texts that then constituted the corpus of knowledge in the Islamic world impressed Sir Hans and his circle of learned associates. He became an invaluable assistant to scholars and virtuosi interested in matters oriental and was elected to the Gentlemen's Society of Spalding on 6 June 1734. That society numbered among its members many distinguished scholars, antiquaries, scientists, and men of letters, three of the best known being Alexander Pope, Sir Isaac Newton, and Sir Hans Sloane himself.

In his house at Bloomsbury, Sloane kept a large collection of birds, stones, Egyptian and Roman antiquities, coins, medals, and some forty-two thousand books and manuscripts. Job most probably assisted Sir Hans in translating some Arabic texts and inscriptions. Sir Hans's collection later became the nucleus of the British Museum.[98]

Job's profound knowledge of the Koran and his unwavering faith in the precepts of Islam recommended him to his English hosts as a remarkably devout and moral person. Bluett states in his biographical account that Job could recite the entire Koran before he was fifteen, and that, while he was in England, he made three copies of that book without any reference to a text.[99] Job engaged his hosts freely in discussions of religious doctrine and belief, although (perhaps to the dismay of his evangelical friends like Bluett) he could not bring himself to accept the idea of the Trinity.

Moving freely as he did among the great and powerful, Job did not fail to extract some tangible advantages from them on behalf of his fellow Moslems in Gambia. He secured from the Royal African Company an undertaking that they would release any Moslems sold to them in Gambia in exchange for two other non-Moslem Africans. The company duly instructed their agents on the Coast to honor the terms of that agreement.[100]

There is a strange irony in Job's relationship with the company. Throughout the entire fourteen months he spent in England, he remained technically their legal property. For some time, his friends feared for his safety, suspicious that he might be resold into slavery after all. Yet the company, on its part, spared no effort to see that he was properly accommodated while he remained in its custody. Although his final departure was long delayed—the fitting out and provisioning of a ship for Gambia was a complicated operation—they seem to have sent him home as soon as they could. When Job finally sailed on 15 July 1734, he took with him many gifts and tokens of his English hosts' appreciation. The company gave specific instructions that he be treated with all deference and hospitality during the voyage. They were anxious that the bond of friendship they had formed with Job should enhance their commercial and trading interests in his country.

The presence of a person of such excellent moral and intellectual qualities could not but transform the climate of English opinion about Africa and her sons. Job Ben Solomon consciously disabused the English of many of their prejudices and misconceptions; unconsciously his gifts of mind and person added to the tradition of Black learning that this chapter has aimed to illuminate. His noble character and irreproachable manners helped pave the way for the more radical revaluation of African humanity that Sancho, Cugoano, and Equiano were later to vindicate in literary terms. Job was a living antislavery document; he was perhaps the nearest human equivalent to the intellectualized image of the "noble Negro" that was to be used so forcefully by antislavery writers in the coming years of abolitionist agitation.

The Black presence in eighteenth-century England, then, spurred a literary reaction that was at once dual and complementary: it generated a species of writing from sources within and without itself whose impact was part favorable and part unfavorable. Each point of view attracted an audience sympathetic to its particular premises and tendencies; together both points of view set in train a philosophical debate about the Black man and slavery that was to give these two subjects a place in the broader domain of the history of ideas.

As we have seen, the English public did not accord Blacks automatic human value on their first appearance among them as a group; the Blacks themselves were forced to contrive forms and expedients that would ensure their survival as individuals and solidify them as a nation in exile. The strategies they adopted were dictated by impulses that are in fact cognate with the most primordial of human faculties—the creative instinct—and operated insensibly to prepare the English mind for a literature celebrating these uniquely human attributes in the African.

Just as the community created its own meaning in the practical terms of survival, so Sancho, Cugoano, and Equiano (as well as those talented African figures described in this chapter) transfigured those terms into a literary and intellectual expression that would present Black life wholly and truth-

fully. The elevation of the Black experience to the level of art lent credibility
to the image of the Black as creator. It furthered the debate over the moral
and intellectual equality of the African race, thereby calling more firmly into
question the legality of slavery itself.

But the Black response, while it was born of impulses towards racial au-
tonomy and of circumstances peculiar to African life in Britain, neither
developed independently of, nor was likely to succeed isolated from, the
broader currents that circulated in the mainstream of eighteenth-century
intellectual life. The following chapter will examine the interaction of these
forces and so extend the contextual framework of Black writing during this
period.

2

The Intellectual Milieu:
Contexts for Black Writing

(A) PHILOSOPHICAL

Eighteenth-century Black writing confronted the conventional mind of Britain with a radical proposition. It asked that mind to exchange its stereotyped conceptions of Africa and Africans for a new intellectual system, in which Africa would attain her equal "place in nature" and Africans their full authentic humanity. This challenge to the received assumptions of collective thought would hardly have found an audience, had it not been for its fortuitous coincidence with sympathetic developments in the wider intellectual milieu of the Western world.[1] The literary works of Sancho, Cugoano, and Equiano contained enough of fashionable sentiment and religious fervor to assure them at least a temporary celebrity with liberal Englishmen, but they needed the propitious climate of the European Enlightenment to corroborate their more profound moral and political implications.

The Enlightenment represented the interaction of a wide range of forces for change and reform in eighteenth-century civilization. Among the ranks of its thinkers were to be found moral and ethical philosophers, writers on history and political economy, scientists and theologians, and the forerunners of sociological theory.[2] Their methods of inquiry often raised sharply diverging opinions about the nature of the universe and humanity's place in it.

A movement for spiritual revival in private as well as public life spurred a reexamination of chronic social problems on the grounds of a stricter morality. At this time also, England saw a rapid growth in periodical literature; many journals dedicated their pages to defending or condemning slavery; nearly all took at least objective notice of the debate about the condition of African slaves on the West Indian plantations and explored the larger question of their place in the human order. The Enlightenment was reflected also in the works of eminent jurists, philosophers, and other persons interested in reforming the laws to make them consistent with the new principles of universal liberty and equality. And in politics, for the first time, a full-scale propaganda machinery was set in motion by abolitionist forces to influence public opinion and to enlist the support of many of England's greatest statesmen in the cause of antislavery. Black literature of this period must therefore be seen not only as a literature of social protest, but, more significantly, as bearing an integral relation to the history of ideas.

For centuries jurists and moral philosophers had accepted Aristotle's doctrine, enunciated in the *Politics,* as the legal basis for slavery. According to that doctrine, some people were naturally fitted to be masters while others were naturally fitted to be slaves. Individuals could lose their personal freedom either by virtue of their natural inferiority or by captivity in a "just war."[3] This axiom came to be known as the "classical" theory of slavery—classical because it was predicated on a very rigorous system of natural law and rationalistic thought, and because the tradition of its validity remained virtually unchallenged until the late seventeenth century.

It should have been relatively easy for supporters of the slave trade to find philosophical justification for it in the pronouncements of two prominent intellects of the Augustan Age. Broadly interpreted, the thoughts of Thomas Hobbes and John Locke could have been made to buttress the logic of merchant and plantation interests involved in the Guinea trade.

Hobbes's vision of society as a continuous struggle for dominance between the powerful and the powerless was an apt rationalization for the sociopolitical premises on which slavery was instituted. Further, Hobbes endorsed Aristotle's captor-captive theory, which gave the master absolute power over the life of the slave. In one detail he diverged from the stern immutability of Aristotle's political order: he allowed for the possibility of political reversal whereby slaves, motivated by a primal urge to dominate (similar to their master's and common to all animals), could overthrow and in turn subject their oppressors.[4]

Locke, in his *Two Treatises on Government* (1689), also reaffirmed the Aristotelian theory by defining slavery as "a state of war continued between a lawful conqueror and a captive."[5] But Locke dissented partially by allowing the captor only limited power over the captive, on the principle that no man can voluntarily deliver himself over to the absolute power of another, since no man has the power over his own life: "Nobody can give more power than he has himself, and he that cannot take away his own life cannot give power over it."[6] The ambiguity in Locke's philosophical theory is clear enough; it is even more glaring in his actual life. Locke was an investor in the Royal African Company and drafted the "Constitution of Carolina" (1699), a document that implicitly tolerated slavery.[7] However, Locke's fundamental belief in individual freedom and in the individual's right to pursue "enlightened" self-interest, unfettered by arbitrary restrictions, identified him with the later spirit of the Enlightenment.

Still, neither Locke nor Hobbes took particular cognizance of the unique circumstances of the African slave trade. Both men kept their pronouncements narrowly restricted to slavery as a consequence of conquest or as a form of restitution for personal damages or debt. Both stayed on the hard, cold ground of theory, disapproving of slavery only on the basis of natural rights.[8] It was left to two principals of the benevolistic school to advance antislavery objections to a higher plane and to describe a higher motive for condemning slavery: namely, that it was unethical, antisocial, and inhumane.

The first decade of the eighteenth century ushered in an uncompromising humanitarian reaction to the egotistic hedonism of Hobbes and the rationalistic ethics of Locke. Lord Shaftesbury, founder of the new school of benevolism, insisted in his *Characteristics* (1711) that human beings possess an innate "moral sense" which impels them to seek the general rather than their own narrow interest. "Man is naturally a virtuous being," Shaftesbury maintained optimistically. "To be good, he needs only to be natural." Shaftesbury stressed that humanity's noble, benevolent passions naturally restrain individuals from causing harm or pain to their fellows, whether natives or foreigners, and that to subject another to torture or personal injury is "wholly and absolutely unnatural, as it is horrid and miserable."[9] Thus, although Shaftesbury did not explicitly take up the case of the African slave, he implied that the Black man was both sensible of pain and capable of noble passions. The proslavery publicists had consistently propagated the myth that the African was insensible to the cruelty of slavery. The *Characteristics,* accordingly, laid the earliest moral foundations for the refutation of that myth.

Francis Hutcheson, an equally significant benevolist, reflected even more clearly the critical shift that was taking place in intellectual attitudes. In his *System of Moral Philosophy* (1734–38, 1755), Hutcheson attacked the classical theory of slavery and the rationalistic view of human nature more explicitly than any ethical philosopher before him. His position is palpably humanitarian. He credits humankind with "a stable, calm Universal Goodwill to all, or the most extensive benevolence," and elevates the sympathetic instincts above the self-serving: "When we see or know the pain, distress, or misery of any kind which another suffers, and turn our thoughts to it, we feel a strong sense of pity, and a great proneness to relieve, where no contrary passion withholds us."[10]

Hutcheson took sharp issue with Aristotle's theory of natural inferiority, contending on the contrary that "all men have strong desires for liberty and property, have notions of right," and that no man has a right to impose arbitrary power over another.[11] Consequently, Hutcheson opposed slavery as absolutely abhorrent to humanity, refusing to qualify his position even with Locke's exception that an aggrieved person had the right to enslave his aggressor. Hutcheson's importance, then, is that he is the first to bring to the antislavery debate a distinct system of humanitarian ethics based on pity and compassion, rather than on classical notions of reason and right.[12]

By attacking the traditional theory of slavery as a right of conquest, Hutcheson struck at the political arguments for the enslaving of Africans. By allowing every human creature the qualities of benevolence and sensibility, he paved the way for greater receptivity in Europe of the idea of African humanity and self-consciousness, later to be exemplified in the personalities and writings of Sancho, Cugoano, and Equiano. As the century progressed, successive Enlightenment thinkers continued to generate discourse about the natural rights of every human being. Their discourse had the common effect of rousing individuals out of their settled habits of orthodox thought. By taking up the advocacy of people hitherto disenfranchised in the traditional arrangements of Western society, the Enlightenment helped to pave the way for the humanization of the African. This was one of the surest foundations on which future objections to slavery and the slave trade would be based.

It was the *philosophes*, the ideologists of the French Enlightenment (principally Montesquieu, Raynal, and Rousseau), who established and popularized the validity of the common person's right to self-possession and the belief in personal perfectibility. But even among the *philosophes* themselves, there were those who had difficulty admitting Blacks to full human equality. Some solved the dilemma by ignoring them in their discussion, others by assigning them an inferior rank in the order of nature. Rousseau's celebration of the "noble savage" is often fallaciously construed as an expression of symapthy for the African slave. In actual fact, Rousseau makes no specific reference to this pathetic human creature. Rousseau's reflections on bondage are often highly abstract and generalized, largely because he had no first hand familiarity with slaves.[13] It is significant that both he and Voltaire held the African inferior in mental ability to the European. And although both men abhorred and condemned slavery, their attitude to Black intellect connects them, paradoxically enough, with the more fully systematized traditionalist theories about race and creation that were adverse to Blacks.[14]

Eighteenth-century Western Europeans commonly assumed that the peculiar physical characteristics of Africans and the topography and culture of Africa itself somehow predisposed Blacks to slavery. In the popular mind, Africans were physically repulsive, morally degenerate by nature and custom, and incapable of higher spiritual sensations. Their enslavement and transportation to America were therefore deemed a merciful deliverance from savagery and darkness.[15] Writers on natural history still arranged living things according to the traditional idea of the Great Chain of Being. Almost invariably, they placed the Europeans at the top of the scale, on the ethnocentric premises that their white skins were aesthetically more pleasing and that their cultural achievements were superior to those of other races. Conversely, they relegated Africans to the lowest ranks because of their dark skins and the Western perception that Africa was backward in the arts and sciences.

The image of Africans was further prejudiced by theories then current about the origin of the races. One major theory, monogenesis, proposed that God performed a single act of creation, making one man and one woman at a specific moment in history. That original pair was presumed to be white. Some monogenists described Blacks as a degenerate variation from the original stock, and they reasoned that the exotic, inhospitable character of the African neighborhood was a fit place of banishment for human beings who had found disfavor with their "normal" counterparts. A second theory, polygenesis, used the evidence of wide variety in the human species to suggest that God created each race separately. This view, sometimes known as "diversificationism" emphasized the differences among humankind. It assigned Blacks the lowest rank on the human continuum and generally related them to the orangutan. Predictably, it found favor with the proslavery publicist, Edward Long, who expounded it with the authority of a field observer (Long lived in the West Indies), although not with the empirical logic of a true scientist.[16]

Thus the apologists for slavery, by ascribing to Blacks one of the lowest ranks in the order of creation, rationalized that slavery was not only fitting but desirable for them. It took some of the most discerning minds of the Enlightenment to expose the inherent fallacies of European racial chauvinism and to propose Africa as a primitivistic image of pure nature and Africans as noble, perfectible, and human.

Adam Smith was one of the earliest Enlightenment thinkers to suggest that standards of beauty were relative. "A fair complexion is a shocking deformity on the coast of Guinea," Smith cautioned soberly. "Thick lips and a flat nose are a beauty."[17] Smith lauded the heroism of "savage" nations, chiefly the North American Indians, and announced that Africans possessed moral virtues that belied their Western image: "There is not a negro from the coast of Africa who does not, in this respect, possess a degree of magnanimity which the soul of his sordid master is often scarce capable of conceiving."[18]

A German ethnologist, Johann Friedrich Blumenbach, brought to the argument the gifts of a mind more scrupulous than the minds of the proslavery detractors and used the tools of rigorous scientific inquiry to show that Africans' differences did not make them inferior to Europeans but merely reflected variations typical of the whole human species.[19] Blumenbach maintained that Africans could improve themselves if given the opportunity: "The Blacks have for the most part head and understanding enough: they comprehend easily and correctly, and their momory is of a tenacity almost incomprehensible; for even when they can neither read nor write, they still remain in their places amidst the greatest bustle of business and traffic and seldom go wrong."[20] As evidence of African intellectual capability, he cited the examples of Benjamin Banneker, the self-taught Black American astronomer and mathematician; of Sancho, with whom Blumenbach corresponded; and of Equiano, whom he knew personally. He had high praise for the literary achievements of Phillis Wheatley and commended the scholarship of Amo and Capitein: "There is no so-called savage nation under the sun which has so much distinguished itself by such examples of perfectibility and original capacity for scientific culture, and thereby attached itself to the most civilized nations of the earth, as the negro."[21]

Across the Atlantic, the Princeton scholar, Samuel Stanhope Smith, stoutly defended the monogenetic theory and its implicit assumptions of African equality. Smith's work, *An Essay on Complexion* (1787), was written in answer to *Sketches in the History of Man* (1774), a polygenetic document written by Henry Home, Lord Kames, arguing, among other things, that race and climate were irreversible causes of the morality and intellect of Africans. Smith was an environmentalist. He believed that the chief causes of the variety in the human race were climate, the state of society, and the manner of living.[22] From this position, he contended that racial characteristics were not of themselves prescriptive of superiority or inferiority but were adaptive features that fitted individuals for their environments. He asserted that the African, like all humankind, retained an innate capacity for civilization which could be improved, but that that capacity was frustrated by poverty and despotism at home and by brutality and prejudice in the New World.[23]

The ideas of improvability and perfectibility were central to progressive thinking of the eighteenth century and fully consistent with the tenets of the Enlightenment. One of the most illustrious exponents of the intellectual and cultural spirit of the age was the French philosopher, Montesquieu. His was to be the most pervasive influence on antislavery thinking on both sides of the Atlantic. Montesquieu's earliest representations against slavery were made in his *Persian Letters* (1721) where, under the guise of the fictitious Usbek, he deplored American slavery and the depopulating effect it had on Africa.[24] But his most definitive treatise on the subject, from which every major antislavery writer drew, was his *Spirit of the Laws* (*De L'Esprit des Lois*, 1748). Montesquieu dismissed all the the leading arguments of the classical theory basically on the principles of universal equality and natural rights.[25] He found slavery repugnant to the natural law and to the institution of liberal democracy. He went further and suggested that slavery demoralized master and slave alike and undermined the integrity of the state, an objection echoed by many critics of plantation society.[26] In a passage that has often been misconstrued as a rationalization for slavery, Montesquieu ridicules the stock proslavery arguments for the enslaving of Africans.[27] His attitude was, finally, uncompromising—"The state of slavery is in its own nature bad"—and egalitarian: "As all men are born equal, slavery must be accounted unnatural."[28]

The distinctive spirit of Montesquieu's thought permeated the works of British Enlightenment thinkers. The renowned English legal authority, Sir William Blackstone, drew heavily on *L'Esprit* in his *Commentaries on the Laws of England* (1765–66). His first edition established unequivocally that "as soon as a negro comes to England he becomes free," a maxim on which the question of slavery's legality was ultimately to be resolved. Regrettably, Blackstone succumbed to pressure from vested interests during the Somerset trial and compromised his opinions in the third edition.[29]

James Beattie, professor of moral philosophy at the University of Aberdeen, was deeply indebted to Montesquieu (as was the whole Scottish Enlightenment) in his arguments against slavery, presented in the *Elements of Moral Science* (1793). This work became one of the most widely read in both Britain and America. In his examination of slavery, Beattie preferred humanitarian objections to rationalistic method. He thought that a slave's right to freedom and self-possession was axiomatic and consistent with natural human rights; and so he concentrated on the moral aspects of slavery, declaring that it is "detrimental to virtue and industry; that it hardens the heart to those tender sympathies, which form the most lovely part of the human character; . . . in short, that it is utterly repugnant to every principle of reason, religion, humanity, and conscience."[30]

In a work written some twenty years ealier, Beattie had exposed the fallacies inherent in Aristotle's and Hume's positions on slavery. To Aristotle's doctrine that men of great genius are born to rule over men of lesser genius and greater physical strength, Beattie counterposed the fact that the Greeks, for all their intellectual excellence, later became slaves. To Hume's assertion that Africans were savage and incapable of civilized achievements, he submitted the facts that the inhabitants of Britain were once savages themselves and that Africans had produced "ingenious manufactures and arts which Europeans would find it hard to imitate."[31]

The subject of antislavery is a complex study in the dynamics of ideological transfer. The English abolitionists were indebted to the French philosophers but did not receive the French ideas directly from that source. Instead, the transfer followed a devious course: from France ideas traveled further north to influence the Scottish intellectuals, then across the Atlantic to the American abolitonists, and finally back to England.[32] It was th Philadelphia Quaker, Anthony Benezet, who was the main source of supply for the English.

Benezet was born in France in 1713. He received his early education in England and, in 1731, moved with his family to Philadelphia. There he became a schoolmaster in a girls' academy and, much later in life, in a Quaker school established to instruct Blacks and prepare them for freedom.

Benezet kept up a steady flow of correspondence with abolitionists on either side of the Atlantic and was fully acquainted with the vast body of literature motivated by slavery and the slave trade. He worked both inside and outside Quaker ranks to promote antislavery opinion. In 1762, he published *A Short Account of that Part of Africa Inhabited by Negroes*. In that pamphlet he countered proslavery misrepresentations of Africa and documented his own humanitarian and rationalistic arguments with the authoritative evidence of travelers like Adanson, Bosman, Smith, and Moore.[33] He insisted that Africans were the human equals of the Europeans; that they were honest, hardworking people whose tranquillity and traditional morality were disrupted by European depredations on the Guinea Coast. The positive aspects of African character were further stressed and elaborated in his longer work, *Some Historical Account of Guinea* (1771). Benezet showed that the European contact had a devastating effect on Africa; that the slave trade and the regimen of plantation life brutalized Africans, as they gave no incentive for the exercise of their higher faculties and sensations. His impassioned descriptions of distressed Africans being separated from their kin are a classic of antislavery sentimentalism: "Mothers are seen hanging on their daughters, bedewing their naked breasts with tears, and daughters clinging to their parents, not knowing what new stage of distress will follow their separation, or whether they shall meet again."[34]

By combining egalitarian with humanitarian and sentimentalist attitudes, Benezet synthesized the major strains of Enlightment thought. His profound impact on British abolitionist leaders is reflected in the writings of John Wesley, Granville Sharp, Thomas Clarkson, and Ottobah Cugoano. This fusion marks the point at which Sancho and Cugoano came to public attention. Benezet therefore played a highly significant role in fostering a climate of receptivity for antislavery ideas, more particularly in facilitating the credibility of African spokesmen.

If Benezet's work laid the foundation of abolitionist agitation in England by dissemination the ideas of the French and Scottish Enlightenment, it also contributed indirectly to the growth of British humanitarianism, again by a curious method of oblique transfer. Benezet regularly corresponded and exchanged antislavery pamphlets with the *philosophe*, the Abbé Guillaume Raynal.

Raynal's *Histoire de Deux Indes (Philosophical and Political History of the East and West Indies)* (1770) shows evidence of this collaboration, especially in its appreciation of the native African virtues of heroism and generosity.[35] Raynal evokes the same sense of trauma the slaves suffered at their sudden removal from home, the rigors of the long voyage, and the stultifying conditions of plantation life. Like Benezet, Raynal found slavery entirely repugnant to humanity, reason, and justice. With an enthusiasm typical of the age, he declared: "Whoever justifies so tedious a system, deserves the utmost contempt from a philosopher and from the negro a stab with his dagger."[36]

The influence of the *Histoire* was as profound as it was extensive. The book ran through some thirty-eight French and eighteen English editions. Clarkson judged it to be one of the primordial agents in promoting antislavery ideas in England during the 1770s. Horace Walpole and Sir Samuel Romilly both acknowledged its part in raising their consciousness about slavery and the slave trade. William Robertson, Edward Gibbon, Samuel Johnson, and Mrs. Vesey were some of the leading intellectuals of the day who read this important work.[37]

Raynal's emphasis on the Africans' humanity urged the horror of their sufferings on the sensibilities of a British public that was, in the latter half of the eighteenth century, highly susceptible to humanitarian reasons. His delineations of the prospect of heroic insurgency on the part of Blacks enslaved in the West Indies was not only an accurate prefiguring of things to come but also an expression of faith in the capability of Blacks. "Where is this great man to be found, whom nature, perhaps owes to the honour of the human species? Where is the new Spartacus who will not find Crassus? Then will the *black code* be no more, and the white code will be a dreadful one, if the conqueror only regards the right of reprisals."[38] Raynal's vision, thus expressed, was to become an optimistic image to crusading abolitionists and a terror to slavery interests.

Not all Enlightenment objections to slavery were based on natural right or humanitarian or religious grounds. The economic doctrine of utilitarianism, coupled with a new liberal ideology about the conduct of commerce, discredited the profitability of slave economies. Adam Smith, another of the Scottish intellectuals and professor of moral philosophy at Edinburgh, published his widely influential book, *The Wealth of Nations*, in 1776. In it he asserted that slavery violated all the laws of utility and morality. He compared the high cost of maintaining slaves with the low return derived from their labor. He attributed that disparity to the fact that slave labor was forced, unskilled, and uninventive.

Although Smith made no special plea for Black slaves, his critique challenged the very basis on which plantation slavery was founded: he called for a more rational and enlightened approach to managing labor and running the sugar economy of the West Indies. He demonstrated an urgent concern for the working classes as a whole and proposed that improved facilities for their education and social well-being would redound to the greatest good of the whole nation.

(B) RELIGIOUS

But while the leaders of the secular Enlightenment were condemning slavery on the grounds of natural rights and utility and the ethical philosophers were deploring its inconsistency with humane principles, the Church as an institution remained strangely impervious to this growing agitation. In the early years of the slave trade religious protest came mainly from nonconformist groups. As far back as the the middle of the seventeenth century, the Quakers had taken the lead in the antislavery struggle. In 1657, George Fox, founder of the Society of Friends, urged slaveholding Quakers in the Americas to show compassion to Africans and Indians in accordance with Quaker belief that all men were equal brothers in the Fatherhood of God.[39] While on a visit to Barbados in 1671, Fox appealed to slaveholding Friends "to cause their overseers to treat mildly and gently with the negroes, and not to use cruelty towards them."[40] He envisaged an eventual emancipation after years of service. Another visitor to Barbados, the Reverend Morgan Godwyn, maintained that although slavery was not expressly forbidden in Holy Writ, it was most certainly in violation of the spirit of religion.[41]

The Quakers in America continued to press the slavery issue and to persuade slaveholding Friends to manumit their slaves voluntarily. Both in America and in England, they began to discuss the slave trade at every yearly meeting. In 1717 the Society's yearly meeting in London took a firm stand against the importation of slaves. In 1758 the London Society again enjoined Quakers against participation in the slave trade on humanitarian grounds. In 1761 and 1763 they went further and resolved to expel any Friends who persisted in the trade. So successful was Quaker antislavery strategy that by 1780 there were no slaveholding Quakers remaining in fellowship in either England or America.[42]

Growing religious doubt and outright denunciation still failed to stir the established Church of England. As Eric Williams suggests, the Church in the eighteenth century could not rise above the limitations of the society of which it was a part.[43] Certain individuals and groups within the Church sought to temper slavery's severity by promoting the idea of Christianization as a more feasible priority and one less disruptive of the vital economic structure of colonial society.[44] Many churchmen subscribed to the view that Africans, as an "uncivilized" group, had to be prepared gradually for emancipation. But , by and large, the Church supported, even openly defended, the status quo. It took the Methodist and Evangelical revivals of the 1730s to protest the Church's failure to recognize the need for broad social reform. These two movements offered hope to the masses by admitting them to fellowship as equals in Christ; and, in this gesture of Christian egalitarianism, the Black became enfranchised. The Evangelicals adopted the issue of slavery as a matter deserving Christian concern and compassion.

The Methodist Revival was calculated to espouse the cause of freedom for the slaves. Methodists were committed to the relief of suffering and their charitable ministry extended to all manner of poor and destitute people.

They carried on an extensive social service program from which many of London's impoverished Blacks must certainly have benefited. Further, as the Methodists believed in the common depravity of all humanity, they made no distinction in declaring Blacks eligible for salvation. Both George Whitefield and John Wesley, the leaders of the Revival, had lived and traveled in America and were acquainted with the conditions of the slaves on the plantations there.

In a "Letter to the Inhabitants of Virginia and Maryland, etc. . . ." (1740), Whitefield remonstrated with American slaveholders for abusing the slaves and failing to provide for their material well-being. He reaffirmed that Black slaves were the spiritual equals of the white colonists, and he pleaded for more humane treatment: "Think you that your children are any better by nature than the poor Negroes? No, in no wise. Blacks are just as much and no more, conceived and born in sin, as White Men are."[45]

Yet Whitefield stopped short of urging full cessation of the slave trade. In fact, he convinced himself that hot regions could only be cultivated by slave labor, and he was instrumental in forcing the repeal of Oglethorpe's original edict against slavery in Georgia. He rejoiced at the opportunity to own slaves himself and to instruct them in the "nurture and admonition of the Lord."[46] Whitefield's overall attitude, therefore, was a mixture of the selfish interests of the property holder and the benevolent paternalism of the missionary.

Wesley, on the other hand, had no vested interests that might have dictated such deceit or temporizing ambivalence. Wesley unequivocally denounced the slave trade as "that execrable sum of all villainies." He preached several sermons against slavery in the 1720s and 1730s, before the Methodists had taken a concerted position against it.[47]

Although Wesley was essentially a conservative in his theology and his politics, he was a staunch liberal on questions of personal liberty. His *Thoughts on Slavery* (1774) harmonizes his own religious principles with Enlightenment thinking on natural rights, the slave trade, and the image of the African.[48] In the *Thoughts,* he upheld these axioms: "Liberty is the right of every human creature, as soon as he breathes the vital air; no human law can deprive him of that right which he derives from the human law can deprive him of that right which he derives from the law of nature."[49] He also refuted the claim implicit in Whitefield's "Letter," and widely retailed by slave apologists, that whites were constitutionally unsuited for plantation labor. Wesley was able to oppose to that specious argument a personal testimony. He and eight members of his family had labored in Georgia felling trees; his neighbors, a German family, had toiled likewise.

Both internal evidence and his own testimony show that Wesley's *Thoughts* was influenced by Benezet. On 12 February 1772, Wesley noted in his journal that he had been reading Benezet on the slave trade. The two men exchanged letters on the subject, and it seems likely that Benezet, tireless campaigner that he was, persuaded Wesley to throw his own support behind the work of the British Abolition Society (founded in 1787). Wesley's *Thoughts* was widely distributed in abolitionist circles: in 1787 he reprinted a special edition for the society.[50] The Methodist publication, *The Arminian Magazine,* carried regular articles on slavery and thus spread among Methodists knowledge of the trade's evils and of the excesses of punishment on the plantations.

Wesley also collaborated closely with William Wilberforce, later to be hailed as the Great Emancipator. Through this association, the Methodists came to play a key role in British abolitionist agitation. On 24 February 1789, Wilberforce had a private interview with Wesley and established the basis for the cooperation his parliamentary party was later to enjoy from Methodist members of the House of Commons during the years of struggle.[51] Shortly before he died, Wesley wrote to Wilberforce commending him for his work and urging him to continue the fight for abolition in Parliament "till every American slavery (the vilest that ever saw the Sun) shall perish before it."[52] When the Methodists held their annual conference in 1791, Wilberforce sent each of the one hundred delegates a copy of the document, "Evidence that appeared before a Select Committee of the House of Commons Relative to the Slave Trade," and asked them to use their influence to get the abolition bill passed in Parliament. From this time on, the Methodists kept up a steady stream of petitions urging abolition. The alliance of the Methodists with "the Saints" (Wilberforce's Evangelical party in Parliament) added religious fervor to intense political activism. Antislavery was transformed from a purely philosophical debate to a movement of moral commitment for a pressing humanitarian cause.

Although the Evangelicals did not have the institutional support of the Established Church, their opposition to slavery was backed by individual clergymen whose private courage and sense of slavery's unchristian nature made them outspoken advocates of abolition. The Reverend James Ramsay, vicar of Teston in Kent, was one such antislavery churchman. Ramsay had spent twenty years in the West Indies and so was able to make an authentic contribution based on his firsthand experiences and observations. In 1784 he published an *Essay on the Treatment and Conversion of African Slaves in the British Sugar Colonies,* in which he deplored the indignities Africans suffered in those parts. He defended the Africans' claims to full human rights as well as their capacity for spiritual and intellectual improvement. Ramsay opposed slavery on the grounds of morality and "general utility." He was concerned that its unnaturalness was contributing to degeneration of colonial society. He adduced evidence to show that slave labor was more costly than free labor.[53] On the question of intellectual capacity he took

Hume to task for asserting that the white race was the superior and the more civilized.

Ramsay's actual contacts with slaves had impressed him with their wide range of skills, which were in fact being exploited in such plantation activities as rum distilling, sugar production, and a variety of mechanical trades. Ramsay stated that slaves had evidenced distinctive talents in music and useful crafts: "As far as I can judge, there is no difference between the intellects of whites and blacks, but such as circumstances and education naturally produce."[54] He failed to see how slaves could be expected to develop their mental abilities when the whole tenor of their lives was so clearly calculated to stultify them and kill any inclination to independence. With fair-minded perceptiveness he reasoned: "These are weights sufficient to crush a first-rate human genius."[55]

Ramsay's *Essay* enjoyed wide circulation and credibility in abolitionist circles, chiefly because it was the factual evidence of an eyewitness on West Indian slavery. Likewise the Reverend John Newton's *Thoughts upon the African Slave Trade* (1788) bolstered the abolitionist argument and complemented Ramsay's evidence. Newton had been an actual participant in the slave trade and so could provide details about slaving on the coast of Africa and the scandalous conditions under which slaves were transported.

Newton's life story, recorded in his *Authentic Narrative* (1763–64), is a classic in Evangelical spiritual autobiography. His was the type of Pauline conversion that Evangelicals and nonconformists generally rejoiced in offering to the world as a token of the redeeming power Christ's love for the vilest of sinners. For here was the record of a man whom nine years in the slave trade had so hardened to the groans of Africans and the atrocities of the slaving crews that he could make this confession: "During the time I was engaged in the slave trade, I never had the least scruple as to its lawfulness."[56] Yet the pangs of conscience and the awakening of a religious sense filled him with repulsion for the instruments of torture and captivity (chains, bolts, and shackles) that his work as a captain showed him every day. After his miraculous conversion, he abandoned seafaring, took holy orders, and became an ardent foe of the infamous traffic in human flesh.

Newton's *Thoughts* charged that the English were the most brutal of slaving nations. They crammed their human cargoes in holds that were uncomfortable, unsanitary, and often pestilential. Newton records the Africans' deep despondency at being suddenly uprooted and subjected to the power of strange men. He documents the high mortality rate among both slaves and crews and the atrocities the slaves had to endure:[57] "I have seen them sentenced to unmerciful whippings, continued till the poor creatures have not had the power to groan under their misery, and hardly a sign of life has remained. I have seen them agonizing for hours, I believe for days together, under the torture of the thumbscrews; a dreadful engine, which, if the screw be turned by an unrelenting hand, can give intolerable anguish."[58]

Clarkson and his co-workers on the Abolition Committee could hardly have desired a more valuable ally than Newton proved to be. His unique experiences served them persuasively in councils where credibility and authenticity were of paramount importance. In 1789 Newton testified before the Privy Council, and in 1790 he gave evidence before a committee of the House of Commons.[59] Thus, at the height of abolitionist agitation, the quality of evidence available to public tribunals as well as to private concerned persons was hard, factual, and unassailable. The authentic records of a slaver's journals coupled with the spiritual testimony of a repentant captain were now added to the flood of economic, philanthropic, and religious objections to slavery.

At least one other Anglican churchman was to break the established church's code of silence and play a leading role in the abolition movement.[60] He was Dr. Peter Peckard, vice-chancellor of Cambridge University and a strong advocate of liberty and human rights. His sermons came to the attention of the French abolition society, the *Amis des Noirs*, who used them as part of their propaganda in the African cause. But Peckard's most lasting contribution to antislavery was made in 1785 when he set as the subject for the undergraduate Latin prize essay the proposition: "Anne liceat invitos in servitutem dare?" (Is it right to enslave persons against their will?) Among that undergraduate class was the young man who was destined to become one of the most tireless campaigners on behalf of the poor Africans. He was Thomas Clarkson, the winner of the prize.

Clarkson had heard Dr. Peckard's sermon the year before and was stirred to learn more about the facts of the trade. For his essay he relied heavily on Benezet's *Historical Account:* "In this precious book," he wrote in a later work, "I found almost all I wanted. I obtained by means of it, a knowledge of, and gained access to great authorities."[61] Clarkson supplemented Benezet's evidence with the personal reports of retired slave trade sailors and with particulars of Africa contained in the writings of travelers like Adanson and Moore. Clarkson was horrified by the excesses, "the enormities," as he called them, of the African trade. His discoveries tormented him to the point of deep melancholy and inner turmoil. He completed his Latin dissertation, entitled *An Essay on the Slavery and Commerce of the Human Species* in 1785 and eagerly resolved to commit his life to ending the Africans' sufferings. He therefore sought immediately to expand the audience of his essay by translating it into English. The translation was published in 1786 by James Phillips, official printer to the Quakers and member of the London Quaker Abolition Committee. This event not only widened the essay's audience but also launched Clarkson into the center of abolitionist politics. He soon became acquainted with leading Quaker activists like William Dillwyn, pioneer of the British abolitionist movement, and other non-Quaker collaborators like the Reverend James Ransay and Granville Sharp. On 21 May 1787 Bennet Langton, a friend of Dr. Johnson's and a "zealous coadjutor in the cause," invited Clarkson to a dinner where his circle of antislavery acquaintances was further enlarged. He was introduced to William Wilberforce, Sir Charles Middleton, William Windham, and Sir Joshua Reynolds, among others.[62] On 22 May 1787, the Society for the Abolition of the Slave Trade was formed in London. It was made up entirely of Quakers, except for Granville Sharp, Thomas Clarkson, and Philip Sanson.

The London society delegated to Clarkson the job of traveling through ports like Bristol, Liverpool, and Manchester, as well as other provincial towns, to gather information concerning the slave trade. He was also to organize local abolition committees and disseminate information about the African cause. Clarkson interviewed some two thousand seamen. He examined the holds of ships and studied their records. Between 1787 and 1794 he made seven journeys and covered thirty-five thousand miles.[63] He uncovered the subterfuges used by unscrupulous slaving interests to decoy English seamen into the trade and the barbarity with which the slaves were treated on shipboard.

Clarkson presented his researches in the *Essay on the Impolicy of the African Slave Trade* (1788). He gave evidence before the Privy Council on 27 July 1788 and tried to persuade a government committee that Britain's relations with Africa should be based upon a wholly new foundation—the foundation of a legitimate commerce mutually beneficial to both Africa and Britain. He offered as proofs of the profitability of this new plan specimens of polished woods, pepper, ivory, musk, gum, spices, and food crops. Clarkson's research cost him great exertions both of body and mind; his health was severely impaired. On one occassion he came very close to violent death when a gang of ruffians tried to push him off a pier in Liverpool. He retired from the committee in 1794 but continued his work in various capacities right through to Emancipation. His friend Thomas De Quincey described him as a "son of thunder, that Titan, who was in fact the one great Atlas that bore up the slave Trade Abolition cause."[64]

The formation of the Abolition Society in 1787 illustrates the Quakers' continuing dedication to antislavery leadership. The work of the seventeenth-century forerunners was unswervingly prosecuted into the eighteenth century when, in 1783, the London Friends set up two committees to prepare a strategy against the slave trade.[65] In that same year they also presented their first petition to Parliament. One of the committees worked almost exclusively disseminating antislavery literature and promoting public relations both in London and in the provinces.[66] That committee was responsible for distributing the influential pamphlet, "The Cause of our Fellow Creatures, the Oppressed Africans . . . etc.," a production of William

Dillwyn and John Lloyd, copies of which were sent to the king and queen, to members of Parliament, and to other powerful dignitaries.[67]

Not only did the Quakers penetrate the corridors of power to press their case, they also worked closely with Blacks like Equiano and Cugoano who were more directly in touch with poor Blacks in London.[68] David Brion Davis points out further that their influence extended into abolition committees outside the Quaker network, and that they were powerful forces behind the work of Clarkson and Sharp and instruments in the organization of the Paris abolitionists, the *Amis des Noirs*.[69]

It is important to emphasize here that the Quaker committee had determined early that its most productive strategy would be to work first for the abolition of the slave trade; that is, to bring an end to the importation of slaves, as against the later goal of emancipation, which was to be the work mainly of abolitionist parliamentarians. The Quakers had reasoned that cutting off the source of supply would force the planters to treat their slaves more humanely, to encourage their natural increase, and to provide for the improvement of their moral and social condition. But as it became evident to the Quakers that the plantocracy would hardly be persuaded to do these things by reasoned appeals, they decided that abolition would be achieved only by hard political lobbying inside Parliament itself.[70] The Quakers' association with Clarkson and Sharp linked them with a group of like-minded humanitarians and religious enthusiasts in Parliament. They found a fruitful alliance in the Clapham Sect and an able champion in William Wilberforce.

The Clapham Sect, or "The Saints," as they came to be known, was a group of Evangelical Anglicans.[71] They brought to bear on the abolitionist movement a consuming passion for philanthropic causes and a fervid commitment to religion in public life. The success of their work underlined the complete failure of institutionalized Anglicanism to address itself to the urgent moral and spiritual issues of the day. The origins of the sect can be traced to the early life of Wilberforce himself.

Wilberforce was born at Hull in 1759. At the age of fourteen, he wrote a letter to a Yorkshire paper condemning the "odious traffic in human flesh." He also did research on slavery in Antigua and had an interview with James Ramsay in 1783. That same year, while on the Grand Tour of the Continent, Wilberforce experienced his spiritual conversion. How fortuitous that Wilberforce's personal awakening should fall in the same year when Clarkson's researches awakened him to the invidiousness of slavery and inspired him to work ceaselessly to stamp it out. In the spring of 1787, Clarkson met Wilberforce and broached to him the idea of collaborating with the Abolition Committee by representing the cause of the Africans in Parliament. Wilberforce relates that he had discussed the slavery question with the prime minister, William Pitt, shortly before his meeting with Clarkson, and that he had decided, on Pitt's recommendation, to raise the issue in the House of Commons.[72] In 1797 Wilberforce married and took up residence at Clapham, on the estate of his uncle, John Thornton.

The Thornton family was wealthy, influential, and well known for unstinting contributions to a wide variety of public charities.[73] It was in John Thornton's great house that the Clapham Sect was born. Nearly all of the members lived at Clapham at some time or other, and between many of them there existed the further bond of marriage. They assembled regularly in each other's houses to discuss the great issues that occupied the contemporary public mind and to plan strategy for parliamentary debate. In the House of Commons they were always unanimous. Reginald Coupland says of them: "The voice of the 'Saints' in Parliament or in the press, was as the voice of one man. It was indeed, a unique phenomenon—this brotherhood of Christian politicians. There has never been anything like it since in British public life."[74]

The members of the Clapham Sect were some of England's greatest statesmen and the chief parliamentary leaders in the crusade for abolition. James Stephen, a young man who had practiced law in the West Indies, returned to England in 1794 with the horrors of slavery fresh in his mind, determined to work for its extinction. Zachary Macaulay, a plantation overseer, whose daily encounters with the inhumanities of the slave system had bred in him a kind of self-preserving indifference, left the West Indies in 1789 and returned to England to gather facts and prepare forceful antislavery arguments on behalf of the Brotherhood. There were Thornton's three sons, Samuel, Robert, and Henry, who all became Members of Parliament. There was Granville Sharp, whose dogged persistence and skill in legal research guaranteed the freedom of Blacks in England. And then there was Thomas Fowell Buxton, Wilberforce's staunchest ally in Parliament, later to become his successor and the finisher of the emancipation fight.

"The Saints" began their parliamentary activities in the closing years of the 1780s. In February 1788 George III had appointed a committee of the Privy Council to hear evidence concerning the slave trade. Pitt and Wilberforce had apparently agreed that this procedure would provide valuable support for the motion when it came before the Commons. In March 1788, when the sessions were to begin, Wilberforce was taken grievously ill and could not attend. It was feared that he would not survive, but he recovered and came back to present his first motion for abolition in May 1789. His speech was a historic three hours long. He sought to prod the conscience of the entire English nation to recognize its collective responsibility for the barbarities of the African trade and for the moral condition of plantation society: "We are all guilty—we ought all to plead guilty, and not to exculpate ourselves by throwing the blame on others; and I therefore deprecate every kind of reflection against the various descriptions of people involved in this wretched business."[75]

Wilberforce clearly demonstrated the Clapham Sect's preoccupation with the need to extend humanitarian principles to improve the lower orders; the sense of outrage "the Saints" felt at the inhumanity of slavery suffuses this part of his speech:

> When we consider the vastness of the continent of Africa; when we reflect how all other countries have for centuries past been advancing in happiness and civilization; when we think how in this same period all improvement in Africa has been defeated by her intercourse with Britain; when we reflect that it is we ourselves that have degraded them to that wretched brutishness and barbarity which we now plead as the justification of our guilt; how the slave trade has enslaved their minds, blackened their character, and sunk them so low in the scale of animal beings, that some think the very apes are of a higher class, and fancy the orang-outang had given them the go-by. What a mortification we feel at having so long neglected to think of our guilt, or to attempt any reparation.[76]

A detailed chronicle of the Clapham Sect's parliamentary struggle for abolition under Wiberforce's persevering leadership exceeds the scope of this study. The process was long and arduous. It also had its moments of high drama and excitement. Wilberforce introduced his motion every year, often laboring under circumstances that would have daunted the stoutest heart. The Clapham Sect continued their campaign by intensifying extra-parliamentary activity. They mounted an unprecedented program of mass propaganda that brought floods of petitions to Parliament. They increased their circulation of antislavery literature and established their own political organ, the *Christian Observer*. The religious fervor that characterized all these initiatives immediately recommended them to a numerous body of middle-class Evangelicals. Support from this quarter of the British population helped to ensure the eventual triumph of the abolitionist cause; for here, for the first time, the interests of plantocratic power were shown to be at variance with the interests of the commercial-industrial elite at home and, philosophically, with those of the whole nation.[77]

In an age of humanitarian sentiment, "the Saints" represented the highest impulses toward the extension of natural rights to the oppressed and toward the relief of suffering. Their strong concern for the dehumanization of the African and their persistent criticism of the colonial economic order laid them open to charges of anarchy and Jacobinism (identification with the ideals of French revolutionary extremists): "At a time when the doctrine [of humanitarianism] was not only trite and commonplace, but novel and dangerous, they valiantly preached the brotherhood of man and the fundamental rights of man, and the shame of permitting for the benefit of commerce what was inherently degrading to humanity itself."[78]

(C) LITERARY

The antislavery movement did not win the concerted advocacy of belle-
tristic writers until the last three decades of the eighteenth century. The slow
response was due to the following three factors. The first was the die-hard
persistence of legalistic doctrines about slavery that helped to shield the
institution from criticism for a long time. The second was that before the
formation of the Abolition Society accelerated the course of antislavery,
literary figures were likely to be as uninformed about the true nature of the
slave trade as ordinary citizens. The third reason was the relation of such
figures to the temper of their times. Like the parliamentarians, the philosophers, and the churchmen, they found it hard to escape the prejudices of
their age: some could accept the idea of Black people's humanity only with
reservation; others might concede kindred humanity but found the thought
of the Black's social equality unpalatable.[79] It is not surprising, therefore,
that the earliest appearance of the African in English literature was as an
abstract literary idealization rather than as a figure of unquestionable
human identity.

The idealized figure of the "Noble Negro," which begins to appear in late
seventeenth-century literature, bears little resemblance to the common
plantation slave who became the consuming preoccupation of abolitionist
writers. The "Noble Negro" is princely, heroic. He is endowed with all the
natural virtues of courage and moral incorruptibility that European primi-
tivists liked to imagine were the distinctive marks of primitive humanity.
This literary ideal clearly informs the vision of Mrs. Aphra Behn's celebrated work, *Oroonoko* (1688).

The hero of that work, Oroonoko, is high-born and high-minded; his
physical features are more Roman-patrician than negroid. Oroonoko is
fearless in the face of his masters' torture and treachery, and faithful in love
to the beautiful Imoinda. Altogether, the lineaments of his origin and character serve to set him apart from the much maligned, downtrodden slave.
Mrs. Behn's fictional portrait conformed more nearly to the artificial models
of conventional heroic tragedy, as exemplified by Dryden, than to the actual
particulars of slavery that a Ramsay or Raynal described for definite humanitarian purposes. Wylie Sypher strongly denies any genuine antislavery
design in Oroonoko: "Mrs. Behn is not repelled by slavery," he perceives,
"but by the enslaving of a prince."[80]

Mrs. Behn's *Oroonoko* went through many editions, translations, and
adaptations. In 1696 Thomas Southerne dramatized *Oroonoko,* and the
subsequent stage history of that production was nothing short of phe-
nomenal; the play was performed at least once every season until 1801. The

relation of the Oroonoko legend to antislavery, however, rests more in the metamorphosis wrought through changing audience interpretation over the years than in what its original authors proposed. It established the tradition of the "Noble Negro," an image that, although highly sentimentalized and unrealistic, stirred most English citizens' consciousnesses to consider more seriously the plight of the African and the ineluctable proofs of Britain's complicity in crimes against humanity.

That Mrs. Behn and Southerne lacked genuine humanitarian commitment in their work must be attributed to the pervasive ambivalences of their age. The Augustans could shed the tear of social sympathy with one eye while winking at injustice with the other. In general, they were too sensible of the inequities on which their Golden Age of progress and stability was built to make any unequivocal stand for enlightened egalitarianism. That had to wait until the next century.

Daniel Defoe was a case in point. In *Reformation of Manners* (1702), a satirical work ranging widely over a multitude of evils, he denounced the slave trade. But fourteen years earlier he had supported the same trade in his *Essay on Projects* (1688). Forty years after *Reformation* we find him urging the continued growth of the slave trade in his *Plan of the English Commerce*. This inconsistency is a consistent reflection of Defoe's tradesman's mentality. His was an unremitting voice for the vigorous promotion of free trade all over the world; his glowing paeans to the virtues of an enlightened commerce are identical with the spirit of proslavery panegyrics appearing later in the century.

Richard Savage, on the other hand, conceived of a colonial enterprise that would yield the best of both worlds—prosperity for the Englishman and liberty for the African. He recognized the value of the plantations to the British economy and supported their development, but he discountenanced the subjugation and enslavement of the Africans:

> Why must I Afric sable children see
> Vender for slaves though formed by nature free,
> The nameless tortures cruel minds invent,
> Those to subject whom nature equal meant.
>
> ("Of Public Spirit" [1737], 141)

Savage was probably the first English poet of mark to devote more than passing attention to the moral implications of colonialism and to plead for compassion for the Black slave. Samuel Johnson, in his *Lives of the English Poets,* particularly praised the tenderness and sympathy Savage displayed in this poem and commended his courage in asserting "the natural equality of mankind" at a time when such ideas were still subject to suspicion.[81]

By midcentury Johnson was stating his own opposition to slavery on the basis of natural rights. He was particularly critical of the Europeans' motives for undertaking voyages of exploration: "The Europeans have scarcely visited any coast, but to gratify avarice, and extend corruption; to arrogate dominion without right, and practise cruelty without incentive."[82] In the same place, he decried the wanton brutality of the Portuguese in firing on the bewildered Africans during their first contacts on the African coast: "We are openly told that they had less scruple concerning their treatment of the savage people, because they scracely considered them as distinct from beasts."[83]

Johnson's biographer, James Boswell, relates that Johnson always hated slavery with a passion, and that on one occasion at Oxford, he made a toast "to the next insurrection of the negroes in the West Indies."[84] Johnson recognized the flagrant irony in the Anerican colonists' revolt against British rule: "How is it," he asked, "that we hear the loudest yelps for liberty among the drivers of negroes?" Johnson's championship of the Black cause is remarkable, for he was a Tory in politics and fundamentally conservative in most things. It was undoubtedly his deeply humane spirit that set his face so firmly against the unjust institution of slavery.

But Boswell was not convinced. He thought Johnson's opinions were the result of "prejudice and imperfect or false imformation." True Whig that he was, Boswell fully appreciated the extensive profits that accrued to the nation from the slave trade and the slave colonies, and so he could muster nothing better than this specious attempt to justify slavery, a claim that it benefited both Englishmen and Africans: "To abolish a status which in all ages God has sanctioned, and man has continued, would not only be robbery to an innumerable class of our fellow subjects; but it would be extreme cruelty to the African Savages, a portion of whom it saves from massacre, or intolerable bondage in their own country, and introduces into a much happier state of life."[85]

And that idyll of slavery would gain credibility as long as the public remained ignorant of the harsh truth. James Thomson, although more enraptured with the pride and beauty of the African wilderness than with the human value of the Africans themselves, pitied the hapless slaves who were unceremoniously uprooted and loaded on to ships bound for strange lands. He provided for the English readers one of the first pictures of the horrors that attended the Middle Passage. Lured by the scent of rotting flesh and jettisoned corpses, a shark stalks the slave ship:

> Behold he rushing cuts the briny flood,
> Swift as the gale can bear the ship along;
> And from the partners of that cruel trade
> Which spoils unhappy Guinea of her sons
> Demands his share of prey—demands themselves.
>
> ("Summer," from *The Seasons,* 1016–21)

That was in 1727. As yet, writers still contrived to subsume their antipathy to the slave system beneath the formal literary ornaments of euphemism and periphrasis. Even James Grainger, who became known as the bard of the sugar cane, was apt to romanticize the West Indian neighorhood and sentimentalize the lot of the slave in his georgic to plantation society, *The Sugar Cane* (1764). His effusions were of this order:

> Nor Negro, at thy destiny repine
> Though doom'd to toil from dawn to setting sun
> How far more pleasant is thy rural task,
> Than theirs who sweat, sequester'd from the day
> In dark tartarean caves, sunk far beneath
> The Earth's surface.
>
> (4, 165–70)

Grainger typified many other Englishmen of his day who, as men of sense, regretted the slaves' suffering, but as men of property could not bring themselves to dismantle the system that inflicted that suffering.[86] Grainger owned slaves on his Saint Kitts estates. His familiarity with African character and manners lends veracity to his delineations of the different tribal types that were to be found in the West Indies. The slave for him always remains a feeling human, albeit an unfortunate one:

> Howe'er insensate some may deem their slaves,
> Nor 'bove the bestial rank; far other thoughts
> The Muse, soft daughter of Humanity!
> Will ever entertain.—The Ethiop knows,
> The Ethiop feels, when treated like a man.
>
> (4, 421–25)

The poetry is not fashioned to serve the ends of truth, nor can it accommodate itself to the urgency of a political moment; but it has benevolism and, as we have seen, this was a necessary antecedent to the more practical humanitarianism of the last years of the century.

Nearly one hundred years after *Oroonoko* was first published, the literary successors of Aphra Behn and Thomas Southerne began transforming the original idealized hero of European myth making into a distinctly political symbol. The "Noble Negro" was not only an enslaved prince, exhibiting the classical qualities of terror and fear and defying his enemies with an indomitable spirit, but he was now being presented as a man of feeling, a benevolist whom slavery scarred and demoralized. In this figure, he was supposed to represent the human virtues of all African slaves, not the overdrawn excellences of a primitivistic ideal. The capacity for feeling, for compassion, and for generosity established the Black's claim to equality with the white. It was the abundance and legitimacy of these virtues that commended the African as a literary figure and Sancho as a literary artist to the reading public. "Beyond any doubt," Philip Curtin observes, "the use of the savage hero as a literary device helped to create a much more favorable emotional climate for Africans than they would otherwise have enjoyed."[87]

Nowhere is the literary myth of the "Noble Negro" more strikingly transfigured than in that minor poetic genre commonly known as the "Dying Negro Poems." Thomas Day was its most worshipful exponent; his poem, "The Dying Negro," its immortal prototype. Although Day has traditionally been given credit for its authorship, the poem was actually a collaborative effort between him and his friend, John Bicknell. The poem is a tragic tale of heroism and natural passion. It seems to have been occasioned by the report of a slave who had escaped his master's custody and planned to receive baptism as a preliminary to marrying a white woman. His master got wind of his plan, recaptured him, and placed him on a ship bound for America. The slave killed himself rather than accept renewed bondage. The sentiments of the poem are noble and the tone high-serious. Day emphasizes the native worth of the African by pointing to his devaluation by European slavery:

> Fallen are my trophies, blasted my fame,
> Myself become a thing without a name
> The sport of haughty lords, and even of slaves the shame.

He makes the Black slave's love for his white bride-to-be as strong as any classical or romantic hero's and certainly superior to any passion of the oppressing antagonists.

> And I have loved thee with as pure a fire
> As man e'er felt, or woman could inspire
> No pangs like these my pallid tyrants know,
> Not such their transports, and not such their woe.
> Their softer frames a feeble soul conceal,
> a Soul unus'd to pity or to feel;
> Damped by base lucre and repelled by fear,
> Each noble passion faintly blazes there.

The hero dies in the hope that Africa will one day triumph over her enemies. He thunders an apocalyptic vision of conquest and revenge. His final utterance is a gesture of triumph and defiance:

> Receive me falling, and your suppliant hear
> To you this unpolluted blood I pour,
> To you that spirit which ye gave restore.

The final two lines were to become the epitome of the Black's unquenchable spirit in "Noble Negro" mythology. They were some of the most frequently quoted lines in abolitionist writing.

Day's poem had its objective equivalent not only in an actual suicide but also in the famous case of James Somerset, the determination of which was to be a milestone in the abolitionists' struggle. Somerset's victory was to furnish the legal precedent on which Blacks in England could thereafter stake their claim to self-possession and resist forcible constraint by slave agents.

Somerset had accompanied his master James Stewart from Virginia to England in 1769 and deserted him there in 1771. Stewart had him recaptured and placed on a ship, intending to sell him into slavery in Jamaica. Granville Sharp and other African sympathizers procured a writ of *habeas corpus* and had Somerset released. They sought to have this case resolved on the principle of the individual's right to personal liberty and to declare that no man could be a slave in England. Much tactical stalling and many procedural complications delayed the course of justice, some of them expressly in the interests of the slave lobby. Finally in June 1772, Chief Justice Mansfield gave his judgment that a slave owner could not forcibly remove a slave from England. Although Mansfield adeptly circumvented the pivotal issue of slavery's legality, his decision was widely interpreted as conferring absolute freedom on slaves in England, and that assumption further intensified literary protest in the decade following the publication of Day's poem.

The Abolition Committee gave active support to writers of antislavery verse, and it devised a thoroughly effective machinery for the dissemination thereof. One of the first productions that was given to the public under the committee's aegis was William Roscoe's poem, "The Wrongs of Africa" (1787–88). Roscoe's poem paints Africans sympathetically and upbraids Britain, the champion of liberty, for its rapacious greed and cruelty in the slavery business. Roscoe's hero, Cymbello, is, like Day's, a fierce, spirited, apocalyptic figure; his deeds presage the imminent collapse of the West Indian system.

The committee was also instrumental in influencing England's most popular poet of the last two decades of the century to wield his pen in the service of the slaves' cause. William Cowper, that poet, was neither by temperament nor by inclination fitted for political movements, but he was a truehearted humanitarian and an intense Evangelical. He found slavery indefensible and censured the ruthlessness of Britain's commercial and imperialistic designs upon African and other primitive peoples.[88] Cowper believed in the equal brotherhood of all men under the fatherhood of God. He also believed that Africans, like all primitive peoples, possessed souls that made them just as worthy of freedom as "civilized" Europeans.

Cowper's earliest attacks on slavery came in "Charity" (1782). There he characterized the slave trade as loathsome and deplored its destruction of the social bonds that knit humankind together as a single race. In *The Task* (1785) He expressed an equally vehement distaste for the idea of slaves as personal property:

> I would not have a slave to till my ground,
> To carry me, to fan me while I sleep,
> And tremble when I wake, for all the wealth
> That sinews bought and gold have earned.
>
> (29–32)

Cowper became an unwitting propagandist for the abolitionist campaign when the committee distributed thousands of copies of his poem "The Negro's Complaint" (1788) all over England. The verses of this poem, along with those of two other Cowper pieces, "The Morning Dream" (1788) and "Sweet Meat Has Sour Sauce" (1788), were set to music and sung as popular ballads in the streets. "The Morning Dream" proclaimed a vision of Liberty, a female figure, sailing to the West Indies to free the slaves. Oppression is vanquished at her sight and thousands of Black voices raises shouts of joy at their release from enslavement.

Among the eminent literary figures of the eighteenth century, Cowper undoubtedly holds first place for the volume of his work specifically addressed to slavery and the impact that it had on the popularization of antislavery. As the wave of abolitionist writing crested in the 1790s, other major poets raised their voices too. The Romantics paid tribute to the humanitarian revolution in modest but memorable tokens.

Coleridge won the Browne Gold Medal at Cambridge University for his "Ode on the Slave Trade" (1792), and he lectured at Bristol on the slave trade in 1795. Southey wrote a series of "Slave Trade Sonnets" (1794) condemning the slave traders and invoking the injured Africans to drive the European intruders out of their country with all their native strength. Wordsworth's enthusiasm was hesitant and belated. He had been disillusioned by the sorry turn in the tide of French revolutionary affairs, after he had thrown his full moral support behind its high ideals at the outset in 1789. In 1792 he confessed a deepening disenchantment with political movements, as the reign of terror and orgiastic bloodshed gripped France. But with the abolition bill bidding fair for passage in Parliament, he wrote a sonnet to Thomas Clarkson (1807) and another to Toussaint L'Ouverture, the black Haitian revolutionary (1807).

As might be expected, the saturation of the mass media with antislavery propaganda satiated the public mind. As enthusiasm for the original ideals of the French Revolution began to flag with the coming into leadership of extremists, so too in the 1790s abolition showed a decline, as slave uprisings

in the West Indies, some of them bloody and terrifying to white supre-
macists, occurred with increasing frequency. Anna Letitia Barbauld, an
uncommonly gifted woman and an earnest campaigner for antislavery,
complained in her "Epistle to Wilberforce" (1791) that the country had
grown impervious and deceitful through its love of ease and pleasure:

> Each flimsy sophistry by turns they try;
> The plausive argument, the daring lie,
> The artful gloss, the moral sense confounds,
> The acknowledged thirst of gain that honour wounds.
>
> (25–30)

Thomas Campbell's "Pleasures of Hope" (1799) reflects the waning of the
"Noble Negro" sentimental fashion. No longer is the sad plight of the enslaved African the burden of poetic song; that theme has diminished to mere
allusions. Campbell strains more toward a vision of universal improvement
as the source of healing for a troubled and imperfect world:

> Where barbarous hordes on Scythian mountains roam,
> Truth, Mercy, Freedom, yet shall find a home;
> Where'er degraded Nature bleeds and pines
> From Guinea's coasts to Sibir's dreary mines
> Truth shall pervade the unfathom'd darkness there,
> And light the dreadful features of despair.
>
> (1, 350–55)

Only James Montgomery seemed not to have lost the old fervor, the revolutionary optimism that characterized abolitionists of the two preceding
decades. Montgomery had long been an uncompromising foe of slavery and
a friend of the Africans. His poem, "The West Indies" (1807), depicts Africans in their familiar surroundings as industrious, peaceful, and hospitable.
Montgomery never doubted the human identity of his subjects:

> Is he not man by sin and suffering tried?
> Is he not man, for whom the Saviour died?
> Believe the Negro's powers:—in headlong will,
> Christian! thy brother thou shalt prove him still;
> Belie his virtues; since his wrongs began,
> His follies and his crimes have stampt him Man.
>
> (2, 107–12)

But even Montgomery, for all his ardor, was forced to acknowledge the
declining enthusiasm for antislavery at this time. He observed that "Public
feeling had been wearied into insensibility by the agony of interest which the

question of the African slave trade excited during three and twenty years of intense and almost incessant discussion."[89] Now in the first decade of the new century, other causes and other issues were claiming priority in politics and literature. The antislavery movement had not died, but it was obviously cooling. The forces of reaction had started to brand abolitionists as anarchists, levellers, whose principles, they feared, would bring on Britain the same political instability and social unrest that were currently rife in France.

It only remains now to consider the role played by periodical literature specifically, in spreading abolitionist ideas, and also generally, in stimulating public awareness about the condition of the African. The eighteenth century saw the rise and flourishing of periodicals and literary magazines. And just as the older literary genres turned increasingly to the defence of common humanity and human integrity, the periodicals likewise reflected the widespread discussion of the problem of slavery. In general, the last three decades of the century saw the same intense agitation and debate in the periodicals as in verse, drama, and fiction.

In no journal were the twin issues of slavery and the slave trade debated with greater animation than in the *Gentleman's Magazine*. Undoubtedly one of the most widely circulated magazines of the day, this journal began noticing the Black presence in 1764. Between 1770 and 1780, as antislavery protest mounted, the magazine's pages resonated with the claims and counterclaims of spokesmen on either side of the debate. When later on, the African became a figure of sentimentality and heroic romance, the *Gentleman's Magazine* also reflected the fashion by printing dozens of the "Noble Negro" poems. The delineations of this idealized African were not significantly different from those described above, but the *Gentleman's* verses seemed to emphasize the idyll of an illustrious past. Snatched from the clinging arms of wife and children, the noble African, who had spent his early years in feats of bravery and adventure, is now dragged away to sea, to a life of fear and coercion:

> Everything I see affright me
> Nothing I can understand,
> With the scourges white man fight me,
> None of this is Negro land.
> ("The African's Complaint on-Board a Slave Ship,"
> *The Gentleman's Magazine* 63[1793]: 749)

The periodicals popularized the image of the African as a child of Nature who felt deeply the pangs of separation from his pastoral haunts, who pined for the felicities of hearth and home, who practiced hospitality to strangers, and whose generosity and innocence were nearly always betrayed by the white man's guile. Thomas Adney's "The Slave," which appeared in the

European Magazine (July–December 1792), vilifies the European by its ironic compliments and humanizes the African slave by underscoring his moral
virtues:

> What tho' no flush adorn my face,
> Nor silken tresses deck my hair,
> Altho' debarr'd of polish'd grace
> And scorn'd by those more haply fair;
> Yet in my veins does honour roll,
> Tho' subject to a tyrant's call;
> Heav'n gave to man a noble soul,
> And not to seek a Brother's fall.
>
> (160–68)

Natural goodness was but one of the Black person's virtues celebrated in
the pathetic verses of the popular journals. Mungo, a stock symbol of the
suffering, abused African, was also capable of feeling:

> I am a slave when all things else are free.
> Yet I was born, as you are, no man's slave
> An heir to all that lib'ral nature gave:
> My thoughts can reason, and my limbs can move
> The same as yours; like yours my heart can love.[90]
>
> ("Mungo's Address," 10–14)

By taking the rhetoric of their cause to the pages of the periodical press,
the abolitionist agents ensured that their ideas received optimal exposure
through the frequent publication and mass circulation of the popular journals. In this way, favorable notions about African character were disseminated and became fixed in the public mind, eventually transforming
themselves into myths useful to abolitionist propaganda. The soul of the
dead slave, for instance, always returned to its native Africa where it was
welcomed in ceremonies befitting a hero. The daring hope of a revitalized
Africa, rising up to visit revenge on her foes and to restore the arts of liberty
and peace to the land, remained a cherished vision in these poems until as
late as 1809:

> Now Christian, now, in wild dismay,
> Of Afric's proud revenge the prey,
> Go roam the affrighted wood;
> Transformed to tigers fierce and fell
> Thy race shall prowl with savage yell;
> And glut their rage for blood.
>
> ("Ode on Seeing a Negro Funeral," 31–36)

The *Edinburgh Review,* in the liberal tradition of the Scottish Enlightenment, lost no opportunity to come to the defense of Blacks, traduced as they often were by proslavery polemicists. One contributor to the *Review* stoutly controverted the claims of a detracting work, in which Africans were stigmatized as foul-smelling, ill-favored and "only one step removed from the state of beasts." The reviewer maintained that Africans, as part of mankind, were capable of improvement like all other members of the human family. He pointed to the Blacks' successful strategy and execution of the Saint Domingue revolt (1791) as compelling evidence of their superior capabilities.[91]

The foregoing survey of the broad intellectual background to abolition illustrates a timely convergence of powerful ideological currents that created a more favorable climate for Blacks to live in and a more receptive audience for Black literary expression than would otherwise have prevailed in eighteenth-century Britain. The cult of benevolism established the principle that all human beings were capable of sensations of pleasure and pain and urged the desirability of working for the increase of the one and the avoidance of the other, particularly on behalf of one's fellow creatures. It forced people to reexamine the proslavery polemicists' rationalization that Blacks were suited to slavery because they were incapable of feeling its rigors. As the Enlightenment promoted the systematic study of humanity and human societies, Europeans began to reconcile themselves to the idea that the African was a legitimate member of the human race and that it would be highly beneficial to universal progress to accept Africa into the community of nations.

Gradually, the pronouncements of leading humanitarians rejected the assumption of Black inferiority and asserted the moral and intellectual equality of the Black slave with the white master. The result was bound to undermine the philosophical foundations on which the colonial slave system was established. For some, the African slave became humanized. Once it was acknowledged that Blacks had a moral nature and intellectual capacity, it was reasonable to believe that they could attain the humanistic ideal of perfectibility.

Enthusiastic negrophiles were fascinated by the thought that the pure blood and robust strength of the African could serve as a potent force in the shaping of a new civilization, the image of which was often mirrored in the mythology of "Noble Negro" poems.[92] Some abolitionist visionaries went further and predicted that European civilization would be eclipsed and eventually supplanted by an Africa revivified and restored to become the center of universal culture and progress. But a great number of abolitionists—and progressivists generally—shared the optimistic view of continuing progress for Africa as well as for Europe. They envisioned the replacement of the lopsided, antihumanitarian trade in slaves by a flourishing trade in more conventional material goods, a system of enlightened commercial relationships and cultural exchange that would ideally yield equal benefits for both Africans and Europeans.

The detailed analysis of the following three chapters will identify each writer in this study with a particular phase in the development of abolitionist ideology. This is intended only to reflect the major emphases and recurrent motifs to be found in each writer's work. It is not to suggest that the full place and meaning of Sancho, Cugoano, or Equiano can be assessed by means of exclusive definitions. The truth is that each writer was motivated by all the dominant impulses that made abolition and emancipation possible. The three Africans were no less products of the Enlightenment than their European counterparts.

3

Ignatius Sancho: Moral Suasion and the Benevolent Self

To appraise the literary merits of eighteenth-century Afro-English writing is to study the acculturation to British life of three highly articulate Black men. To weigh the individual contributions to antislavery of Sancho, Cugoano, and Equiano is to trace the emergence of a special kind of racial and political consciousness in each writer that defined the extent of his acculturation. That measure in turn determined the rhetorical strategies each author employed in his work as a vehicle for abolitionist ideas and as a way of resisting the whole complex of negative images that concerted to devalue the humanity of Blacks everywhere. While Cugoano and Equiano could use their personal recollections of boyhood experiences, family life, and tribal customs to celebrate the validity of African culture, the accidents of Sancho's birth and upbringing denied him all these. He was, quite literally, a child of Georgian England and a creature of Western civilization. These were the two chief formative conditions that constrained him to choose moral suasion as a strategy for abolitionist ideas and sentimental benevolism as a frame for self-portrayal.

Ignatius Sancho was born in 1729 aboard a slave ship that was transporting his mother and father to slavery in the West Indies.[1] Neither of his parents survived the hardships of initial adjustment: his father committed suicide and his mother died soon after arrival. A ship's captain brought the infant Sancho to England at the age of two and presented him to "three maiden sisters at Greenwich." Thus Sancho was initiated early into the ritual of loss and separation that all Blacks, uprooted and transplanted through the slave trade, came to inherit in the New World.

Sancho's guardians refused to educate him. In their ignorance and prejudice, they reasoned that education would almost certainly unfit him for that state of service and obedience to which most Blacks in England were relegated. But Sancho was curious about books. His quick mind and engaging address won him the favor of the duke and duchess of Montagu, neighbors of his guardians.[2] Unknown to them, the duchess nurtured Sancho's interest in learning by giving him books from the duke's library to read. The duke himself pleaded with the squeamish maiden ladies to educate Sancho, but they would not be moved. When Sancho persisted in his quest for knowledge, they threatened to return him to the West Indies as a slave. At twenty, Sancho finally abandoned his mistresses and entered service in the Montagu household in 1749 (the duke, his first patron, had only recently died).

At the duchess' decease, she bequeathed Sancho an annuity of a hundred and thirty pounds. But the loss of a loving and generous friend drove him into a bout of reckless spending, gambling, and wild living. About this time, he met David Garrick and might have started a career in the theater were it not for some defective mannerism in his speech.

After that heady interlude, Sancho returned to the Montagu household to become personal attendant to the third duke, George Brudenell. From this time on, his life ran a rather more steady course. At Montagu House he learned the manners of polite society and cultivated a taste for literature, art, and music. There, too, he met Laurence Sterne, who was to become his lifelong friend and idol. He also met and married Anne, "a deserving young woman of West Indian origin."[3]

Advancing middle age brought upon Sancho the miseries of gout and the discomfort of overweight. He was forced to leave the Montagus' service and set up house on his own in Charles Street, Westminster, where he also opened a shop and raised a family of six children.

The shop quickly became the focal point not only of Sancho's domestic life but also of his diverse social and intellectual interests. Now humoring the persistent prattle of a toddling child, now scribbling a letter of friendship between serving customers or receiving the visit of a duchess or an artist friend, he was as likely to be reading a Voltaire tragedy as to be composing a minuet of his own. Several light musical compositions and a *Theory of Music* have been attributed to him.[4] His knowledge of painting won him the respect of the painter John Hamilton Mortimer, who came regularly to consult his opinions on painting. He sat for Gainsborough at Bath. The Gainsborough portrait is now the property of the Canadian National Gallery in Ottawa. Sancho died on 14 December 1780.

After his death, a friend and regular correspondent, Mrs. F. Crewe, collected his letters and published them in 1782. Sancho himself had made no such request, but Mrs. Crewe conceived the idea to express her loyalty to his memory and to announce to the world the exceptional accomplishments of this specimen of African improvability. A subscription list of over six hundred names attests to the interest that this literary event generated. The reviewer in the *European Magazine* recommended the *Letters* to all those desirous of "promoting the common elevation of the human race" and cited them as testimony that "endowments of the mind are not restricted by any accidents such as race or geographic origin."[5]

That reviewer (and undoubtedly other readers of like discerning) quickly grasped the significance of public accessibility to the thoughts and sentiments of a man "whose species philosophers and anatomists have endeavoured to degrade as a deterioration of the human species." But Sancho himself, living and writing in an earlier time, was restrained from exploiting the full power of his facility with the written word by two important conditions that circumscribed his life continually. He had to be wary of alienating the sympathies of an audience that was decidedly not yet ready for abolition, although it might have subscribed to many of the liberal clichés of the age. But he also could not ignore his need to express the private tensions he felt as a Black man, born in slavery and partially assimilated to the values of European civilization. It was, in short, a chaos out of which Sancho had to order a personal and authorial identity.

Sancho endeavored to satisfy both demands by carefully modulating his rhetorical strategy to harmonize with the fashionable currents of thought and feeling with which his readers identified. He had to select a language that would stir the social conscience of his audience without arousing their Augustan distaste for radical causes. To fulfill these requirements, he chose the language of the heart, identifying himself passionately with the cult of benevolism and religious enthusiasm, the broadest bases from which early antislavery objections were launched in England. These choices are indicative not only of Sancho's spiritual identification with his time, but also of his ability to manipulate his audience's impulses to general liberalism and philanthropy.

The letters are replete with high moral sentences, reflecting the general moral philosophy of the age. Sancho consistently expresses an unshakable faith in the possibility of a brighter world, even though his middle years were marred by ailing health and the relative security of his life in England troubled by the enslavement of Africans in the New World and the destitution of Blacks in England. He put his trust in "hope" and "self-love" that the future would usher in an era of universal amelioration (Letter 28, p.58).[6] To a friend anxious about material success, he counseled, "Time and patience conquer all things" (Letter 113, p.229). And a deep faith in the biblical promise of a new heaven and a new earth nurtured in him the vision of a golden eternity: "I am convinced in our next habitation there will be no care—love will possess our souls—and praise and harmony—and ever fresh rays of knowledge, wonder, and mutual communication will be our employ" (Letter 109, p.222). His was a distinctly Augustan frame of mind. It exemplified that "stability of settled desires and tempered ambitions"[7] which English people devised as a useful myth to defend themselves against anarchy. Sancho adopted this fiction to help him sublimate his natural anxieties about the powerlessness and suffering of his Black brothers and sisters beneath the profession of a widely shared enlightened faith in human perfectibility. A 1772 letter to Julius S[oubis]e, whose giddy life often prompted Sancho's sober admonitions, demonstrates his concern for the improvement of the Black condition: "Look around upon the miserable fate of almost all our unfortunate colour—super-added to ignorance—see slavery, and the contempt of those very wretches who roll in affluence from our labours. Superadded to this woeful catalogue—hear the ill-bred and heart-wracking abuse of the vulgar. You S[oubis]e, tread as cautiously as the strictest rectitude can guide ye—yet must you suffer from this—but armed with truth—honesty—and conscious integrity—you will be sure of the plaudit and countenance of the good" (Letter 14, pp.31–32).

Sancho seems to have taken the position that Blacks could hardly expect any sudden alleviation of their adversities as long as white society remained virtually impervious to the dire conditions of their own kin, while ironically paying lip service to benevolence and the cult of sympathetic feelings. One historian describes the chilling irony of that enlightened age thus: "Effusions went hand in hand with exploitation; men who piously lamented the lot of the slaves, coolly sent their children to the mines at home. . . . Yet this myopic humanity was the fumbling response to unprecedented social changes; it was the piecemeal, often painful attempt to construct a coherent attitude appropriate to a new society struggling to be born."[8] The age of blessed philanthropy was also the age of blissful contradictions.

Inevitably, Sancho understood and shared these limitations and inconsistencies. Adopting the manners and assumptions of the English helped him to enjoy a high measure of security among them; but the immutable legacy of his birth and racial origin divided his psychic allegiance permanently. The forced migration of his parents had alienated him from Africa, and the vagaries of the displaced life equally alienated him from a true sense of place in European culture. Yet, paradoxical as it may seem, he belonged to Europe in a very special and inalienable way. He was a creature of its infamous system of economic relations with Africa and a product of its system of patronage towards a privileged number of "darling Blacks" like himself.[9]

Whatever might have been his private feelings about the English people's shortcomings, he was usually tactful enough to couch his objections in the broadest terms of support for liberty in political life, egalitarianism in social life, and toleration in matters of religion. "I thank God," he rejoiced in a letter setting out his reflections on these subjects, "that I am no bigot—but honour virtue—and the practice of the great moral duties—equally in the turban—or in the lawn sleeves—who think heaven big enough for all the race of man—and hope to see and mix among the whole family of Adam in bliss hereafter (which perhaps some may style absurd)" (Letter 58, p.126).

Some critics are inclined to see this as weak-spirited, temporizing rhetoric. Edwards and Walvin call these effusions "a self-indulgent sentimentalism more concerned with virtuous acts of charity than with the cruelties it claims to alleviate."[10] But in associating himself with these widely approved liberal principles, Sancho was placing himself safely within the respectable pale of the Enlightenment—safely, because, up to the 1780s, the Enlightenment was perhaps the only intellectual citadel from which dissidents could attack traditional values and institutions.

It is perhaps fairer to Sancho and more realistic to his time to see his attitude as identical with the gradualism of early abolitionist leaders.[11] It must be remembered that during the years of Sancho's early manhood, 1750–60, there was as yet no organized political opposition to slavery and, further, that those leaders like Benezet and Clarkson, who led the debate in following decade, did so from a fundamentally religious and humanitarian standpoint. Even statesmen as active in the later struggle for emancipation as Buxton, Canning, and Wilberforce, who held more political power than Sancho or any other Black leader of the time, were still urging a policy of gradualism as late as 1824. Besides, Sancho knew what he must do to preserve his special relations with the privileged classes. For them he fashioned a self-conscious image of himself as a literate, social being, genial and urbane, dedicated to the Augustan values of individual wholeness and goodwill to all.

Lifelong admirer of Uncle Toby's affectionate good nature as depicted by Sterne in *Tristram Shandy*, Sancho spent his life studiously cultivating the art of friendship. With Edward Young, he believed that friendship was the "balsam of life," and he drew deeply from the accumulated experience of the ages, combining that with his personal and spiritual gifts to place them all at the disposal of his correspondents and friends. Sometimes, as in this letter to J——W——E, a young man seeking his fortune in colonial India, he counseled like a father, in the manner of Lord Chesterfield to his son:

> You will of course make Men and Things your study—their different genius, aims and passions:—You will also note climes, buildings, soils, and products, which will be neither tedious nor unpleasant—If you adopt the rule of writing every evening your remarks of the past day, it will be a kind of friendly tête-à-tête between you and yourself, wherein you may sometimes happily become your own monitor;—and hereafter those little notes will afford you a rich fund, wherever you shall be inclined to retrace past times and places. (Letter 1, p.3)

Sometimes we find him studiously advancing the interests of a friend, as in a letter to Mr. I—— whose influence he courts to promote the "hobby horses" of a fledgling artist "speedily into the world" (Letter 65, p.142).[12] When a young lady friend is forced to travel by night on her return journey from London, Sancho recaptures for her in a letter the shifting sensations with which his mind followed her progress. His emotions run the gamut from anxious care, while she is on the road, to warm relief when she arrives: "Well, now she is above halfway—Alas: she will not get home till Saturday night—I wonder what companions she has met with, . . . Well, night arrives and now our friend has reached the open arms of parental love—excess of delightful endearments gives place to tranquil enjoyments—and all are happy in the pleasure they give each other" (Letter 33, p.65).

Nothing gratified him more highly than the conversation of true friends. He was lavish in his invitations for their company, and they requited with gracious visits and edifying discourse. The fashionable coffeehouses of London had little to boast over the shop at the southwest corner of Crown Court where Sancho sold laundry blue, soap, and candles. Sancho played host to patrons as diverse as the duchess of Queensberry; David Garrick, the actor; Joseph Nollekens, the artist; and John Hamiltion Mortimer, the painter. A veritable lust for the uses of conviviality burns through these lines from a letter to Mrs. F——, whom he wants to come and share the joy of Mrs. Sancho's convalescence: "Come, do come, and see what a different face she wears now—to what she did when you kindly proved yourself her tender, her assisting friend.—Come and scamper in the meadows with the three ragged wild girls.—Come and pour the balm of friendly converse into the ear of my sometimes lowspirited love. Come, do come, if you mean to see the autumn in its last livery" (Letter 6, p.16).[13]

While Sancho gave generously from his rich storehouse of sociability and loving-kindness, he also drew freely from the bounty of his privileged acquaintances. Although his pension and the modest profits from shopkeeping shielded him from the abject poverty of his less fortunate brothers and sisters, he was still straitened to provide for a wife and six "Sanchonetas" (as he fondly called his children). The patronage of friends in affluent circumstances regularly supplied his miscellaneous personal and household needs. Whether it was a side of venison or a fawn from Mr. M——; a bottle of wine from I——S——, Esq.; or the gift of a "sweet and highly finished portrait of my dear Sterne" from Mr. S——; Sancho received every one with the humble thanks of a sensible heart. He had the ironic gift of effusively praising his benefactors so that they could feel the correct measure of self-righteous virtue for having dispensed charity and he a disarming sense of obligation to the beneficiary for affording them the opportunity to be beneficent:

> I have been well informed there's a Mr. S——at Bury—and I think I have seen the gentleman—who lives in a constant course of doing beneficent actions—and, upon these occasions, the pleasure he feels constitutes him the obliged party.—You, good sir, ought of course to thank me—for adding one more to the number you are pleased to be kind to—so pray remember, good sir, that my thanks (however due in the eye of gratitude) I conceive to be an act of supererogation—and expect that henceforth you will look upon the Sanchos—as a family that have a rightful call upon you notice. (Letter 57, p.124)

This artful use of wit and rhetorical virtuosity to subvert the conventional decorums associated with acts of giving and receiving recurs in at least three other letters.[14] In the passage cited above, the Mr. S—— referred to is the very recipient of the letter, but, by a tactful shift into the objective third person and a thrusting of the sardonic tongue into the authorial cheek, Sancho anticipates from his correspondent the artificial modesty people commonly evince at having their virtues sung and masks his own ambivalence about this form of civilized deceit. There is a discreet subversiveness about the whole structure of irony here that only a certain kind of Black, with a certain kind of relationship to English society, could practice with impunity. Sancho was sufficiently assimilated to that society to observe its codes of civilized conduct; but he was also enough of an outsider to subvert those very codes. It is clear, then, that the letters spoke another language to which Sancho's essentially preabolitionist audience was not attuned.

Literacy bought Sancho a series of advantages that very few, if any, of his less fortunate Black brothers and sisters enjoyed. That irresistible passion for knowledge, which had caused his mistresses so much anxiety when he was still a youth, opened up for him the great treasury of English letters and of the Western intellectual heritage as a whole. His reading in familiar authors gave him a point of reference and a common ground on which to meet his own epistolary audience. It expanded his mind to greater self-awareness; it liberated his imagination to fashion the world in his own ideal image and to propose that image for the approval of his readers.

In his private Parnassus of literary gods, Sancho placed Sterne first among his favorite authors. He considered Sterne's sermons as the catalyst by which the world could be transformed into a community closely knit together by universal philanthropy. Sterne was also the model for the benevolence Sancho practiced in his life and for the mock-seriousness with which he sprinkled his letters.

On the whole, what he seemed to crave most in books was their classic twin functions of instructing and improving. The *Letters* are widely suffused with the spirit and idiom of the Bible and the Prayer Book. When he quotes or alludes to major secular authors like Shakespeare, Pope, or Thomson, it is almost always to extract some moral precept, some parable of practical wisdom that he would commend as a rule of life.[15] In an age that tended to distrust novelty and venerate the collective wisdom of the past, Sancho's letters were bound to win approbation, for they promoted an ethic of stability and optimism that was highly valued among his correspondents.

Ironically, the letters draw their sharpest censure from modern critics for those very features that made them palatable to an eighteenth-century audience. Where the former deprecate his lack of invention, Sancho's contemporaries and several of his later readers must have found his flair for imitation remarkable for a member of a race from which little was expected in the way of intellectual attainments. Although we have very few of his correspondents' letters to him, we can infer from the unreserved effusiveness of his manner in his letters, from his propensity to assume every posture from the solemn moralist to the frolicsome buffoon, that he felt secure in his audience's tolerance and esteem.

Sancho could assume all the drollery, the whimsy, above all, the affecting sentiments, of Sterne without losing any personal value or authority in the bargain. A letter to a friend in low spirits recommends Young's *Night Thoughts* for soul cheering but also salutes an old horse (himself also ailing) in this vein: "My best respects and kind enquiry to your old horse. Tell him I wish him better—and am a real friend to honest brutes—some I could almost envy" (Letter 53, p.110). And Sancho carries it all off with the greatest of ease: there is not the slightest note of discord or diminishment, even though this deference to a dumb animal stands cheek by jowl with a lavish compliment to his human audience: "What Sterne said of himself, that think I of you—that you are as good a gentleman as the king."

To accommodate the fleeting alternations of such an agile mind, Sancho's epistolary art had to be flexible as well as inventive. At a flash it could be called upon to soar in a flight of fancy, as in this excursion into the pastoral genre: he expresses his happiness that some friends visiting Suffolk will be able to "enjoy the beauties of this sweetest of seasons—with its attendant dainties—fresh butter—sweet milk—and the smiles of boon nature on hill and dale—fields and groves—shepherds piping—milkmaids dancing—and the cheerful respondent carolings of artless joy in the happy husbandmen" (Letter 62, p.135).

And yet that same mind was capable of graver reflections. Some letters are complete meditations, evocative of the awesome wonder the psalmist David felt before God or of the dark melancholy of Samuel Johnson in the moral essays. Sancho speculated often on the nature of human existence, on humanity's place in the universe and relation to God. The speculations were never abstract dissertations on Scripture or morality: they typically begin with a sober inspection of immediate temporal things and culminate in the sublime regions of transcendent thought: "Smoking my pipe, the friendly warmth of the air—the cheerful glow of the atmosphere—made me involuntarily cry, 'Lord, what is man, that thou in thy mercy art so mindful to him!'" (Letter 45, p.90). In such peregrinations, the spirit invariably comes to rest on the solid bedrock of Christian faith in the promise of a glorified life hereafter, "the promise of never, never-ending existence and felicity—to possess eternity—'glorious dreadful thought': to rise, perhaps by regular progression from planet to planet—to behold the wonders of immensity—to pass from good to better—increasing in goodness—knowledge—love—to glory in our Redeemer—to joy in ourselves—to be acquainted with prophets, sages, heroes, and poets of old times—and join in symphony with angels" (Letter 45, p.92).

But pervasive as are imitation in his writing and orthodoxy in his belief, these features do not constitute the full measure of his mental faculties. The letters also show him to have been a discriminating reader and a discerning critic. When a correspondent charges Sterne with imitating Fielding, Sancho is anxious to clear the critic's judgment of the cobwebs of cant in order to install truth. He counters the charge with calm rationality and self-assurance: "Fielding and Sterne both copied nature—their palettes stored with proper colours of the brightest dye—these masters were both great originals—their outlines correct—bold and free—Human Nature was their subject—." The concluding remarks of this letter reveal a hint of impatience; they suggest that Sancho determined the critic's flaw to have been a lack of thoroughness and range in his reading. Accordingly, Sancho sends him back to reread and reconsider. He is even less sparing in his candor and directness about a painting sent to him by a friend. A concern for artistic integrity over dilettantism and for substance over formal beauties causes him to set the painter's hackneyed conventionalisms at nought. He begins his critique with a brief note of approval: "I enjoyed content at least in the vortex of smoke and vice—and lifted my thoughts no higher than the beauties of the park or—gardens." But he ends with a sharp sneer at the painting's clichés and a withering attack on the painter's style:

> What have I to do with rural deities? with parterres—field—groves—terraces—views—buildings—grots—temples—slopes—bridges—and meandering streams—cawing rooks—billing turtles—happy swains—the harmony of the woodland shades—the blissful constancy of rustic lovers?—Sir, I say you do wrong to awaken ideas of this sort:—besides, as I hinted largely above, you have no talent—no language—no colouring—you do not groupe well—no relief—false light and shadow—and then your perspective is so false —no blending of tints—Thou art a sad fellow, and there is an end to it.
> (Letter 110, pp.223–24)

Apart from courting his audience's favor by displaying a familiarity with official literary culture and a capacity for higher reason, Sancho impressed continually on his readers the liberal complexion of his views and his staunch patriotism to their country. As night be expected, he maintained an intelligent interest in public affairs and kept himself well informed by reading the leading journals of the day. The letters abound with references to public events and current affairs. The trial of Mrs. Butterfield, a noted socialite; the paper war between the duchess of Kingston and Samuel Foote, the playwright; the birth of a prince to the queen; and the defeat of Washington's army are all relayed to correspondents with the absorbing interest of one who was more than a passive observer.

Not only did Sancho read the papers regularly, he also wrote letters to the

editors, the substance of which reflected his civic loyalty and his discern-
ment in matters of public moment.[16] On 12 March 1778, he wrote a letter
to the *General Advertiser*, "actuated," he declared, "by zeal to my prince,
and love to my country," proposing a plan for reducing the national debt.
It was an appeal to the ostentatiously wealthy to demonstrate their noble
spirit and true patriotism by donating all their superfluous plate to be
melted down by the state. Sancho reasoned that this gesture would relieve
merchants, tradesmen, and other members of the middle class of the dis-
proportionate share of taxes that they were then carrying. In another letter
to the same paper, he outlined a three-point plan for improving the efficiency of the navy. It would provide attractive wages and pensions for the
sailors; establish educational opportunities in shipbuilding and navigation
for their young sons; and put an end to the infamous practice of kidnapping
men into service, a practice that Clarkson had denounced (Sancho, *Letters*,
pp.81–83).[17]

Although Sancho seemed anxious in both his private and his public representations to identify himself with the growing number of proponents of
liberal reforms in England, he was equally anxious not to be mistaken for
a freethinker or, worse, an anarchist. While his attitude on political and
religious issues was generally one of tolerance, he shunned fashionable
ideologies because, as he confided to a a friend, "I love not a multiplicity
of doctrines" (Letter 67. p.152). He took a firm stand for law and order
in the 1780 disturbances known as the Gordon Riots.

Between 2 and 7 June that year, Protestant mobs, instigated by the de-
magogic Lord George Gordon, demonstrated for the repeal of an act intended to mitigate the disabilities English Catholics suffered under old penal
legislation. The extremists burned the properties of prominent Catholics,
and citizens sympathetic to the rioters' cause plundered shrines and
assaulted members of the nobility. The letter in which Sancho recalls these
events seethes with outrage and contempt for the unruly masses. He calls
them "the maddest people that the maddest times were ever plagued with."
The excesses of a mob composed largely of fanatics and the chronically
dispossessed, wielding clubs and destroying property, made him pause to
reconsider the British ideals of liberty that he had so long cherished. He
writes to the moment: "This—this—is genuine British liberty: This instant
about two thousand liberty boys are swearing and swaggering by with large
sticks—thus armed in hopes of meeting with the Irish chairmen and labour-
ers." At one moment he attempts to dissociate himself from the "insanity"
and "barbarity" of the rioters by pleading his racial identity: "I am not
sorry I was born in Africa." Then, toward the end of the letter, he resumes
his liberal British identity and becomes once more conciliatory: "I am forced
to own that I am for universal toleration. Let us convert by our example and
conquer by our meekness!" (Letter 134, p.273). He identifies himself with

the traditional British liberal impulses of toleration and restraint, supporting the Catholics' right to religious freedom and condemning the rioters' fanaticism. But he also expresses dismay that a people who were capable of evolving such high principles of civilized conduct should also be capable of spawning such bitter anarchy and discord. Torn between identification with and repulsion from defferent aspects of the British ethos for most of his life, Sancho commonly used the attitudes described above as defence mechanisms whenever he was faced with similar hard choices.

Just as the sectarian squabbles of British domestic life provoked ambivalence in Sancho, so too did Britain's conduct in foreign affairs aggravate the internal divisions of his psyche. A report in 1779 that the British fleet had acquitted itself honorably in an encounter with the French, under Admiral D'Estaing in the West Indies, stirred his national pride: "We fought like Englishmen, unsupported by the rest:—they fought till they were quite dismasted and almost wrecked—and at last gave the French enough of it—and got away all" (Letter 105, p.213). But in the same letter we find him deploring the lack of discipline in the navy and the seeming collapse of the British Empire. Sancho was not unaware of these contradictions within himself; indeed we find him often struggling to reconcile them through a pattern of dissociation and retreat. When social and political issues tax his patience, he disclaims any personal interest and typically puts an end to his reflections on the woes of the British Empire thus: "For my part, it is nothing to me—as I am only a lodger—and hardly that" (Letter 105, p.214). The earlier example ("I am not sorry I was born in Africa"), illustrates how he used retreat to his African origins to defend himself against these conflicts and to remind himself of his status as an outsider.

His statements on the American Revolution seem to betray a reactionary's antagonism toward the colonists. He seems to view the rebels as recalcitrant Englishmen who should be dealt with firmly. Wars, like riots and other internal broils, repelled him; he thought them the "bitterest curse" (Letter 56, p.119). But he also thought he saw in the Americans' bid for self-determination, as in the sporadic rebelliousness of Ireland and Scotland, a retributory judgment on England's abuse of power and prosperity: "Oh, this poor ruined country:" he lamented, "ruined by its success—and the choicest blessings of the Great Father of Heaven could shower down upon us—ruined by victories—arts—arms—and unbounded commerce—for pride accompanied those blessings—and like a canker-worm has eaten into the heart of our political body" (Letter 111, pp.225–26).

What seems to emerge, then, is that as Sancho approached middle age, he felt more keenly the affliction of his double identity. As the vagaries of England's national and international affairs engendered disenchantment and confusion, he found it increasingly difficult to sustain his old posture of the compliant, assimilated Black. Social upheavals like the Gordon Riots and

the steadily unfolding scenario of Britain's role as an imperial power high-
lighted for Sancho contradictions in her practice that were irreconcilable
with her much-vaunted principles. He reacted by assuming the persona of a
timid, marginal man who little understood the forces around him and who
could not possibly have any opinions about them: "But let me return, if
possible, to my senses.—for God's sake: What a poor starving Negroe,
with six children to do with kings and heroes, and armies and politics?—
or artists—of any sort?" (Letter 56, p.120). And so, even though his life
among the English never became untenable, the impact of various trans-
formations at work in the society intensified for him the ironies of his double life as an African and a "naturalized" Briton.

It is tempting to see in the examples of retreat and self-mockery cited
above an abatement of Sancho's sprightly wit and a negation of self and
race. The truth is that retreat frequently afforded Sancho a safe haven for
attack, and self-mockery a deceitful persona for self-affirmation. Sancho's
tendency to rail at himself, to jest at his family ("the hen and chicks"), and
to make his Black brothers and sisters in general the butt of inoffensive jokes
is almost always good natured. Often what appears as ridicule is seen, on
closer inquiry, to carry a double edge: on the one side a structure of accom-
modation intended to appease the myths of his white audience, on the other
a structure of sarcasm intended to resists them. Letter 108 apologizes to Mr.
M—— for Sancho's delay in replying to his letter. It employs an ingenious
irony by which Sancho pretends to absolve himself on the grounds of some
fictional and irreversible racial traits and blame his correspondent for be-
friending him in spite of those traits:

> Such beings, I say, as the one I am now scribbling to—should make
> elections of wide different beings than Blackamoors for their friends—
> The reason is obvious—from Othello to Sancho the big—we are either
> foolish—or mulish—all—all without a single exception. Tell me, I
> pray you—and tell me truly—were there any Blackamoors in the
> Ark?—Pooh:—Why there now I see you puzzled—well—be that as
> the learned shall hereafter decide.

Here Sancho turns the rhetoric of self-mockery into a tool that is at once
appeasing and resistive to his audience. The allusions to Othello and to
Noah and the ark are a sarcastic attempt to anticipate the unspoken
thoughts of Mr. M—— as a representative of the British mind and to de-
bunk the authoritative basis of the Bible and literary myth. The allusions
undercut traditional biases in Western thinking about the Black's place in
history and scoff at the conventionalized images of him in literature. By
seeming to ridicule himself and his race, Sancho forces his white audience to
redefine his relationship to them and to revamp their traditional conceptions

of all Black people. Lloyed Brown notes that Sancho, being both an "outsider" and a culturally assimilated Black, was well placed to "subvert the standard images of the uncivilized Negro." Brown explains that "Sancho's ironic insinuations are so effective because his intimate knowledge of his society enables him to subvert its prejudices and ambiguous values from within."[18]

There are instances in the *Letters* where ironically disparaging references to African racial traits are employed to further a personal ambition or to advance the interests of a friend. Letter 25 supports the application of a fellow Black for a place in a white gentleman's service. It announces the friend playfully as "a merry—chirping—white tooth'd—clean—tight—and light little fellow;—with a woolly pate—and face as dark as your humble," but Sancho is quick to dispel any impression that he is recommending his friend solely on the basis of his physical features: "I like the rogues looks, or a similarity of colour should not have induced me to recommend him." He implies that he is neither bigoted nor partial to his own kind; elsewhere he proudly proclaims that Africans have their own stock of human qualities which have survived despite malicious vilification and the scars of slavery. He expresses confidence in the African's continued capacity for truth, honesty, and integrity: "I have observed a dog will love those who use him kindly—and surely, if so, negroes in their state of ignorance and bondage, will not act less generously, if I may judge them by myself—I should suppose kindness would do anything with them;..." (Letter 13, p.30)

Sancho was not averse to describing himself by self-conscious epithets such as "a poor Blacky grocer," "a coal, black, jolly African," or "a poor thick lipped son of Africa" to awaken the sympathies of his audience for his personal ambitions. In Letter 118 he applies to a person, clearly well-to-do and influential, to help him obtain a franchise to operate a general post office on his premises at Charles Street. The pervasive tone is deferential and supplicatory; it combines the proper measure of respect due to a potential patron with Sancho's double-edged irony: "Figure to yourself, my dear Sir, a man of convexity of belly exceeding Falstaff—and a black face into the bargain—waddling in the van of poor thieves and penniless prostitutes—with all the supercilious mock dignity of little office—what a banquet of wicked jest and wanton wit—" (Letter 118, p.238).

Sancho had learned both to cater to his audience's deceit and to practice the arts of dissembling for his own ends. Years of acculturation had taught him to address white Englishmen with the deference and self-effacement they naturally expected of an "inferior" race. He knew that even those who acknowledged his sensibility and intelligence expected of him a certain degree of prostration to preserve the caste lines unbroken and a certain display of outlandish buffoonery to reaffirm their deep-rooted suspicions that the

African race was not susceptible to complete civilization after all. While his rhetorical deceit helped him to fulfill the expectations of the white world, it also helped him to sustain a positive valuation of Blackness. In its overt manifestations, his self-raillery accommodates the personal prejudices of his correspondents. On the private level, it becomes an affirmative statement of the author's self and a vindication of the whole Black race, for the performances are highly self-conscious and deliberately deceitful.

The audience that read the *Letters* as a public document was vastly different from the audience which received the letters as private correspondence between 1768 and 1780. Almost all of the original recipients were Sancho's close friends who found his wide philanthropy affecting without necessarily being swept along into an active struggle for Black liberation by the letters' moral and political undercurrents. There simply was not sufficient public awareness about the facts of the slave trade or urgency about the conditions of Blacks on the West Indian plantations to stir their Georgian complacency. On the other hand, the later reading public, living in the heyday of abolitionist agitation (between 1782 and 1803, when the first and fifth editions of the *Letters* were published respectively), could hardly escape the political implications of a published work authored by a Black man, who had been born in slavery, exposed to Western modes of thought and feeling, and who showed himself to be literate, cultivated, and improvable. These tangible proofs, coupled with all those attributes that won him the respect of his private friends, were now to serve as evidence of the improvability of the whole African race and to establish Sancho's credibility as a spokesman for the Black claim to freedom.

The content of the *Letters* and the character of their author effectively refuted three main proslavery strictures against the African. The allies of the West Indian plantocracy held that (1) the slave was not capable of feeling the afflictions of slavery, (2) his life of bondage in the New World and his marginal situation in Europe were preferable to the savage freedom of his native Africa, and (3) he was morally and intellectually inferior to the white man. Sancho was fully aware of these detractions; his color and appearance were often the object of slurs and derision. Accordingly, the excesses of sensibility that abound in the *Letters* seem to function as compensatory defences; they are as much statements of conventional sentimentalism as they are expressions affirmative of human value.

Abolitionist readers who had been educated in the tradition of humanitarianism that evolved from Shaftesbury and Hutcheson through to the political propagandism of antislavery sentiment could find in the *Letters* eloquent proofs to counteract the proslavery calumnies. Sancho suffered the miseries of gout and dropsy, complications of which finally caused his death. The teething troubles of little Billy, his son, elicited the tenderest emotions of compassion and paternal care. He knew the grief of losing an infant daughter to early death, and he and Mrs. Sancho lived together in perfect conjugal solicitude for the changing states of each other's mind and body—so perfect indeed that Sancho could write: "I am her barometer—if a sigh escapes me, it is answered by a tear in her eye.—I oft assume a gaiety to illumine her gay sensibility with a smile—which twenty years ago bewitched me:—and mark: after twenty years enjoyment—constitutes my highest pleasure" (Letter 54, p.113). Two hundred years of human intellectual progress must no doubt make these illustrations of Sancho's sensibilities seem gratuitous or trite; but a timely reminder should suffice to dispel hasty assumptions. Two hundred years ago, widespread credence in the myth of African insensibility, whether based on genuine ignorance or genuine deviousness, was still one of the most impregnable barriers to the admission of Black people to full status in the human community.

Coming as it did in one of the most prolific decades of antislavery writing, the publication of the *Letters* also coincided with a period of profound social changes in British institutions that made the public more conscious of the needs of the poor and the oppressed. Moral forces in England had begun to translate the public passion for benevolence (well-wishing) into a passion for beneficence (well-doing), basically the two major phases in the evolution of British humanitarianism.

Abolitionist readers could find both phases exemplified in Sancho's work. We know that Sancho esteemed Sterne highly; the *Letters* show that the African claimed the great leader of the sentimentalist cult as his chief spiritual mentor and accorded him the accolade of genius of the age (see Letter 54, p.112). Just as Sterne apotheosized the worship of feelings in his anecdote of a poor old man weeping over his dead donkey (*Sentimental Journey*, "The Dead Ass"), so Sancho pours out his compassion for that poor, benighted object of perennial human scorn and abuse. In a letter entitled "Jack Asses," he excoriates a number of potato vendors who pass his shop daily riding on donkeys already overburdened with produce. The letter is an appeal for a friend to use his influence to prevent such cruelty: "I am convinced we feel instinctively the injuries of our *fellow* creatures, I do insist upon your exercising your talents in behalf of the honest sufferers. I ever had a kind of sympathetic (call it what you please) for that animal—and do I not love you? Before Sterne had wrote them into respect I had a friendship for them—and many a civil greeting have I given them at casual meetings" (Letter 48, p.97). This is the kind of passage that typically provokes charges of insincerity from those modern critics who find Sancho's sentiments tiresome because cultivated. Admittedly, there is a degree of mawkishness, even whimsy, in the whole thing. But there is the danger that in censuring such excesses of feeling, critics may become unconscious conspirators with those who would deny him any capacity for feeling at all. And that would be to put him just where the Longs, the Humes, and the Jeffersons relegated him in their hierarchy of human types.[19] That would signal a failure to separate the fashionable myth from the authentic mind.

When we look beyond the rapturous transports and the fits of feeling, we discover that Sancho had perhaps an equal appreciation for the practical forms of philanthropy, even if that appreciation was always mediated by a candor about the good feelings he derived from doing good deeds: "Blessed Philanthropy," he rhapsodized, "Oh the delights of making happy—the bliss of giving comfort to the afflicted—peace to the distressed mind—to prevent the request from quivering lips of indigence." (Letter 34, p.67). It is conceivable that Sancho hoped to exploit contemporary fashions in feeling and the apparently nonpolitical manifestations of benevolence to further the ends of social justice for his people. He may have reasoned that if the English people could be caught up fully in this mass movement of minds towards a universal philanthropy, then some of that movement's energy could be harnessed to relieve the sufferings of his own fellow Africans. In this idea, his thinking was at one with the spirit of similar utterances by moral philosophers of the age. Adam Smith wrote: "The influence of our good offices are circumscribed by our physical limitations, but that of our good will may embrace the immensity of the Universe."[20]

This hidden dimension of the Letters might have eluded his private correspondents, but it was sure to register with an audience becoming increasingly politicized by abolitionist propaganda. To that audience, any expression of powerful feeling, whether by heroic slave or cultivated African, strengthened the arsenals of antislavery forces against the attacks of proslavery publicists. Any single gesture, such as Sancho's appeal for clemency in the case of Dr. Dodd, pleaded powerfully the cause of African humanity in the minds of abolitionists.[21] The combination of sensibility and practical humanitarianism urged the integrity of the author as a creature of mind and soul and provided eloquent proofs that the African slave had the right to possess his own body and to determine the disposition of his labor.

In short, Sancho's Letters, like "Noble Negro" literature in particular and abolitionist literature in general, reflects the Black man's search for place in an alien and hostile world, offering the qualifications of rationality, love, courage, loyalty, and compassion as evidence of his moral right to participate equally in the human community. Even though these assumptions are often unstated or partly subconscious in Sancho's work, the implicit strategy has a validity sanctioned by the age's presiding philosophy. Robert Nicklaus writes this appreciation of it: "In the quest for happiness, sentiment and reason combine to reconcile anarchical man and social man. . . . It is the power of reason in individual man, whatever the nature of the factors that can lead it astray or distort it, that is the condition of his very real, if limited freedom. For only the man who thinks can feel and therefore be free."[22] The Enlightenment had enunciated the concept of that quest in general ideological terms. It was left to antislavery to implement those terms, to buy a reprieve for the African from the sentence of moral and spiritual death which Europe had pronounced on him.

Sancho makes very few outright references to slavery and the slave trade and fewer still that match the candor and intensity of Cugoano, Equiano, or any of the other major abolitionist writers. It is not that he was incapable of intensity and candor: the *Letters* provide ample proofs that he could use both when it was politic or innocuous to do so. But many of his correspondents were persons of more or less liberal persuasion who were largely sympathetic to the African cause. Some, like Laurence Sterne and Edmund Rack, shared Sancho's views on slavery and the wrongs it inflicted on Blacks. Sancho saw no point in preaching to the converted. As typical middle-class people, Sancho's intimates were more likely to think of liberty, equality, and fraternity as abstract ideas than as the rallying cries of an emergent social revolution. They shunned the fanaticism of extreme causes and were hardly minded to change what many saw as the providential disposition of things. With such people one does not fight. Sancho chose not to assault their complacency head on.

That he chose a nonmilitant, conciliatory posture has caused disquiet among certain readers and drawn censure from some critics. They are impatient with his "warm ebullitions of African sensibility"; they are skeptical about his faith in benevolence as an instrument for correcting universal injustice; they are disenchanted by his apparent compromise with the status quo. And so they ignore the fact that he wrote in an age when abolition was still an idea whose time had not yet fully come, that the British public was not to feel the transforming impact of abolitionist agitation until the publication of Clarkson's researches and the parliamentary activities of Wilberforce and the Clapham Sect. Moreover, Sancho's critics underestimate the value of moral suasion and the technique of masking—the only safe and palatable ways Blacks (and even some whites) had of expressing themselves about the condition of the masses on the West Indian plantations and the plight of the Black poor in England itself.

Because Sancho understood the limitations and the sensitivities of his audience, he chose to mask his protests against the evils of slavery behind the generalized terms of an attack on the widespread decadence and immorality he was witnessing in English life as a whole. Just as he hoped that the universal diffusion of the benevolist cult might eventually ransom the African from oppression, so he wished that Sterne's sermons would rekindle in the public a sense of moral duty and become the catalyst for a more socially conscious church—a church that would resolutely assume leadership in the fight against injustice. In July 1777 he wrote to Mr. M——: "I would to God my friend that the great lights of the Church would exercise their oratorical powers upon Yorick's plan:—the heart and passions once lifted

under the banners of blessed Philanthropy, would naturally ascend to the
redeeming God—flaming with grateful rapture.—Now I have observed
among the modern Saints—who profess to pray without ceasing—that they
are so fully taken up with pious meditations—and so fully absorbed in the
love of God—that they have little if any room for the love of man" (Letter
43, pp.84–85). By uniting with those critics then upbraiding the church for
its dismal failure to defend the weak and minister to the poor, Sancho could
express his genuine discontent without fear of being identified with dangerous opinions. The mask of general philanthropic intention would provide
him with anonymity, and the mask of enlightened toleration would lend
respectability to his rhetoric. Together both would render him immune to
counterattack. He could blend the conciliatory tone of the sentence beginning "I would to God, my friend. . ." with the oblique satirical tone of the
allusion to "modern Saints—who profess to pray without ceasing" and still
manage to stay within the pale of acceptable dissent. That strategy was
calculated to consume the establishment powers with guilt rather than confront them with a hollow militancy. Sancho shrewdly perceived that Blacks
would do more for their cause *at that stage* if they wore a mask of meekness.
He supposed that the exercise of personal virtue on their part would compel
at least a palliation in British prejudice.[23]

Besides the church, Sancho also made an undisguised assault upon the
political establishment that authorized the slave trade and upon the economic interests that benefited from it. In the privacy of a letter to Mr. J——
W——E——, he denounced the rapaciousness of the British in India, in the
West Indies, and on the Guinea Coast, observing quite openly that "the
Grand object of all Christian navigators is money—money—money" (Letter 68, p.149). The Whig faith in commerce as an instrument for promoting
universal harmony was strong in him, but he regretted that the Europeans
had perverted the noble ideals of that faith by not basing their commercial
relations with nonwhite nations on equity and mutual progress.

Although in one letter he makes specific mention of Europe's offenses
against Africa, it is remarkable how he assumes a tone of objective detach-
ment, being careful to avoid any suggestion of vested interest or special
pleading. He refrains from identifying himself in any way with the injured
Africans, taking the rather more moderate stance of indicting both the
Christian traders for buying and the corruptible African chiefs for selling:

> In Africa the poor wretched natives—blessed with the most fertile and
> luxuriant soil—are rendered so much more miserable for what Provi-
> dence meant as a blessing:—the Christians' abominable traffic for
> slaves—and the horrid cruelty and treachery of the petty kings—
> encouraged by their Christian customers—who carry them strong
> liquors, to enflame their national madness—and powder and fire-

arms to furnish them with the hellish means of killing and kidnapping."
(Letter 68, p.150)

Sancho chose to see slave trading and slave holding in the larger context
of an age when the lust for power and for control of the world's wealth had
become the ruling passion, both within the highest councils of the state and
in the hearts of individuals. He shared that critical platform with Wesley,
Ramsay, Clarkson, Wilberforce, and the whole panoply of antislavery
forces who were to succeed him. And so, by the time his *Letters* reached the
hands of an abolitionist audience, his references to "these wretches who roll
in affluence from our [African slaves'] labour" (Letter 14, pp.31–32) must
have assumed greater poignancy and moment. That audience must have
appreciated his attack on the decadence and infamy of an age which could
applaud the genius of a Phillis Wheatley and yet not muster the moral re-
solution to liberate her to achieve full selfhood. Sancho wrote:

> It reflects nothing either to the glory or generosity of her master—if she
> is still his slave—except he glories in the low vanity of having in his
> wanton power a mind animated by Heaven—a genius superior to him-
> self. The list of splendid—titled—learned names, in confirmation of
> her being the real authoress alas! shows how very poor the acquisition
> of wealth and knowledge is—without generosity—feeling—and
> humanity." (Letter 58, p.126)

Those few letters that touch directly on the slavery question do so with
sensitivity and concern, although deep inside Sancho found the subject an
intractable one (he confessed that "it is a subject that sours my blood") and
one that disturbed him with a sense of his own powerlessness to do anything
about it. Reading abolitionist writers like Benezet, possibly (Letter 58,
p.125), and Sharp, certainly (Letter 96, p.197), he must have felt the familiar anxieties springing from the well of his double consciousness, galling
him that white Europeans were taking up the struggle for liberation of his
Black brothers and sisters, while he was compromised by his special relationship to British society to wage his campaign by irony and indirection.

The much-quoted letter to Sterne, in which Sancho petitions that author
to use his "striking manner" to condemn slavery, betrays a sense of inade-
quacy as well as a humanitarian compassion for the millions who lan-
guished on the plantations and perished in the Middle Passage: "Dear Sir,
think in me you behold the uplifted hands of thousands of my brother
Moors.—Grief (you pathetically observe) is eloquent:—figure to yourself
their attitudes: alas:—you cannot refuse.—Humanity must comply— . . ."
(Letter 36, p.72). He hoped that what he could not do in the limited scope of
private letters, Sterne could, because that author had established his name in

the official literary culture and distinguished himself as a kind of cult figure of universal philanthropy.

The *Letters of Ignatius Sancho,* then, as far as they can be considered abolitionist in content, belong to the benevolistic and religious phase of antislavery. The author's death occurred just when the major abolitionists were gathering their forces to launch a sustained attack on the slave trade. Sancho was therefore prevented from playing any active part in the public political campaign for Black liberation. In the vigorous years of his youth, the patronage of the great had sheltered him from want and the other adversities that hedged the lives of Blacks in England. In his mature years, the domestic responsibilities of caring for a family and running a small business claimed his time. Gout and physical afflictions plagued his later years, effectively restricting his activities to the Charles Street shop and residence.

Even if these personal circumstances had been different, Sancho might still not have been any more political in his writing. It is well to remember that there was no significant Black leadership or antislavery protest until the decade of the 1780s. The temper of Georgian England was not propitious for open revolt. Sancho himself shared too fully the philosophical assumptions of his time that universal goodwill and optimism were sufficient to right the world's wrongs. But despite his perfect assimilation to British values, he never lost sight of what it meant to be Black in an eighteenth-century white world, nor did he disclaim his kinship with those other Black men and women whose lot was less fortunate than his own.

By expressing his attitude to injustice in universal terms, he identified himself with the moral positions of greater literary figures, like Johnson and Pope, who opposed all those forces that would impoverish the human spirit. By preferring his concern for the total condition of humanity to the immediate troubles of his race, he projected a liberal-mindedness that made his position more secure and his plea more persuasive. His disguised intention was to siphon off support from the general tolerance for humanitarian ideas and direct it toward ameliorating the conditions of African slavery. Through the generous effusions of feeling in his epistolary art and beneficence in his practical life, he sought to justify himself to his private correspondents and later won the applause of abolitionist readers. Through his skillful mastery of the written word, he made an essentially political statement on the lower registers of moral rhetoric. The audience in 1782 was ready for that hidden axiom that lies at the heart of all his sentiments: that the mind is the measure of the human being, and that Blacks, because they were rational and sensible, were whole beings. Semiconsciously, Sancho spoke the earliest language of abolition.

Ottobah Cugoano: The Appeal to Religion and the Intellectual Self

The subject of slavery might well have "soured" Sancho's blood. Shackles, thumbscrews, and muzzles are anathema to the benevolent heart and an offence to the delicate sensibility. However passionate his sympathies were for the suffering Africans, he could write about their condition only at second hand, because a timely providence had rescued him from that "hell in the sunshine" to which they were condemned. Cugoano, on the other hand, was not so favored. Kidnapped at thirteen from his native village of Ajimako in Ghana, he heard with his own ears the groans of African captives as they waited in the coastal forts to be transported to the West Indies. The rattling of their chains alarmed him. Their anguished cries with every lash of the whip made him tremble with anxiety for what his own fate might be. In the West Indies, he was introduced to further "dreadful scenes of misery and cruelty." He saw slaves "cut to pieces" for trivial offenses, beaten mercilessly, their teeth knocked out for eating a mere piece of sugar cane. Slavery was a memory too palpable for him to sentimentalize, the slave trade a traffic too immoral for him to condone.

Cugoano refused to compromise with either of these institutions. Unlike Sancho, he had no sensitive audience of private friends to divide his loyalty. His comparatively greater independence from patrons freed him to attack slavery and the British institutions that supported it. Where Sancho was forced to temporize, Cugoano was able to defend his race fearlessly from the slavocrats' slanders, because he took with him into the West Indies an ineradicable fund of memories about his carefree boyhood and a solid sense of native African values. These precious possessions saved him from the powerful inducements to self-negation that encompassed Blacks in the slave societies of the New World and from the forces of cultural assimilation which threatened them in the metropolitan civilizations of the Old.

Born among the Fantee people of Ghana in 1757, Cugoano was raised in the Fantee royal household, his father apparently a man of some status in the king's service.[1] Having one day ventured farther into the woods than was prudent for their safety, he and a group of playmates were abducted by a band of marauders who sold them into slavery down the coast. A slave ship took him to Grenada where he spent some nine months as a slave, witnessing firsthand the most horrifying facts of slave life. After spending a further year in other parts of the West Indies, he was taken to England by a gentleman named Alexander Campbell at the end of 1722.

Cugoano seems to have made almost immediate contact with the Black community in England. In a brief biographical note appended to the "General Contents" of his book's 1787 edition, he records having been advised by "some good people to get myself baptized, that I might not be carried away and sold again." We know that baptism was a common defensive strategy urged on both free Blacks and escaped slaves by those of their fellows who were more knowing about the hazards besetting the liberty of Africans in free England. Accordingly, he was instructed and later baptized by a Dr. Skinner at Saint James's Church in 1773, taking as his Christian name John Stewart. His master also provided for his education in reading and writing. Exactly when he left Alexander Campbell is not clear, but in the 1780s he entered the service of Richard Cosway, chief painter to the Prince of Wales, and remained in that capacity at least until 1788.[2]

Cugoano readily appreciated the power of literacy as a necessary tool in the struggle for personal and collective liberation. He firmly resolved to use his own education chiefly to provide effective leadership for the powerless Black community, and in the 1791 edition of his book he revealed that his purpose in publishing his work was "to convey instructions to his oppressed countrymen."[3] Cugoano considered a plan to provide instruction in reading, Christianity, and the laws of civilization. Although there is no evidence that the plan was enacted, the language of the proposal suggests that Cugoano appreciated the need for political education among Blacks and for raising their consciousness about the injuries they suffered in a country where their legal status was still unsettled and therefore subject to frequent violation. Cugoano no doubt also understood the subversive power of teaching. He observed that Blacks had been unceremoniously snatched from their native lands by people who professed Christianity. Their subsequent masters and mistresses often kept them deliberately ignorant of true Christian teaching "through motives of Avarice" (*Thoughts,* 22). If Blacks could have been instructed in the true spirit of Christ's teaching, they would have been intellectually prepared to act as a community of informed persons and challenge the contradictions of their social and political status in a free, Christian land.

By 1786 Cugoano had assumed a position of leadership among London Blacks. On his arrival in England he had been distressed by the community's vulnerability to continuing harassment and violation of civil liberties, despite the provisions of the 1772 Mansfield decision. The realization that Africans in England were a dispossessed people, lacking the conventional benefits of diplomatic representation, forced him to assume the role of an unofficial ambassador, intermediary, and political representative.[4]

The first two decades of Cugoano's life in England fully exercised his capacity for social and political activism. The most celebrated of legal cases involving the violation of Africans' human rights—the Somerset case (1772), the Knight case (1788), and the Zong case (1783)—claimed the attention of the courts and the public press during those years. The opportunity to observe the treatment of Blacks before the law provided Cugoano with a measure of the grave disabilities burdening Blacks in their struggle to survive in alien lands. These experiences corroborated his later charges that the law as an institution was corrupt and discriminatory towards Blacks. Cugoano worked closely with Sharp to assert and defend the legal rights of Blacks. In 1786, he helped to rescue Henry Demane, a Black who had been kidnapped and was about to be shipped back to slavery.

Edwards, the modern editor of Cugoano's *Thoughts,* has brought to light four letters that evidence the initiative Cugoano took in promoting awareness of the African question at the highest levels of British political power. The letters were all originally sent to prominent people in public life, together with abolitionist tracts and copies of the *Thoughts.* Two letters, dated 1786 and 1787 respectively, were addressed to the Prince of Wales, specifically petitioning him to stop the slave trade. A third was sent to Edmund Burke, probably in 1787, and a fourth to King George III himself.[5] The letters are all properly respectful, but they also attempt to impress strongly on their recipients the moral urgency of the slave question. They indicate that Cugoano possessed sufficient political maturity to recognize that redress had to be sought at the prime sources of power, since the slave trade was being carried on under royal assent and parliamentary approval.

Very little is known about Cugoano's life after the publication of the 1791 edition. Shyllon states that he married an Englishwoman but that no records of their family life have been found.[6] There is evidence that he may have known James Albert Ukawsaw Gronniosaw, another ex-slave of the period, who wrote a spiritual autobiography that Cugoano mentions in his own book.[7] Cugoano collaborated closely with Equiano in matters concerning the Black community. They volunteered together to go exploring for the African Association; and, in 1791, Cugoano wrote Sharp that he was planning to go to New Brunswick to recruit skilled labor for the Sierra Leone colony from among the Loyalist Blacks who had settled in Canada after the American Revolution.[8] Shyllon suggests the possiblity that Cugoano may have gone to Sierra Leone himself.[9]

The first edition of Cugoano's book, *Thoughts and Sentiments on the Evils of Slavery,* was published in 1787, the year in which the London Committee for the Abolition of the Slave Trade was formed. It is not unreasonable to conjecture that the work was produced under the auspices of the committee. The dedication to "The inhabitants of Great Britain" reflects a definite propagandistic intention that is the hallmark of the abolitionists' tactics, and the book's debt to the great canon of abolitionist works of that decade—Clarkson's *Essay on Slavery,* Wesley's "Thoughts on Slavery," and Ramsay's *Treatment and Conversion of Africans*—identifies it with the best in the antislavery intellectual tradition.

Cugoano draws liberally from these authors' works, as he does from Sharp's *Just Limitation* and Benezet's *Account of Guinea,* often without acknowledgment. This relationship served not only to connect him to the best in antislavery but also to bring respectability to the image of the Black man by presenting him to his detractors as a thinking, articulate, intellectually improvable person. Such purposes were quite consistent with the Abolition Committee's endeavor to make the cause of the Negro a credible concern of more than sentimental significance.

Although Cugoano's book was influenced by a wider intellectual tradition, some critics have questioned its authorial integrity. Because the work's style and rhetorical qualities are not consistent throughout, it has been suggested that Cugoano may have written his book in collaboration with some very highly trained, knowledgeable antislavery publicist.[10] Several theories have been proposed. One is that Cugoano was the titular author, receiving specialized assistance in marshaling the biblical and historical arguments concerning race and slavery. A second theory is that someone, perhaps Equiano, made emendations of substance to Cugoano's text but neglected to correct many of the grammatical and syntactical infelicities. A third theory is that both Cugoano and Equiano collaborated in the broad subject matter, and that a third contributor supplied the passages of florid rhetoric and advanced argumentation.

None of these speculations can be conclusively verified; none can be maintained without qualification. If Cugoano's collaborator was a native English speaker, it is curious to find in those very passages supposedly contributed by the collaborator or third contributor errors more typical of the the portions attributed to Cugoano. In the absence of more decisive evidence, only this much may be concluded: in a decade that turned out to be the most sympathetic to the African cause and the most prolific in abolitionist literature, a production marked by uncommon erudition in scriptural, legal, and historical authority could be easily attributable to an ex-slave. It was imperative to the success of antislavery for its propagandists to supplant the old myth of African brutishness with a new myth of noble Negro progressivism, of African virtue and African intelligence. The friends of the African must have thought the fiction involved in ghosting a work under the guise of an ex-slave's authorship a lesser evil than permitting the falsehoods of proslavery spokesmen to go unchallenged. Still, in spite of the allowances that must be judiciously made for the possibility of purposive collaboration, the main narrative sequences and a high proportion of passages devoted to analyzing the slave trade and slave practices in the West Indies are identical with the authorial character of Cugoano evidenced in the prefaces and letters. This chapter will therefore treat the *Thoughts* as a work written and approved by Cugoano, with assistance from a collaborator or collaborators.

Working under the aegis of the powerful Abolition Committee, Cugoano could afford to announce himself publicly as the author of the *Thoughts*. His personal experiences as a slave in Grenada authenticated the narrative portions of the work and those particulars of slavery that only an ex-slave could relate with candor and realism. The memory of his native Ghana in particular and his knowledge of and patriotism for Africa as a whole served him well in his assumed rhetorical role as corrector of slanders and misrepresentations popularized by prejudiced commentators.

Cugoano displayed a shrewd sense of the historical moment at which he wrote and of the audience his book was nost likely to influence. He saw clearly that antislavery was taking a new direction, evolving from the essentially passive phase of benevolistic ethics to the more active phase of political agitation and propaganda. The rhetorical strategies of his book suggest that he aimed to appeal to an audience mentally prepared by the Enlightenment and morally stirred by Evangelical revivalism to face the truth about the slave trade. And so he does not mince his words nor moderate his attack. The overriding motive of Cugoano and his associates was to garner sympathetic opinion for the injured Africans and to use that opinion to influence public policy for the eventual abolition of the slave trade.

Cugoano adopted a variety of voices in order to appeal to the wide-ranging interests and persuasions of the British public as well as to enhance the authority of his discourse. He chose an unvarnished sentimental naïveté in relating the details of his early life and in recounting the circumstances of his enslavement. The romantic image of innocent African boys roaming freely in the woods, gathering fruit and catching birds, then suddenly kidnapped and spirited away from the security of their home by a band of fearsome ruffians (*Thoughts*, 6–7), recalls the pseudo-Africa of the earlier "Noble Negro" phase of antislavery:

> Let it suffice to say that I was lost to my dear indulgent parents and relations, and they to me. All my help was cries and tears, and those could not avail; nor suffered long, till one succeeding woe, and dread, swelled up another. Brought from a state of innocence and freedom, and, in a barbarous and cruel manner, conveyed to a state of horror and slavey: This abandoned situation may be easier conceived than described. (*Thoughts*, 10)

This primitivistic mode of narration was no doubt calculated to enlist the sympathies of readers inclined to sentimentalism and to reflect the purity of feelings they associated with "savage" nations.

The plain style of these earlier sections gives way to the more formal manner of those sections in which Cugoano examines the legal and historical arguments of the proslavery apologists (59–77). In those passages the style is one of practiced eloquence, full of learned allusion and incisive analysis. The method of refutation is distinctly rationalistic and enlightened, in many respects similar to Montesquieu's method in *L'Esprit*. One could safely assume that here the theoretical second intelligence, more scholarly than Cugoano, might have interposed his or her insights and opinions.

Similarly, those parts of the argument which draw their evidence from historical and scriptural authority display a comparable erudition. They seem specifically directed to middle class Evangelical readers. Such readers were gradually becoming a prime target for abolitionist propaganda and could be most counted upon to support abolition, if they could be persuaded that slavery was contrary to God's law and commandment and emblematic of humankind's fallen, depraved nature.

Cugoano also exploited the reformist tendencies of the commercial classes who were anxious to break the monopoly capitalism of the plantation interests. He presented himself as a progressive supporter of a new economic order that would challenge the entrenched status of the sugar barons and extend the opportunities for trade and commerce with Africa and the New World on a broader, more equitable basis to a larger number of entrepreneurs.[11] In courting the political support of this group, Cugoano was astute enough to show himself a responsible spokesman for reform. He recognized that sudden abolition would dislocate the British economy, and therefore he proposed the alternative of expanding the African trade so that manufactures could replace the traffic in human beings.

Just as in his public life Cugoano saw himself as a kind of ambassador and intermediary for a stateless people, in his literary character he assumed the identity of a nationalist, emphasizing the constructive, human face of Africa. The major thrust of his representations was to restore luster to the tarnished image of Africans and to reaffirm the integrity of their native culture. All in all, Cugoano sought to build an antislavery argument on the solid foundations of a respectable intellectual tradition, thus offering himself as a rational, well-informed polemicist in a cause of broad humanitarian and progressive implications.

Having first established his credibility with that segment of the reading audience from which he could logically expect sympathy and support, Cugoano turned next to that quarter from which he could naturally expect calumny and detraction. From the earliest years of the century, spokesmen for slave-trading and plantation interests had put the case for slavery with all the deceitful persuasiveness that would ensure their continued economic security.

One of the most notable apologists for the colonial plantocracy was

James Tobin, himself a planter at Nevis, who had sought to controvert the Reverend James Ramsay's account of West Indian slavery in an essay entitled, "Cursory Remarks upon the Reverend Mr. Ramsay's Essay on the Treatment and Conversion of African Slaves in the British Sugar Colonies" (1785). Tobin had offered all the stock proslavery defenses of plantation slavery. He had repeated all the aspersions against the character of the African slave. He had begged to submit that the African was better off in slavery than the British poor were in freedom; that the lot of the former was more tolerable than that of the American slave; and that slavery might, after all, be a fitting condition for Africans since, as he alleged, the Africans were slow of interest, backward in civilization, and contentious in their tribal relations.

In taking this "cursory remarker" to task, Cugoano exposes him as an apologist for the colonial status quo, who was attempting to defend a patently evil system on the basis of lies, misrepresentations, and contradictions. Where Tobin feigns common cause with Ramsay, in hoping "the blessings of freedom will, in due time, be equally diffused over the globe," Cugoano shows him to be more disingenuous and apologetic on the slave traders' and masters' behalf than philanthropic on the slaves'. Cugoano bluntly calls the slave dealers, for whom Tobin speaks, robbers, thieves, and vagabonds whose crimes should be punished with the same severity as those of highwaymen, banditti, and pirates. He finds Tobin's comparison of the slaves' lives with those of the British poor a false one. While Cugoano concedes that the latter suffer social and economic distress similar to the slaves', he finds the severe limitations on the slaves' basic human freedoms to be the single most differentiating condition that invalidates Tobin's analogy. Likewise, Cugoano dismisses Tobin's allegation that the West Indian slaves were treated better than American slaves. Slavery, he objects, could not be justified on any such relative ground. To Tobin's slurs against African intelligence, Cugoano counterposes the argument that slavery could never be an acceptable substitute for ignorance and savagery: "This specious pretence is without any shadow of justice or truth, and, if the argument was even true, it could afford no just and warrantable matter for any society of men to hold slaves. But the argument is false; there can be no ignorance, dispersion or unsociableness so found among them, which can be made better by bringing them away to a state of a degree equal to that of a cow or a horse" (*Thoughts*, 21).

It was clear to Cugoano that the proslavery rationalizations for enslaving Africans were based on a pervasive disrespect for African humanity and on the Europeans' presumed hegemonic right to expropriate and subvert Africa itself. Cugoano believed firmly in the essential human value of his people and in Africa's right to govern itself according to its particular laws and traditions. Consequently, he made the next order of business in the

Thoughts an extension of his remarks, beyond discrediting Tobin's special pleadings, to disproving the myths and theories about race and color that had managed to gain respectability with even better minds.

The explicitness with which Cugoano challenges the pseudointellectual proponents of racial theories unfavorable to Africans reveals much about his mental acuity and about his sense of the necessary direction of antislavery. The tendency of his discourse concerning the spurious misrepresentations of African character is distinctly corrective in motivation. Cugoano appeared to have discounted any strategy that relied on impulses as transient as sentimentalism or benevolence. He chose to establish the African's place in the order of humankind by applying the sterner and more exacting methods of exegesis and confutation to the rational principles of the law, ethics, and religion, rather than repose any confidence for the success of abolition in the momentary fervor of fashionable cults. Some concession must be made to the strong indications in the exegetical and polemical sections of the text that a highly trained (even scholarly) mind at least collaborated in constructing or contributed outright such excellent arguments against those proposed by slavery's defenders.

Among the theories regularly advanced by propagandists to rationalize slavery were two based on biblical precedents. Through a tendentious reading of the Old Testament, they managed to implicate Blacks in the curse pronounced by Noah on his son Ham. In the first instance, the propagandists theorized that the "mark of Cain" (Genesis 4:15) was a black skin, and from that they deduced the origins of Black Africans. But the text does not specify the nature of the mark: it merely states that the mark was a sign to protect Cain from being killed on sight.[12] Cugoano quickly seized on this fallacious reading of the text and pointed out that Cain's punishment was not eternal damnation, as the slaves' enemies pretended, but rather a sentence to the ceaseless wanderings of a fugitive and a vagabond. Furthermore, Cugoano perceived that it was impossible for Cain to have had any direct postdiluvian descendants, since God had destroyed the whole human creation in the flood, saving only Noah and his sons (who had together won his special favor) and subsequently replenishing the earth's population through the offspring of Noah's sons.

In the second instance, Cugoano showed the apologists for Black slavery to have been in error in their theory that Africans were the latter-day heirs of the Hamitic curse (Genesis 9:22–27). He refuted the popular but erroneous notion that Noah had pronounced a curse on his son Ham after Ham had allowed his son Canaan to look on Noah's nakedness as he lay sleeping in a state of inebriation. Adhering to historical evidence that Ham's descendants migrated to various parts of Africa, the proslavery polemicists had logically inferred that Africans must therefore be the inheritors of the curse. But, as Cugoano demonstrated, Noah did not curse Ham but Ham's son Canaan.

By a faithful tracing of the historical record, Cugoano delineated the subsequent dispersion of Canaan and his descendants, and he documented their defeats by successive armies of Assyrians, Chaldeans, Persians, Greeks, Romans, and Turks in the various Canaanite kingdoms of Asia. Cugoano further weakened the proslavery identification of the Africans with the Canaanites by citing historical sources to show that Canaanite migration was not confined to Africa but extended probably into Europe itself. This introduced a whole new range of ironic possibilities that Cugoano uses with telling effect:

> Many of the Canaanites who fled away in the time of Joshua, became mingled with the different nations, and some historians think that some of them came to England, and settled about Cornwall, as far back as that time; so that, for anything that might be known to the contrary; there may be some of the descendants of that wicked generation still subsisting among the slave holders in the West Indies. (*Thoughts,* 36–37)

Cugoano was familiar with proslavery arguments justifying slavery on the evidence of various forms of bondage among ancient peoples, particularly those biblical references to the practice of slavery among the ancient Israelites. Like Locke and Montesquieu before him, Cugoano made a clear distinction between the temporary (often informal) arrangements under which persons served as bondsmen or slaves in antiquity and the long-term, more coercive conditions under which slaves toiled in the New World. Cugoano showed by methodical inquiry into the ancient systems that it was customary for refugees from wars of tyranny or conquest to enter into bonds to exchange their personal service for protection and sustenance. This kind of relationship he viewed as voluntary: he rejected any comparison between the bondage covenants of Mosaic law and the repressive legislation of West Indian slave societies. The status of the bondsman in Israel and the terms and conditions of his service were radically different from the West Indian slave's. It was customary for one man to buy another who was being held captive for personal debts, but the man so bought could be held only until such time as he had worked out the original terms of his bond. Cugoano pointed out a further dissimilarity: while West Indian slaves were bought and sold at the whims of their masters, bondsmen in Israel were not treated as chattels or goods. On the whole, Cugoano's purpose was to demonstrate that servitude in biblical times was more akin to vassalage in medieval Europe, a state which "rather might be termed a deliverance from debt and captivity, than a state of slavery" (*Thoughts,* 40).

It is significant that in the course of this comparative analysis, Cugoano suggests that slavery systems are proper and tolerable only in the ruder and more primitive phases of human social evolution. He speculates that provisions for bondage in Mosaic law were ordained by God as emblems of that nobler relationship of service in which human beings stood to their divine Creator: "Whoever will give a serious and unprejudiced attention to the various things alluded to in the language of sacred writ must see reason to believe that they imply a purpose and design far more glorious and important, than what seems generally to be understood by them; and to point to objects and events far more extensive and interesting, than what is generally ascribed to them" (*Thoughts*, 45).

In thus subjecting the arguments of abolition's foes to the rigor of searching historical analysis, Cugoano exposes the characteristic flaws in their method of defending the slave system. His strategy calls attention to the serious lack of reliable information about Africa in the England of his day and to the deliberate falsification and suppression of evidence about European slaving practices. He attempts, in effect, a kind of historical revisionism to shatter myths unfavorable to Africa and to uncover the true motives of the slave traffickers. He invalidates the European imperialists' deterministic assumptions that Africans were a degenerate species marked out by some iron law of nature to serve a superior race. If they would relinquish their bigotry, Cugoano suggested, and study diligently the social and political behavior of African tribes, they would find among the Africans an extraordinarily high respect for the universal principles of liberty and patriotism, loyalty to their chiefs, and reverence for their family ties.

Cugoano based his final assurance for the validity of his Old Testament exegesis in the fact that there is no support for human slavery in the New Testament. This extension of the scope of his proof invalidated any attempt on the part of the slaveholders to rationalize their latter-day slavery on a pre-Christian practice, arguably intended by God as an emblem for the spiritual edification of his people at that particular phase of their history, rather than as a literal sanction to be adopted by successive generations (*Thoughts*, 33–34).

This section of the *Thoughts* makes further use of the emblematic critique to address the popular myths about the black color of African skin. The author rejects as spurious those ethnological theories which construed variations in the human race as evidence of some predetermined ranking system, devised by nature or the divine Creator. Physical features are seen purely as superficial differences with no more ability to alter the essential human nature beneath than a black or white coat: "The external blackness of the Ethiopians, is as innocent and natural, as the spots in the leopards, and that the difference in the colour and complexion which it hath pleased God to appoint among men, are no more unbecoming unto either of them, than the different shades of the rainbow are unseemly to the whole, or unbecoming to any part of that apparent arch" (*Thoughts*, 47).

In this interpretation of the diversificationist theory of complexion, Cugoano rewrites the symbolic equation of the African's black skin with sin and evil. Whereas previously that equation was invoked as an index of the African's moral character, it is now conceived as a universal emblem to remind all people of their original sinful nature and of their inability to change it of their own volition. Thus, in Cugoano's new mythology, the African is elevated from the status of an object of scorn and disparagement to that of an icon with a positive moral designation in the divine scheme of things.

Having demonstrated by the most scrupulous inquiry that proslavery appeals to the biblical and historical precedent were both based on misconceptions of the texts involved and motivated by the need to preserve a profitable but immoral activity, Cugoano next examined slavery in the light of a more general secular philosophy.

Fully one third of the discourse so far has been polemical in character, expressly directed against the natural opponents of antislavery. At the same time, however, Cugoano acknowledged that their use of the Bible was liable to influence not only individuals of their peculiar mentality but also others who might have been inclined to believe the literal truth of the Bible. The next movement in his discourse, therefore, reinforces the objections from religious morality with objections from the popular secular philosophies of the day. In this respect, Cugoano looks back to Sancho and the moral culture that informed his *Letters*, as well as to the audience to which that collection was addressed.

A strong case for the African capacity to feel pain and suffer the woes of enslavement gave point to Cugoano's appeal to contemporary fashions in sensibility. In one of the earlier narrative sequences of the *Thoughts*, he painted a most affecting image of his own desolation as the terror of forced abduction from the warmth and security of his familar environment engulfed him. But the weight of his personal despondency was not enough to repress his natural sympathies for the other equally hapless captives he saw around him; nor now, removed by time and space and changed fortunes, is he any less mindful of slavery's unabated afflictions: "The grievous thoughts which I then felt, still pant in my heart; though my fears and tears have long subsided. And yet it is still grievous to think that thousands more have suffered in similar distress, under the hands of barbarous robbers, and merciless task-masters; and that many even now are suffering in all the extreme bitterness of grief and woe, that no language can describe" (*Thoughts*, 10–11). This kind of noble-minded empathizing achieves a dual rhetorical effect. It presents the author as a man of sensibility, manifesting the quality his race was accused of lacking. And, conversely, it insinuates that the slave dealers lacked sensibility because they had refused, so far, in spite of ceaseless entreaty, to abandon the inhuman traffic altogether, even though the

evidence was overwhelming that the Africans suffered profound psychological distress from the experience of cultural dissociation and personal loss.
Cugoano could have found no more positive proof of slavery's antithesis to
sensibility than this description of the landing and auctioning of slaves at the
end of a perilous Middle Passage:

> Here daughters are clinging to their mothers, and mothers to their
> daughters, bedewing each others [sic] naked breasts with tears; here
> fathers, mothers and children, locked in each others arms, are begging
> never to be separated; here the husband will be pleading for his wife,
> and the wife praying for her children, and entreating, enough to melt
> the most obdurate heart, not to be torn from them, and taken away
> from her husband; and some will be still weeping for their native shore,
> and their dear relations and friends, and their endearing connections
> which they have left behind, and have been barbarously tore away from
> and all are bemoaning themselves with grief and lamentation at the
> prospect of their wretched fate. (*Thoughts*, 95–96)[13]

The author of the *Thoughts* wanted to persuade his readers that, to be
unmoved by such scenes, the slave dealers must of all men be the most bereft
of human feeling. His unstated assumptions are that, since the ability to feel
injury is such a universal human trait, any failure to avoid causing pain to
one's fellow must be a sure sign of diminished humanity.

From the axiom that slavery was against sensibility, Cugoano moved next
to enunciate the axiom that slavery was against humanity. It was the coercive nature of the European practice that made slavery such a heinous crime
against human beings. He was skeptical about the state of human progress
that allowed such flagrant violation of human liberty. Without the faintest
deferential suggestion, he characterized man stealing as robbery, a crime
against humanity, because it disregarded the sanctity of the person and
violated the essential bonds of kinship that linked all human beings to God.
Significantly, Cugoano invoked in his argument the principle of general philanthropy so central to Sancho's humanitarian thesis. He proposes it as the
touchstone of all the other virtues, using this occasion discreetly to attack
the implicit cultural chauvinism that shaped the European view of Africa
and the treatment of her people:

> And those who go on to injure, ensnare, oppress, and enslave their
> fellow creatures, manifest their hatred to men, and maintain their own
> infamous dignity and vassalage, as the servants of sin and the devil: but
> the man that has any honour as a man scorns their ignominious digni-
> ty: the noble philanthropist looks up to God and Father as his only
> sovereign and he looks around on his fellow men and his brethren and
> friends; and in every situation and case, however mean and contempt-

ible they may seem, he endeavours to do them good. . . . (*Thoughts*, 61)

There is a similar primitivistic proposition in this very rhetorical structure. A denial of natural kinship with one's fellow humans must necessarily precede a decision to enslave those same humans. The denial itself is a sign of corrupted reason, the flawed foundation on which the myth of European racial superiority was built.

A third axiom in this stage of Cugoano's argument that challenged the eighteenth century's image of itself is the assertion that slavery was inconsistent with civilization. Cugoano seems to take as his basic assumption the view that a love of liberty and a desire to extend its benefits to one's fellows without discrimination should be an indispensable rule of conduct for an enlightened, civilized people. As he could not reconcile slavery—the taking away of freedom—with these high expressions of human social progress, he concluded that slavery must necessarily diminish the vaunted achievements of a supposedly rational people. Indeed, he went further to question by implication whether nations that practiced slavery could be considered civilized or progressive at all. In Cugoano's formulations, slavery, as it was then being practiced in the New World, belonged more properly to a barbarous, preenlightened age, more identifiable with the predatory moral universe of Hobbes than with the benevolent conceptions of a Hutcheson or a Shaftesbury: "Slavery can no where be tolerated with any consistency to civilization and the laws of justice among men; but if it can maintain its ground to have any place at all, it must be among a society of barbarians and thieves and where the laws of their society is [*sic*] for every one to catch what he can" (*Thoughts*, 114).

Such scathing strictures indicate a strong sense of unease in the author's mind about the limitations of reason and enlightenment—a perception that their sole guidance could not be counted upon to steer individuals into paths of consistent moral responsibility. Unlike Sancho, Cugoano was clearly not susceptible to the cant of optimism and perfectibility that were so much the public assumptions of the age in which he lived. He was more forcefully impressed with the myopic tendency of people to seek shelter for their bad principles by associating them with the presumed perfections of an unimpeachable past.[14]

Thus far the aim of Cugoano's discourse has been to establish a clear line of division between the uncompromising standards of Judaeo-Christian ethics and the expedient morality of proslavery dogma. Cugoano could also use the most commonly retailed scriptural and historical arguments to indict a whole civilization, because those arguments conflicted so blatantly with that ideal standard of moral conduct with which most virtuous-minded eighteenth-century Englishmen would readily have associated themselves. Having once established these basic contradictions, he could now show, by a logical process of rational inquiry, that the major British institutions were knowing accessories to a corrupt system. He therefore directed his central antislavery attack against the four great pillars of the British state: the law, the monarchy, Parliament, and the church.

The unmasking of the powerful institutional authority on which slavery had been legitimized and supported was a major landmark for such an early abolitionist work. That the exposure should appear in a work of protest penned by a representative of the oppressed slaves was nothing short of revolutionary. Other writers before Cugoano had challenged the inequities that poor people suffered before the British law, but none had so far urged violent overthrow of the plantocracy or called the integrity of the legal system into question with such withering reproach.[15] While Cugoano does not advocate anarchy—he fully admits the necessity of law to govern the variable passions of human beings in society—he shows himself openly contemptuous of those laws which protected the narrow interests of special classes. He believed that the actions of individuals could be efficiently governed by the equal application of "the universal law of love, honour, righteousness and equity" (*Thoughts*, 61), but that when the Golden Rule, which was the essence of Divine Law, was infringed, especially as in the case of man stealing, the transgressors should suffer the full severity of the secular penal laws:

> And with regard to that law of menstealers, merchandizers, and of slaves found in their hands, that whatever mitigation and forbearance such offenders ought to meet with, their crimes denote a very heinous offence, and a great violation of the law of God; they ought, therefore, to be punished according to their trespasses, which in some cases should be death, if the person so robbed and stole [*sic*] should die in consequence thereof, or should not be restored and brought back; and even then to be liable to every damage and penalty that the judges should think proper. . . . (*Thoughts*, 66)

Cugoano's guiding thesis is that man stealing, slave trafficking, and slave holding were manifest criminal activities that could not be reconciled with the Golden Rule of love and reciprocity in human relations enjoined in the Christian Gospel. His contention was that if the legal codes of England provided such harsh penalties for minor offenses like petty theft and in general were so protective of the right of private property, they should prescribe a penalty commensurate with the serious crime of depriving human beings of their personal freedom. He found the institutionalized laws of European nations inequitable, in that slaves hardly ever escaped their rigor even for the mildest offenses, while their masters and their masters' accomplices seemed to escape with scandalous impunity.

Thus, Cugoano's critical commentaries cast a dark shadow of suspicion and distrust on the lawmakers and law enforcers of civilized nations. In an extended disquisition on Western secular penal codes, he exposes some of the most blatant paradoxes of a civilization purportedly guided in its social and political arrangements by the infallible light of reason:

> But all the laws of civilization must jar greatly when the law of God is screwed up in the greatest severity to punish men for their crimes on the one hand, and on the other to be totally disregarded. When the Divine law points out a theft, where the thief should make restitution for his trespass, the laws of civilization say, he must die for his crime: and when that law tells us, that he who stealeth shall surely die, the laws of civilization say, in many cases, that it is no crime. In this the ways of men are not equal; but the wise and just determine whether the laws of men are right. (*Thoughts*, 71)

Cugoano exercised the unique critical perspective that alien status confers to unveil the inperfections of this "enlightened" system, so patently discriminatory to his fellow Blacks. Having weighed the laws of God and the laws of civilization, he concluded that humankind could not be trusted to devise laws to protect the interests of all equally, and so he proposed that the laws of God should take precedence over human laws. He seemed to believe that humans should observe and enforce God's laws faithfully rather than arrogate to themselves the tyrannical powers of life and death applied in regimes like the slave colonies.[16]

A mixture of apocalyptic prophecy and revolutionary rhetoric marks the concluding terms of this appraisal of British law. Cugoano's vision of the ultimate collapse of slavery's empire over the African is informed by a fiery eloquence. It echoes the spirit of ancient Hebrew prophecy and freely adapts Micah's denunciatory text (delivered against the rich and powerful exploiters of Israel) to the immediate conditions of African oppression:

> Yet, O Africa: yet poor slave: the day of thy watchmen cometh, and thy visitation draweth nigh, that shall be their perplexity. Therefore I will look unto the lord; I will wait for the God of my slavation; my God will hear me. Rejoice not against me, O mine enemy; though I be fallen, I shall yet arise; though I sit in darkness, the Lord shall set a light unto me. . . . Then mine enemies shall see it, and shame shall cover them which said unto me, Where is the Lord the God, that regardeth thee: Mine eyes shall behold them trodden down as the mire of the streets. In that day that thy walls of deliverance are to be built, in that day shall the decree of slavery be far removed. (*Thoughts*, 76)[17]

The translation of the Jewish experience into a parallel image of the Africans' sufferings under slavery underlined Cugoano's conviction that God had specially favored Blacks because of the grave injustices they suffered. Further, the espousal of open revolt against an immoral system signified his belief in the rightness of the Africans' cause and the sinfulness of the European regime of slavery over them. By conceptualizing slavery in the terms of a forcible constraint and slave masters therefore as robbers, Cugoano gave moral support to any attempt by slaves to free themselves of an unlawful yoke. Significantly, he makes resistance a moral duty with clear biblical foundation: "However much it is required of men to forgive one another their trespasses in one respect, it is also manifest, and that we are commanded, as noble, to resist evil in one another in order to prevent others doing evil, and to keep ourselves from harm" (*Thoughts*, 73). It is true that he does not formulate any specific plan of political action for the overthrow of the slave system; but, just as the prophet Micah had proclaimed a future of hope and national restoration for Israel's masses, so Cugoano draws on the copious examples of history to assure himself that a dialectical pattern of tyranny followed by retaliation would utimately break the Africans' bondage.

Cugoano was one of the few early abolitionists to identify the British monarchy as one of the major state institutions giving active support to slavery. In tones of prophetic gravity he charged the monarchy with complicity in crimes against Africa. He recalled that one of the first English expeditions to the slave coast was made by the Royal African Company, a corporation of traders commissioned by Charles II. While Cugoano respected the traditional divinity ascribed to the office of monarch, his criticism of the royal family's connections with the slave trade raised questions about the moral integrity of God's vicegerents on earth; it indicated to a barely half-informed public that some of the slave trade's chief beneficiaries must have been men of great power and influence in the councils of state:

> Nothing else can be conceived, but that the power of infernal wickedness has so reigned and pervaded over the enlightened nations as to infatuate and lead on the great men, and the Kings of Europe, to promote and establish such a horrible traffic of wickedness as the African slave trade and West Indian slavery, and thereby to bring themselves under the guilty responsibility of such awful iniquity. The kings and governors of the nations in general have power to prevent their subjects and people from enslaving and oppressing others, if they will; but if they do not endeavour to do it; even if they could not effect that good purpose; they must be responsible for their crimes, . . . (*Thoughts*, 106)

Cugoano discerned that Britain's failure thus far to abolish the slave trade was occasioned by a crisis in leadership, because the monarchy had been compromised by its own economic interest in slavery, and by the interests of the plantocratic and trading classess so closely allied to it. He therefore called on the king to exercise the moral and legal authority of his office, to stand firm against corruptive inducements, and to exercise a restraining influence on the rapacious appetites of those who speculated in human property (*Thoughts*, 105–6).

As abolitionist politics intensified within the legislatures in the next two decades, Cugoano's strictures against the monarchy were to be justified by the pronouncements of certain royal figures. On 11 April 1793, during the debate in the House of Lords on the abolition of the slave trade, the duke of Clarence came out firmly in support of the trade and scathingly against the abolitionists. He stated plainly that it would be "impolitic and unjust" to abolish the trade, since England's economic well-being was so extensively bound up with it. He leveled a stinging attack on the characters of Ramsay and Wilberforce, labeling them and their associates as "fanatics and hypocrites," and insinuating (quite spuriously) that they were colluding with republican ideologues in France to bring a regime of terror and anarchy to England.[18] Writing to Lord Grenville on 27 June 1804, Wilberforce was distressed to see four members of the royal family "come down to vote against the poor, helpless, friendless slaves."[19]

From the monarchy, Cugoano turned his attention to the next most powerful institution—Parliament. He bluntly denounced that body's members as connivers in the evil of slavery and patrons of the unjust traffic, basing his charges on the fact that they were not using the power they had to repeal the laws which legalized slavery and that they had done nothing so far to discourage the actions of "those planters and merchants, and of all others who were the authors of African graves, severities, and cruel punishments. . . ." (*Thoughts*, 110). Cugoano's critique ascribes to the British Parliament the responsibility for moral leadership, not only in Britain itself, but also among all the civilized nations of europe. It weighs that serious duty against the legislature's actual countenancing of man stealing and slave holding. From such assumptions and observations, it proceeds logically to accuse Parliament of failing to protect the oppressed Africans and of compromising the very standards of civilized justice and equity for which it stood, by not bringing pressure to bear on other nations to desist.

Cugoano gave so much force to this principle of collective moral obligation that he suggested Parliament should have committed Britain to a kind of crusading posture against the other colonial powers in an attempt to terminate slavery:

> For it might be to the universal rule of duty to all men that fear God and keep his commandments, to do good to all men wherever they can and they find any wronged and injured by others, they should endeavour to deliver the ensnared whatever their grievances may be; and

should this sometimes lead them into war they might expect the protection and blessing of heaven. How far other motives may appear eligible for men to oppose one another with hostile force, it is not my business to enquire. (*Thoughts*, 115)

In harmony with some of the best antislavery thinkers, from Benezet to Clarkson, Cugoano pointed to the ultimate danger that a heedless perpetuation of slavery would diminish the British nation as a whole. The despotism, cruelty, and oppression embedded in the ethos of plantation society struck him as a positive threat to the continuance of free institutions in Britain itself. It seemed to him that, given the right conditions, the supporters of slavery were capable of abridging those very freedoms which the English cherished so zealously for themselves and that "the most generous and tenacious people in the world for liberty, may at last be reduced to slaves" (*Thoughts*, 90).

The established church was the fourth major body to come under attack in Cugoano's critical survey of instituional cooperation with slavery. With a comprehensive view of their potential moral force, Cugoano incriminates both the Western church and the Eastern church for their silence in the face of these enormous wrongs. Besides the two major branches of Christendom, he includes Islam and attributes to her a proportionate share of guilt for the participation of the Moslems in the slave trade—an important factor little discussed, even among the principal abolitionist writers. To Cugoano, the moral debility of the church seemed to spring from its preferring forms and ceremonies over the real issues that distracted a troubled world. The clergy's reticence and the laity's "passive obedience" implicated the whole communion of God's people in the guilt of the slave handlers (*Thoughts*, 125).

By describing the broadest nexus of institutional responsibility for the instigation and continuing support of the slave trade, Cugoano managed to focus his audience's attention on the pervasiveness of slavery's evil and its moral consequences for their collective national life. By maintaining that the oppression of Africans and the curtailment of their liberty were bound to undermine the progress of European civilization, he appealed to some of the most sensitive instincts in individuals of enlightened pretensions. This strategy shifts the center of concern—temporarily, at any rate— away from what was, for some, a weakly understood condition, affecting a people of lineaments and customs markedly different from their own, to the more frightening possibility that slavery could subvert the whole European way of life.

In another major thematic movement of the *Thoughts*, Cugoano holds up the stated objects of European expansion and colonization to a similar hardheaded inquiry. Again, by systematic analysis of the historical record, he demythicizes the noble intentions that historians often claimed for the explorers and settlers who established Europe's influence in distant lands. He shows by cogent examples how the Spaniards' activities in the New World were characterized by a recurrent motif of treachery, fraud, and atrocity. He delivers a searing attack on the modus operandi of the conquistadors: his clear attitude is that there can be no glossing over what was obviously a very sordid business:

> ...their establishing and carrying on of that most dishonest, unjust and diabolical traffic of buying and selling, and of enslaving men, is such a monstruous, audacious and unparalleled wickedness, that the very idea of it is shocking, and the whole nature of it is horrible and infernal. It may be said with confidence as a general fact, that all their foreign settlements and colonies were founded on murders and devastations, and that they have continued their depredations in cruel slavery and oppression to this day. . . . (*Thoughts*, 77)

Cugoano selected some of the most egregious acts of rapaciousness and cruelty from the saga of colonization in the Americas to underscore his opinions. He called Ovando's attack on and destruction of Queen Anaconda of Hispaniola "truly horrible and lamentable." The betrayal of Montezuma and the ravaging of Mexico by Cortés he found "dreadful and shocking." With considerably more vehemence of language he painted the "treacherous bastard" Pizarro, at the head of a band of miscreant depredators, conquering and subjecting Peru in one of the most barbarous acts of plunder and treachery in the history of humankind.[20]

One vignette from Cugoano's revisionist critique of Spanish colonial history stands out both for the force of its conception and for the insight it affords into the inclusiveness of his political vision. With disarming candor and informed judgment he details how Christian missionaries became accessories to the frauds perpetrated against the indigenous peoples of the Americas. He describes Father Vincent Valverde, "the fanatic monk" in Pizarro's expedition to Peru, as a self-righteous missionary, exuding much civilized religiosity while hypocritically serving the secular ends of Spanish imperialism. At the request of Pizarro, the Inca Atahualpa comes to parley with the Spaniards:

> As he [Atahualpa] approached near the Spanish quarters, Father Vincent Valverde, chaplain to the expedition, advanced with a crucifix in one hand and a breviary in the other, and began with a long discourse, pretending to explain some of the general doctrines of Christianity, together with the fabulous notion of St. Peter's vicegerency, and the transmission of his apostolic power continued in the succession of the Popes; and that the Pope, Alexander, by donation, had invested their master as the sole Monarch of all the New World. (*Thoughts*, 79)

The studied particularity of Cugoano's scene painting here sharpens the sense of dramatic moment, as it penetrates the facade of dissimulation erected by the "crucifix in one hand and the breviary in the other." If Cugoano intends mere distrust by the ironic understones ingrafted in the phrases "long discourse," "pretending," and "general doctrines," he reflects the most scathing cynicism respecting the authority of the Church temporal by his outright challenge to the doctrine of the apostolic succession in the words, "the fabulous notion of St. Peter's vicegerency." By contrast, Cugoano sustains his habitual respect for primitive customs throughout the reenactment of the episode. He portrays Atahualpa as conciliatory to the strangers, dignified in his royalty, and faithful to the traditions of his ancestors. While previous testimony should dispel any suggestion that Cugoano may have forsaken his faith in Christianity, these censorious reflections on the church show clearly that he had no respect for the pseudomissionary adventurers who bulldozed indigenous peoples into exchanging their familiar religious practices for Christianity while promoting the imperialist designs of their European masters:

> Had the Peruvians been visited by men of honesty, knowledge, and enlightened understanding, to teach them, by patient instruction and the blessing of God, they might have been induced to embrace the doctrines and faith of Christianity and to abandon their errors of superstition and idolatry... I would have my African counterparts know and understand, that the destroyers and enslavers of men can be no Christians, for Christianity is the system of benignity and love, and all its votaries are devoted to honesty, justice, humanity, meekness, peace and goodwill to all men. (*Thoughts*, 83–84)

By extending the arc of antislavery protest to encompass the issues of colonization and conquest, Cugoano relates abolition to the wider ethical and political questions raised by the expansion of Europe. By unraveling the intricate nexus of institutions responsible for the continuance of slavery, he aimed to focus his audience's attention on the pervasiveness of slavery's evil and the moral consequences it entailed for their collective national life. The inclusiveness of his critique reflects an uncommon understanding of the essentially economic motive for European contacts with the darker-skinned races of the world. That understanding spurred him to criticize through his writings and to spend a good part of this recorded life agitating against the exploitation of London's Black poor in a scheme to settle and colonize Sierra Leone.

Early in January 1786, conditions among London's Black poor were so distressing that a committee of merchants, bankers, and parliamentarians was formed to launch an emergency fund for their relief. The public response was generous, and Blacks started to receive regular assistance with food, clothing, and medicines from the emergency fund, which reached some eight hundred and ninety pounds in four months.[21]

Notwithstanding the public officials' apparent concern for their plight, Blacks could derive no permanent sense of security from these mere subsistence measures. Many of them grew restive and expressed a desire to return to Africa. The committee energetically supported the idea and between March and May of 1786 discussed a proposal, outlined by Henry Smeathman, for resettling them in Sierra Leone. The House of Commons, too, endorsed the plan and voted over four thousand pounds for the maintenance, supply, and outfitting of the expedition. Cugoano's attitude toward the project was at first one of optimism and support. It seems likely that he was one of nine Black leaders elected as "headmen" or "corporals" during the first week of June 1786 to serve as liaisons between the committee and the Black poor in London and to be group leaders during the expedition and settlement.[22] However, Cugoano found reason to suspect the organizers' integrity and quickly withdrew from the group. Like others interested in the welfare of the Black poor, Cugoano was unhappy about the haste with which the project was conceived. Abolition and rights activists like Sharp and Equiano were deeply disturbed by reports that the authorities were using intimidatory and coercive tactics to lure Blacks into the scheme. They objected to the absence of any firm guarantees for the preservation of the free Blacks' liberty once they arrived in Sierra Leone. In his record, Cugoano uses such terms as "flattering and laudable appearance" and "appearance of honour" to voice his deep misgivings that this might be one more scheme to ensnare and exploit the Black massess in a new kind of slavery:

> This prospect of settling a free colony to Great Britain in a peaceable alliance with the inhabitants of Africa at Sierra Leone, has neither altogether met with the credulous approbation of the Africans here, nor yet been sought after with any prudent and right plan by the promoters of it. Had a treaty of agreement been first made with the inhabitants of Africa, and the terms and nature of such a settlement fixed upon, and its situation and boundary pointed out; then might the Africans, and others here, have embarked with a good prospect of enjoying happiness and prosperity themselves, in return of some advantage to their friends and benefactors of Great Britain. (*Thoughts*, 139–40)

Apparently, Cugoano's objections were effective enough to dampen the enthusiasm of some Blacks for the scheme. Many Blacks stopped turning up at the relief centers to collect their weekly assistance. Out of some 709 who had signed the repatriation agreement, only three hundred embarked in the transport ships in December 1786. And so, four months later, when the four ships sailed for Africa on 10 April 1787, only 441 settlers remained on board. This depletion in numbers was caused by a combination of factors.

Passengers grew tired of waiting on board the ships during the long delays caused by administrative and mechanical problems. Apprehensive about their future security, some changed their minds and returned to land. Sickness, starvation, and death took others. The chicanery and high-handedness of the expeditions' agents also inspired distrust among the deportees and their leaders. Equiano, who was appointed commissary, wrote to Cugoano revealing the greed and self-interest of the agents and repenting that he had ever consented to participate.

Shyllon, drawing heavily on newspaper editorials and reports, has proposed that the repatriation project was conceived not so much out of any humanitarian concern for the destitute Blacks but more out of fear for the impact of their steadily increasing numbers on English society. The government officials were eager to clear the streets of Black beggars and vagrants, and the Africanophobes wished to bid good riddance to the "dingy-faced" offspring of Black-white unions. The contracting agents saw in the project a way to capitalize on human misery, as well as to exploit the resources of the new colony.[23]

The position that Cugoano took of cautious support for the project and open opposition to its movers was conditioned by his habitual insistence on the highest ethical standards in public life and his deep sense of responsibility to a people much abused in the past. Some sixteen years' experience with white prejudice against Blacks made him understandably wary of this sudden goodwill. With his unfailing ability to detect contradictions in official policy, he pointed out an ominous irony in the government's plan to establish this colony in close proximity to forts and garrisons where the sordid business of kidnapping and enslaving was still being carried on against the local population. He drew substance for his stubborn misgivings from the enduring wisdom of the Bible: "Can a fountain send forth at the same place sweet water and bitter?" he asked (*Thoughts*, 141–142).

Although Cugoano devotes the better part of his book to condemning slavery and its supporters, he is mindful of the serious critic's responsibility to propose solutions. In some eighteen pages towards the close of the book (120–38), he outlines a program of reforms. Having examined and refuted the deceitful proslavery arguments and having vehemently opposed any compromise with a system that brutalized human beings, he would rest content with nothing less than an immediate abolition of the slave trade and emancipation of West Indian slaves. He proposed a system of "free and voluntary labour," under which the ex-slaves would work for a wage. Apparently influenced by the thinking of Adam Smith and other antislavery political economists, Cugoano supported the view that an enlightened policy toward plantation labor would foster a more industrious and intelligent work force; that free Black laborers would produce more and therefore increase Britain's prosperity.[24] Progressive reformer that he was, Cugoano recognized the need for a rapid compensatory social development for a people long kept in ignorance. His plan therefore required that masters provide for their slaves religious instruction and training in useful arts and crafts, so that Blacks could eventually build independent lives.

The exact terms of emancipation appear more discretionary than radical. In the light of Cugoano's sustained resistance to the inherent degradation of slavery, they present a sobering paradox. However progressive his reform ideology might have been, Cugoano stopped short of recommending a sudden and complete severance of ties between master and slave. He understood all too well that it would take more than a simple declaration of emancipation to transform a hitherto totally unautonomous people into a confident, self-determined community. He understood that slave owners would violently resist any scheme that threatened sudden collapse to the plantation economy without providing adequate compensation for the loss of their financial investments. He therefore proposed an eligibility plan that carried built-in protection for both white and Black interests. All slaves would have to serve seven years before earning their freedom. In addition, they would have to show themselves religious minded, civil, and generally well behaved. As a provision for their personal protection and support, they were to remain in a relation of "lawful servitude" to their masters, "without torture or oppression."

While most Africans would stay in the West Indies as free Blacks, Cugoano conceived of a scheme to use some of them who had attained a more than common understanding of the Christian faith and all-round personal development to return to teach their brothers and sisters in Africa. In the light of Cugoano's strong views against European missionaries, his plan here may be seen as a shrewd means of christianizing Africa and starting a native pool of skilled Blacks to spearhead the continent's overall development without the attendant problems of cultural imperialism.

Also contained in these proposals was a plan for the legal enforcement of abolition laws. Cugoano suggested that a British fleet should be assigned to police the Guinea Coast and the high seas of the Atlantic, in order to discourage kidnapping, and to inspect merchant shipping for illegal human cargo. The corrupt governors of the coastal settlements and their villainous assistants would be dismissed and replaced by men of higher caliber who would implement a new phase of African-European relations.

Trade was to be the mainspring of this new relationship. Cugoano was aware of the growing agitation among the commercial classes against the monopoly enjoyed by the sugar plantation and West India trading interests. He knew that they desired a larger share in existing markets and control of expanded industries. In a calculated appeal to this emergent bloc within the British economy, Cugoano announced that a substitution of slave trading for manufactures would break the West Indian monopoly and yield ten times more revenue than the trade generated by that quarter. In his view, it would be a trade mutually beneficial to both Britain and Africa. It would give Britain a conspicuous and enviable advantage over her other European competitors: "And were the noble Britons and their august Sovereign, to cause protection and encouragement to be given to those Africans, they might expect in a short time, if need required it, to receive from thence great supplies of men in a lawful way, either for industry or defence; and of other things in abundance, from so great a source, where everything is luxurious and plenty, if not laid waste by barbarity and gross ignorance" (*Thoughts*, 134). Africa, for her part, would stand to benefit from British advancements in arts and sciences, adopting the skills necessary to develop industry and manufacture of her own.

It is remarkable to find Cugoano prefiguring a kind of economic thinking that really did not gain wide acceptance until at least two decades after the publication of his book. While his proposals for restructuring the African trade must have been quite widely discussed in abolitionist circles—as, for example, among the Quakers, who themselves represented substantial commercial interests—it is noteworthy that Cugoano should fasten on such a precise perception of Britain's economic self-interest to promote his own fierce brand of African nationalism. His abolition proposals may be criticized on the ground that they allow slave owners too much latitude in deciding when to liberate successive generations of slaves. Also, they do not provide for any regulatory safeguards against possible infringements of the ex-slaves' rights. But when one considers that Wilberforce and the abolitionist party in Parliament found it necessary to make similar concessions to the propertied interests as late as the 1820s, Cugoano's capacity for shrewdness and compromise in political matters becomes all the more distinct.

Just as the highly polemical character of the discourse is fashioned to expose the corrupting effects of slavery on the Europeans and their civilization, conversely, it develops a more constructive affirmation of faith in the African future. Cugoano believed firmly in the moral integrity and social improvability of his people. He built his case for their eventual vindication from proslavery libels on the asumption that the universe was an ordered creation and that a just God intervened to punish and reward individuals according to the merits of their actions. Since Europe was in this case the aggressor, he was confident that divine justice operating in the inexorable laws of history would bring about her swift demise and set up a revitalized Africa in her place.

It has been shown previously that Cugoano drew much of the inspiration for his historical analysis of slavery from the biblical experience of the Israelites. By a deft adaptation of the scriptural record to the circumstances of African oppression, he develops a metaphorical structure on which he builds a vision of ultimate justice. He invests the metaphor with such elasticity that both the Europeans and the Africans are conceptualized as latter-day Israelites, adverse political relationships notwithstanding. Europe stands for him as an emblem of stubborn disobedience, its people shortly to be visited by God for their transgressions. Africa is the Israel of the Patriarchs, her people chosen by God for their fortitude and faithfulness under suffering to be leaders of the nations. The Africans become symbols of virtue in distress, victims and martyrs in a cruel war against humanity: "For we have been hunted as the wild beasts, and sold to the enemies of mankind as their prey, and should any of us endeavour to get away from them, as a man would naturally fly from an enemy that way-laid him, we have been pursued after, and, by haughty mandates and laws of iniquity, overtaken, and murdered and slain, and the blood of millions cries out against them" (*Thoughts*, 118–19). The Europeans, on the other hand, are conceptualized as a people once blessed with God's favor and endowed with the benefits of civilization, power, and prosperity; but now they have forfeited that special relationship by their active participation in human slavery and by their failure to condemn other nations who followed the same sinful course.

In the broadest intellectual terms, Cugoano's *Thoughts and Sentiments* stands as a work of comprehensive achievement. It participates in all the principal systems of thought that made antislavery such a representative synthesis of Enlightenment values. It harmonizes the objective, more exacting methods of rationalistic inquiry with the subjective, more passionate poetry of religious fervor and outraged emotions. With a judicious subordination of abolitionist tendencies to sentimentalize the African's woes, Cugoano directed the cold light of reason on the problem of slavery, effectively announcing that the proslavery case could be rebutted by an African commanding the most sophisticated methods of debate and championing ideas highly respected in the world of the Enlightenment.

5

Olaudah Equiano: The Appeal to Humanity and the Political Self

With the appearance in 1789 of Olaudah Equiano's two-volume auto-biography, the revolution of racial and political consciousness in Black literature of eighteenth-century England reached its highest form and effectiveness. Published during the climactic phase of abolitionist agitation, *The Interesting Narrative of the Life of Olaudah Equiano, or Gustavus Vassa, the African* was supported by the British Anti-Slavery Trade Society and was proposed to the British public as an authentic document to bolster the abolitionist case and to win the sympathy of Parliament, which was then beginning active formal debate on measures to end the slave trade. Although Equiano was no stranger to antislavery partisans (he had made several political representations on his African brothers and sisters' behalf during the preceding fifteen years), this literary event gave to the world a permanent and inspiring record of a Black man's experience under slavery. It offered a persuasive account of the actual conditions of that economic system which exploited the free labor of Blacks for the material prosperity of whites and of a social system which dehumanized members of the African race through laws and practices that were hostile, discriminatory, and oppressive.

Both Equiano's personal life as depicted in the *Life* and his public activities as attested by independent sources corroborate the thesis that the Africans themselves were a major force in the struggle for and eventual achievement of respect for their human dignity and value. If committed, imaginative leadership consists in using the tools of wide personal experience to seize and transform the circumstances of a given historical moment, Equiano's performance wins that citation deservedly. Many experiences helped to shape his colorful career as an abolitionist and political activist: the rigors and hazards he endured as a seafarer; the resourcefulness he acquired as a small trader; and the spiritual intensity he experienced as a convert to Calvinism. This extraordinary accretion of practical abilities and moral endowments fitted him well for the challenge of verbalizing more explicitly those issues of race and status which Sancho was forced to equivocate about and which Cugoano had inveighed against in a more heavy-handed polemical style. As the third figure in the triumvirate of eighteenth-century Black writers, Equiano joins the moderating impulses of religion

118

and humanitarianism to the sterner techniques of politics and activism to epitomize in himself all that was most ennobling and heroic in the anti-slavery struggle.

Of the three authors covered in this study, none furnishes as extensive a personal memoir as Equiano does in the *Life*. Throughout the narrative, he makes a conscious effort to delineate the principal incidents and experiences of his life as faithfully as memory would allow and to appraise his conduct with honest judgment and sober reflection. The result is a document both thoroughgoing and credible. Since to rehearse all the details would be super-fluous here, only those circumstances that make for continuity in this study and that illustrate important phases of his life will be described in the ensuing discussion.

Equiano was born in 1745 at a place called Essaka, in Eboe, an interior province of the then powerful and wealthy kingdom of Benin. His father, like Cugoano's, held positions of prestige and authority among the elders of his village. He was a chief, a judge, and a senator; young Olaudah was destined in time to inherit those offices of respect, had he not been kidnapped at age eleven and sold into slavery along with his sister. Passing from the hands of his original abductors into the custody of several different masters and sojourning among diverse tribes, he felt deeply the loss of his parents and lamented his eventual separation from his sister. After some six months had elapsed, he finally arrived on the coast, whence he was transported to Barbados with a cargo of other slaves. From Barbados he was shipped to Virginia and sold there to a Mr. Campbell, who put him to work on his plantation. Not long after, Michael Henry Pascal, the captain of a trading ship and a lieutenant in the Royal Navy, bought Equiano from Campbell and took him to England. It was from Pascal that he received the name Gustavus Vassa; and aboard his ship that he met a true friend and teacher, Richard Baker, himself then only a lad of sixteen or seventeen.

Equiano, Baker, and other shipboys spent the spring and part of the summer of 1757 cruising in and out of various ports around the British Isles. During this time, Equiano got his first glimpse of London, visited Holland twice, and saw naval engagements off the coast of France. In London he stayed in the home of the Guerins, relations of Captain Pascal. There he immediately won the affection of the Misses Guerin, who took particular care of him on this and future visits. Equiano was by this time acclimatizing himself to the manners, habits, and physical appearance of the Europeans but still finding many things about them that variously excited, puzzled, and terrified him. In the short space of a year, he had served aboard HMS *Roebuck*, *Preston*, *Royal George*, and *Namur*, following the quick succession of Pascal's appointments and promotions. In 1758, he sailed to North America as part of a "mighty fleet" under the command of Admiral Boscawen. The Seven Years War with France was in progress, and Equiano's

youthful passion for adventure and heroics was fired by several naval skir-
mishes with the French fleet: he was stirred by the siege of Louisburgh, awed
by the presence of General Wolfe aboard their fleet in Nova Scotia (1758),
and flattered by the fond attention of Captain George Balfour (*Life* 1:123).

On his return to England in 1759, Equiano's master sent him to wait on
the Misses Guerin in London. The ladies persuaded Pascal to baptize him,
and the ceremony was performed at Saint Margaret's Church, Westminster,
in February of that year. They took great pains to teach him reading,
writing, and the principles of Christianity, but he was forced to part from
them within a few months when his master set sail for the Mediterranean in
early spring. Fortunately, Equiano was able to continue his education on
board ship and, according to his own report, he was well provided for.
When Pascal became captain of the fire ship *Aetna*, he made Equiano his
steward. The African youth enjoyed the kindness and affection of the
captain's personal attendant, Daniel Queen, a sailor in his forties. Queen
taught Equiano to dress hair and to read the Bible; above all, he instilled in
him a sense of personal freedom and human dignity. Equiano wrote of this
relationship: "In short he was like a father to me, and some even used to call
me after his name; they also styled me the black Christian. Indeed I almost
loved him with the affection of a son" (*Life* 1:172).

In March 1761, after a stay in England, Equiano set sail once more with
the fleet for further naval engagements, this time to meet the French fleet,
which the British finally destroyed at Belle Ile off the Breton coast. This was
to be Equiano's last voyage with Captain Pascal; for in December 1762, on
their return to London, the captain burst into a sudden and unexplainable
rage, accusing him of planning to escape. Equiano pleaded his innocence,
but nothing availed. Pascal sold him to Captain Doran, who took him to the
West Indies in early 1763. Doran sold Equiano in Montserrat to Robert
King, a Quaker merchant who owned ships that plied between the West
Indies and America.

Equiano served his new master faithfully aboard the ships, gradually winning his confidence and respect. He sailed under several different captains,
increasing his knowledge of seamanship and improving the general education he had begun in his navy days. In three years' time he was able to
purchase his freedom, although he willingly agreed to continue working
aboard King's ships as a freeman. Early in 1767, he bade King farewell and
sailed for England.

Arriving in London after an absence of four years, he went immediately to
see the Guerins. They found him employment as hairdresser to a gentleman,
Captain O'Hara, with whom he worked from September 1767 until February 1768. He had a brief association with Dr. Charles Irving, noted for his
desalination experiments. Although Equiano seems to have decided to settle
permanently in England, his love for seafaring and adventure had not by

any means diminished. He continued to ship out on different voyages to the Mediterranean, the Caribbean, and America until 1786. In 1773 he accompanied Constantine Phipps on that explorer's expedition to the North Pole, and two years later he joined Dr. Irving on his voyage to set up a plantation among the Indians of the Mosquito Shore. In 1792 Equiano married an Englishwoman, Susanna Cullen. He died on 31 March 1797.[1]

The foregoing sketch bespeaks a life defined by rapid change, where crucial choices were externally imposed and where adjustment to them had to be as quick as present fortune was variable. Even before he left Africa, Equiano was faced with these uncertainties and had begun to feel their profound psychological effects. He was sold repeatedly in the different communities that lay between his native village and the slave coast. Even though he was treated with affectionate indulgence by some of his masters, the wrenching pangs of loss and the terror of things unknown left him heartsick and distraught. Every youthful dream of happiness and permanence was frustrated by a fresh shift in circumstance: he had become a victim of the inexorable laws of trade in the commodity of human flesh. Equiano thus recalls his distress on being passed from the control of a people whose customs were similar to his own to that of a people whose customs were strange and repugnant:

> At the very moment I dreamed of the greatest happiness, I found myself most miserable; and it seemed as if fortune wished to give me this state of joy, only to render the reverse more poignant. The change I now experienced was as painful as it was sudden and unexpected...but I came at length to a country the inhabitants of which differed from us in all particulars [manners, customs, and language]. I was very much struck with this difference, especially when I came among a people who did not circumcise, and ate without washing their hands. (*Life* 1: 66–67)

But if Equiano's encounter with different tribes of his own race evoked from him responses of prejudice and distrust, his initiation into the culture of the Europeans occasioned him even greater trauma. The long hair and strange language of the white men on board the slave ship intimidated him and intensified his sense of total dissociation from this strange, new world: "I was now persuaded that I had gotten into a world of bad spirits, and that they were going to kill me." The sounds and sights of human misery among the African captives, the unhealthy stench of crowded quarters, and the brutal floggings inflicted on them by the white men all filled him constantly with a fear of his own death.

The manners of the whites and the mechanics of their world were to remain continual sources of fear and puzzlement with Equiano for a long time to come: "I could not help expressing my fears and apprehensions to some of my countrymen: I asked them if these people had no country, but lived in this hollow place [the ship]: they told me they did not, but came from a distant one. 'Then,' said I, 'how comes it in all our country we never heard of them?' They told me because they lived so very far off" (*Life* 1: 76). He was convinced that his new masters must be a race of evil sorcerers to invent and operate something as marvelous to him as a sailing ship, and he relates his confused astonishment in terms of striking self-humour and naivete: "I asked how the vessel could go? They told me they could not tell; but that there were cloths upon the masts by the help of the ropes I saw, and then the vessel went; and the white men had some spell or magic they put in the water when they liked in order to stop the vessel. I was exceedingly amazed at this account and really thought they were spirits" (*Life* 1: 76–77).

Other symbols of Western culture were to stir Equiano's imagination further. On the high seas, he was fascinated by the use of the quadrant; in Campbell's Virginia plantation house, the ticking of the clock on the wall raised in his unsophisticated mind the fear "that it would tell the gentlemen anything I might do amiss"; and on Pascal's ships he conceived the notion, from watching his close friend Dick Baker read, that white people literally conversed with books: "I have often taken up a book, and talked to it, and then put my ears to it, when alone, in hopes it would answer; and I have been very much concerned when I found it remained silent" (*Life* 1: 107).

The relation of incidents such as these carry plural significance. First, it shows that although Equiano was, by the time of writing, a man widely traveled in and knowledgeable about the white man's world, he does not disdain that earlier image of himself as the archetypal innocent, the primitive stricken by fear and amazement at the wonders of an alien world. Then, we are forced to ponder what must have been the heavy emotional costs, not only to Equiano individually, but to all African slaves collectively, of sudden propulsion from their cultural matrix into a vastly different civilization. It is clear that Equiano's confusion was aggravated by his initial inability to communicate in English. After leaving the slave ship, he had met no one who spoke his native tongue, and after less than two years, he was to lose the companionship of Dick Baker to the vagaries of navy life.[2]

As if friendlessness and language difficulties were not enough, Equiano had to suffer the constant humiliation of being called by a different name, according to the whims of successive masters. On the slave ship he was called Michael; in Virginia they called him Jacob; and in England Pascal renamed him Gustavus Vassa. Evidently, Equiano disliked this last appellation and resisted it spiritedly for a time (*Life* 1: 96). On the other hand, he took great pride in Olaudah, his African name, and retained a lasting respect for his people's native tradition of naming children purposefully—as he explains it, "from some event, some circumstance, or fancied foreboding at the time of their birth."[3]

All these changes and chances threatened the integrity of his ego and the survival of his personal cultural inheritance. And although age and maturity would eventually reconfirm his faith in Africa, in her people and their traditions, during these early years among the Europeans, he found himself doubting his own identity and loathing his physical features. From his first observations of the Europeans' manners on the slave ship, Equiano had acquired the notion that they would surely eat him. This notion was unwittingly reinforced by the playful taunts of crew members and, in later years, by his master Pascal and by other sailors in the navy (*Life* 1:99–100). The possibility that this childish fantasy could transform itself into an annihilating reality seemed to increase in direct proportion to his contacts with white people during his early months in England. Again, it is instructive to attempt a speculative analysis of Equiano's psychic state. It illuminates both his individual behavior and the collective behavior of all the slaves under the shock of cultural displacement. We may see Equiano's fear of being cannibalized by the whites as his apprehension of the white master's ultimate prerogative over the Black slave. We may see it further as a death wish through which he hoped to find a speedy issue out of present affliction. But perhaps more revealingly, we may perceive in the coincidence of self-loathing emotions with the fear of cannibalism the logical extremes to which white dominance over Blacks must have driven the slave in those times: just as food, eaten and digested, in time becomes an integral part of the eating organism, so in this fantasy we may perceive an unconscious succumbing to that assimilation which was the fate of the New World slave.

That Equiano's primary self-concept, forged in the security of his African homeland, was beginning to quail under assault from the powerful images of the new world around him is even more vividly illustrated in another recollection. In it, he recalls his despondency about the difference in complexion between himself and a little female playmate he met at Guernsey: "I had often observed that when her mother washed her face it looked very rosy; but when she washed mine it did not look so; I therefore tried oftentimes myself if I could not by washing make my face the same colour as my little playmate (Mary), but it was all in vain" (*Life* 1:109). As his fluency in English improved, Equiano began to feel easier among the English and to repudiate his irrational fears. Greater understanding of English manners and customs, however, only had the adverse effect of depreciating those he had been socialized to in Africa. He strove to remake himself in the white man's image in order to become more acceptable in his society: "I soon grew a stranger to terror of every kind, and was, in that respect at least, almost an Englishman. . . . I now not only felt myself quite easy with my new countrymen, but relished their society and manners. I no longer looked upon them as spirits, but as men superior to us; and therefore I had the stronger desire to resemble them; and to imbibe their spirit and to imitate their manners" (*Life* 1:32–33) Temporarily, at least, we may see in Equiano's fond attachment to Pascal, to Daniel Queen, and to Robert King in particular an orphaned youth's search for a surrogate father. His readiness to embrace English culture may likewise be viewed as the adaptive reorganization of a culturally displaced person's ego-identity to meet the demands of a new life.

Unlike Cugoano's *Thoughts*, Equiano's *Life* poses no significant questions of authorship. The story agrees closely enough with other slaves' accounts of slavery conditions and with the record of independent history. It is written with a simplicity that is the mark of honest truth and with a moral earnestness that is usually lacking, or at best only contrived, in ghostwritten slave narratives. By the time he came to write his narrative, Equiano had received considerable tuition in reading and writing: on the ships from his young teacher, Richard Baker, and from the father figure, Daniel Queen; and in London from the Misses Guerin and from a tutor at the Reverend Gregory's academy. His irresistible curiosity about books is illustrated elsewhere in this chapter. Besides, he makes numerous references to reading the Bible and other devotional books.[4]

In addition to these conscious sources of intellectual stimulation, one must also take into account the unconscious education he derived from his association with Evangelical mentors; from abolitionists like Granville Sharp, Thomas Clarkson, and Peter Peckard; and from prominent persons like Governor MacNamara (whom he served for some months in 1779) (*Life* 2:216), Dr. Charles Irving, and Constantine Phipps, the explorer.

Despite the weight of all this evidence for independent authorship, there have been a few hints, even from reviewers persuaded of Equiano's ability, that he was assisted in writing. Even a reviewer as appreciative as the writer in the *Monthly Review*, who praised Equiano's artlessness profusely and accepted the authenticity of the *Life* ("the narrative wears an honest face," he wrote), still guardedly conceded that he may have been assisted, if only in the proofing. Of course, this is to cavil rather triflingly, for even the work of eminent established writers undergoes some proofing and emendation at the hands of others. A number of grammatical and mechanical errors have been remarked, but in the main they are either identical with those found in other eighteenth-century native English writers or are non-native features common in West African English.[5] There is, then, no serious doubt that Equiano wrote his autobiography on his own: the evidence of personal letters and the testimony of reliable contemporaries establish him as the indisputable and sole author of the *Life*.[6]

The success of Equiano's book was largely due to the timeliness of its publication, the topicality of its subject matter, and the popularity of its literary form. When it appeared in 1789, Parliament was inquiring into the operations of the slave trade. Up to that time, much of the evidence about that traffic was supplied by prejudiced observers and vested interests. Now, the availability to the lawmakers of an ex-slave's authentic account of the indignities he suffered was bound to weigh heavily against abolition's foes. Furthermore, the active promotion of the book by the Abolition Committee soon established it as an authoritative document from which antislavery advocates in Parliament quoted regularly.[7]

Both the volume of the subscription list and the quality of persons whose names appeared on it showed the extent to which all social classes had been sensitized to abolitionist activities. The publication of an eighth edition only five years after the first is proof of the continued interest in Equiano's character and in his point of view on slavery. Nor was the book's appeal confined to metropolitan London. In the decade between 1789 and 1799, Equiano traveled extensively throughout Great Britain speaking on behalf of the Abolition Committee and promoting his book. He was in Birmingham in 1789; Manchester, Nottingham, and Cambridge the next year; Belfast on Christmas Day, 1791; Dublin and Hull in 1792; and at Bath and Devizes, in the west of England, in 1793. In Ireland alone the book sold nineteen hundred copies in an eight-and-a-half month period.

Like Sancho and Cugoano before him, Equiano wrote his autobiography with a clear conception of the readers it would appeal to. In a general sense, also, the identity of his audience was much the same as theirs: readers whose support for broad humanitarian causes encompassed a sympathy for the plight of the African. Yet Equiano's work did not thrive solely on inherited fortune. Certain important distinctions in the charater of his narrative and in the quality of his life served to enrich the African literary heritage and expand the audience for these productions. Sancho's *Letters* was likely to attract mainly the aficionados of sentimentalism and good-natured drollery after the manner of Sterne. Cugoano's *Thoughts*, on account of its more formal rhetorical features, could, by and large, sustain the interest of only the most literate, even erudite, readers. But Equiano's choice of an engaging human story, told in a consistently lucid style, makes the *Life* the most permanently interesting of the three works. What is more, the wider range of experiences he relates and the strategic emphases he places on certain categories of experience gave him a wider scope for audience appeal than either of his forerunners.

Besides profiting from widening popular support for the African cause, Equiano's book also participated in certain important developments favoring the genre of autobiographical writing. The Methodist Revival in religion encouraged converts to give form and validity to their lives by recording their experiences in spiritual memoirs. A marked tendency towards openness about personal feelings (the inevitable result, no doubt, of a corresponding interest in self-analysis) made the interior truth of individual lives a fit subject for conventional literature. And if all these developments point to a concern for depth rather than surface, a preoccupation with essence rather than appearance, it is not hard to see why the African, who suffered so much from prejudice against his external features, should now be rescued from eternal nonentity by a literary form eminently suited to reveal his full humanity to European readers. Shumaker's comments about general autobiography are applicable here: "The truth about character, men began to realize, could not always be observed in outward behaviour."[8]

Equiano was compelled by his troubling self-consciousness in the presence of white people to search deeper within himself to rediscover the meaning of blackness, both in the narrow political terms of eighteenth-century slavery and in the broader terms of his relation to the human race. Autobiography provided a medium through which to recreate that identity which his early encounter with the Europeans had threatened to efface. Also, through the peculiar rhetoric of this literary form, he was able to confront his readers with the proposition that the African was capable of spiritual and emotional sensations which slavery might deny but could not destroy. While his day-to-day life was marked by constant flux, self-doubt, hardship, and change, the intellectual process of transforming these realities into a single object of literary art afforded him a new vision of himself and a new valuation of his people. Any such observation necessarily defines a difference between how an individual perceives the raw materials of daily existence as life hands them to him and how he perceives them after they have been tempered in the forge of recollected experience.

This difference manifests itself in Equiano's work as two contrastive prose styles. When he wants to recapture the bewilderment and ignorance of young Olaudah, the kidnapped victim, his narrative style is naïve, the language plain, almost studiedly simplistic. Take the following recollection of his first days in England: "As I was now amongst a people who had not their faces scarred, like some of the African nations where I had been, I was very glad I did not let them ornament me in that manner when I was with them" (*Life* 1:108). Here, the effect is achieved by reconstructing his mind and tone at that age. The lines occur in the same portion of the text as those expressing his mortification over the immutability of his complexion. They are stylistically of a piece with the pathetic fallacies underlying the "magic" anchor (*Life* 1:77) and the "talking" book (*Life* 1:107). Taken at face value, the passage quoted might prompt the inference that Equiano had come to detest African tribal customs. On closer inspection, however, we discover that Equiano himself recognized these incidents as constituting, collectively, that crucial phase of his life when the cultural values of his untutored mind were under assault from those of a presumably more advanced civilization. Further analysis reveals that Equiano recreates these "spots of time" also to gain balance and perspective on his life, to look on it with soberness and proportion, to hold a mirror up to the past and smile at his simpleminded self with humor, irony, and pathos.

On the other hand, when he wants to show that maturity had taught him to value himself and his cultural heritage, the style is confident and self-affirming. It is strategically significant that those qualities characterize the better part of chapter 1 and a small portion of chapter 2, where he outlines the circumstances of his upbringing and the manners of his people. The following passage not only celebrates Ibo life but manages also to convey a distinct sense of its order and joyousness, attributes that were not compre-hended in proslavery images of Africa as a dark place of irremediable chaos, barbarism, and internecine strife:

> We are almost a nation of dancers, musicians and poets. Thus every great event, such as a triumphant return from battle, or other cause of public rejoicing is celebrated in public dances, which are accompanied with songs and music suited to the occasion. The assembly is separated into four divisions, which dance either apart or in succession, and each with a character peculiar to itself. The first division contains the mar-ried men, who in their dances frequently exhibit feats of arms, and the representation of a battle. To these succeed the married women, who dance in the second division. The young men occupy the third; and the maidens the fourth. Each represents some interesting scene of real life, such as a great achievement, domestic employment, a pathetic story, or some rural sport; and as the subject is generally founded on some re-cent event, it is therefore ever new. This gives our dances a spirit and variety which I have scarcely seen elsewhere. (*Life* 1:10–11)

Through passages like this one Equiano uses the autobiographical form creatively. It becomes not just a journalistic record of events and adventures but a tool to reconstruct his ethnic identity and to raise those nurturing memories which clearly had not died but were only suppressed under the weight of acculturation. In this way, Equiano achieves two vital ends: the necessary imperative of self-discovery and the greater end of establishing the human truth about his race.

Although Equiano shuns the confrontational polemics of Cugoano by giving more space to spiritualized reflection than to political rhetoric, he still challenges directly certain widely published views of Africa and some of the most common misconceptions about her people. Typically, he does this in calm, declarative statements. In the following simple declaration, he answers, without naming his opposition, those detractors of African charac-ter who painted Africans as constitutionally prone to indolence and shift-lessness: "Agriculture is our chief employment; and every one, even the chil-dren and women, are engaged in it. Thus we are all habituated to labour from our earliest years. Every one contributes to the common stock; and as

we are unacquainted with idleness, we have no beggars" (*Life* 1:20–21).
The high incidence of mendicancy and vagrancy in eighteenth-century England makes the last sentence tellingly sarcastic. To those racial chauvinists
who associated physical beauty and intellectual power with fair skins, blue
eyes, and blond hair, Equiano, again unobtrusively, proposes these sobering
thoughts:

> The West India planters prefer the slaves of Benin or Eboe to those of
> any other part of Guinea, for their hardiness, intelligence, integrity, and
> zeal. Those benefits are felt by us in a general healthiness of people, and
> in their vigour and activity. I might have added too in their comeliness.
> Deformity is indeed unknown amongst us, I mean that of shape. Num-
> bers of natives of Eboe now in London might be brought in support of
> this assertion: for in regard to complexion, ideas of beauty are wholly
> relative. (*Life* 1:21)

Now writing as the abolitionist of 1789, Equiano has supplanted the naïve
self-depreciation of the boy of 1757 with a mature apprehension of the
nature of things.

Equiano's life as a slave and seafarer eloquently attested the native virtues
of his people. Jostling daily among men given to drunkenness, swearing, and
bloodthirsty threats, he stood out as a model of virtue and industry, sparing
no effort to perform his duties diligently and winning for himself his masters' respect and his captains' trust. To Robert King he became an indispensable factotum:

> There was scarcely any part of his business or household affairs, in
> which I was not occasionally engaged. I often supplied the place of
> clerk, in receiving and delivering cargoes to the ships, in tending horses
> and delivering goods: and, besides this, I used to shave and dress my
> master when convenient, and take care of his horse, and when it was
> necessary, which was very often, I worked likewise on board of dif-
> ferent vessels of his. (*Life* 1:202–3)

To Thomas Farmer, a captain on one of King's vessels, he proved equally
trustworthy: "better to him on board than any three white men he had"
(*Life* 1:231). Under pressure of many perilous situations at sea, Equiano
showed himself courageous and resourceful. During a shipwreck on a
voyage from the West Indies to Georgia in February 1767, it was Equiano's
fortitude and self-possession that saved the crew from total disaster, the
captain's navigation having proved inept and the crew having abandoned
themselves to drunken desperation: "I could not help thinking that if any of
these people had been lost, God would charge me with their lives, which
perhaps, was one cause of my labouring so hard for their preservation, and

indeed every one of them afterwards seemed so sensible of the service I had rendered them; and while we were on the key I was a kind of chieftain among them" (*Life* 2:48–49).

The diligent reader will detect a generous measure of boastful exaggeration and personal aggrandizement in this passage (note the last eight words) and others. Also, although the calamity described in the first two lines occurred before his conversion, the manner of his remembering it is strongly informed by the religious self-consciousness of his maturer years. Narrative invention notwithstanding, to an abolitionist audience these solid demonstrations of individual integrity affirmed the African's human capabilities and gave point to antislavery agitation for the end of the dehumanizing trade. They gave even greater urgency to proposals for the establishment of a social order that would recognize the Africans' intrinsic dignity and replace the plantation ethos.

So Equiano wrung from the autobiographical mode a positive image of his own personal worth, expressed in terms of his capacity for work. He rediscovered and redefined the self in affirmative images, while implicitly repudiating the slanders of the slavocrats. Although not scored in a strident rhetorical key, such indirect statements are equally effective as protest. Mary Williams Burger calls them "positive protest"—a protest that creates as it eliminates and deals with the opposition's ugliness by concentrating on its own beauty."[9]

Just as Equiano reinterpreted slave labor, which was otherwise only drudgery and a mark of menial status, so that it becomes one of his most sophisticated subversive tools, he used religion (which the colonial establishment used to make slaves passive and obedient) to add greater moral authority to his politics and his writing. That authority was the fruit of long self-searching and of observing an almost unrealistic standard of rectitude in personal conduct.

Equiano endeavored very early in his youth to make a positive protest against slavery, not so much by resisting overtly as by presenting himself as a moral agent in his own right, certainly equal, if not superior, to the whites he worked among. His regular practice of prayer and Bible reading won him the respect of his crew mates. On the *Aetna*, the sailors styled him the "black Christian." In the *Life*, he is confident that his piety was the cause of many a narrow escape from death, both for himself and for his fellow sailors. He claims to have had several premonitory dreams about shipwrecks, one of which was realized much as he had dreamed it during the 1767 voyage alluded to above. He ascribes spiritual significance to the most commonplace events and fosters a firm belief in the universal influence of Providence: "I had a mind on which everything uncommon made its full impression, and every event which I considered as marvellous. Every extraordinary escape or signal deliverance, either of myself or others, I looked upon to be effected by the interposition of Providence" (*Life* 1:154). G. A. Starr remarks on this tendency in spiritual autobiographers to spiritualize every aspect of their common experience: "Since mere trifles can have the gravest consequences if allowed to pass unheeded, it follows that nothing is beneath the notice of the alert Christian."[10] And the Abbé Gregoire, in specific reference to Equiano, viewed his spiritualizing tendency as a result of the African's peculiar social condition in the world of the eighteenth century: "The effect of adversity is to give more energy to religious sentiments. Man abandoned by his fellow man and unfortunate upon the earth, turns his looks towards heaven, to seek there consolations and a father."[11]

A great majority of the mishaps and emergencies recounted in the narrative precede Equiano's conversion. While the genuineness of his spiritual faith, as it emerges in this situation, is umimpeachable, it is obvious that Equiano was highly self-conscious about the moral leverage which his profound spirituality gave him over the white men. There is noticeable religious conceit in his self-portrait as it appears in the description of the shipwreck off Cadiz in March 1775. He is the image of resignation and self-composure, secure in the knowledge of God's will, while the rest of the crew are thrown into panic and confusion: "Although I could not swim and saw no way of escaping death, I felt no dread in my then situation, having no desire to live. I even rejoiced in spirit, thinking this death would be sudden glory. But the fulness of time was not yet come. The people near to me were much astonished in seeing me thus calm and resigned; but I told them of the peace of God, which through sovereign grace I enjoyed. . . ." (*Life* 2:162).

At the start of the narrative, Equiano prefaces his life story with words skillfully chosen from the repertoire of rhetorical convention. He courts the interest of his readers by modestly characterizing himself as a "private and obscure individual, and a stranger too," disclaiming any interest in literary sensationalism ("I offer here the story of neither a saint, a hero, nor a tyrant.") and any desire for personal glory ("I am not so foolishly vain as to expect from it [the narrative] either immortality or literary reputation").

But Equiano displays considerable technical capacity in creating, through these disclaimers, an illusion of artless autobiographical writing while fulfilling the less obvious political designs of his abolitionist sponsors. While it may be assumed that a sympathetic audience and a more reliably informed public would have been willing to generalize on the basis of Equiano's proven capacity for hard work and intense spiritual faith, Equiano did not leave it entirely up to his readers to reshape their received images of Africans solely on the evidence of his exemplary life. He devoted significant space to a deliberate description of Ibo life in particular and to a spirited defence of African culture in particular.

The examples from chapter 1 of the *Life*, discussed earlier, show that

Equiano was anxious to erase those negative images which some accounts of unimaginative travelers and spokesmen for special economic interests had implanted in the popular mind. He chose to present the hard facts, implying rather than naming his opposition outright. But the intention is clear enough and the impact persuasive. Ibo society emerges as a culture regulated by its own set of traditions, laws, and customs. In emphatic denial of the myth of barbarism and misrule, he cites the existence of a distinct code of laws that governed human relations. He shows, for instance, that polygamy, as practiced among his people, was not synonymous with adultery; he emphasized that they celebrated marriage in ceremonies uniting ritual order with festive joy and human dignity.

In a few blunter statements, obviously directed at the stubborn misconceptions of European chauvinists, he compares the manners of European society directly and indirectly with those of Africa. Given the low standards of personal hygiene and community sanitation that prevailed in England at the time, Equiano had no doubt seen many Englishmen eat without washing their hands. In favorable contrast to this, he counterposed the extreme scrupulosity the Ibos practiced in matters of personal hygiene: "Before we taste food we always wash our hands; indeed our cleanliness on all occasions is extreme" (*Life* 1:13). Equiano endows these "purifications and washings" with such high religious significance that he draws the obvious favorable analogy with Jewish custom (*Life* 1:32; 1:39).

He speaks in equally proud affirmative terms about Ibo women, contrasting by implication their modest, staid way with the immodest, desperate lives many lower class Englishwomen were forced to live by adverse social conditions (witness DeFoe's Moll Flanders). He paints Ibo women as beautiful, hard working, industrious: "Our women too were in my eyes at least uncommonly graceful, alert and modest to a degree of bashfulness; nor do I remember to have ever heard of an instance of incontinence among them before marriage" (*Life* 1:22).

It is remarkable that several of these comparative statements occur in reminiscences about Turkey. Equiano cherished very fond memories of his visits to that country and retained high admiration for its people. Indeed, at a time when the Turks were almost universally considered marauding barbarians whose very existence threatened the continuance of civilization in western Europe, it is ironic to find an African forcing the Europeans to reexamine their prejudices and confront some of the more positive aspects of Turkish character. "I always found the Turks very honest in their dealings" (*Life* 2:194), Equiano writes of his commercial transactions with them. And in another context he remarked: "I really thought the Turks were in a safer way of salvation than my English neighbours" (*Life* 1:119).

By such strategies of indirection and implied criticism, Equiano debunked the myths of Western European cultural superiority. He corrected some of the impressions white people had about Africa by affirming Africa's authentic cultural validity and by showing that difference or strangeness was not a criterion of value, since ideas of progress and civilization were all relative to time and place. Paul Edwards and Ian Duffield, in a joint article examining in greater depth Equiano's appreciation of Turkey and Africa, assess his achievement thus: "The picture Equiano draws of Ibo society seems a generally accurate one, and without extravagance, but with understandable pride he shows us a society which is, within its own terms, rational, pious, virtuous, frugal, hygienic, industrious. Equiano offers us the earliest defense of African social order to be written by an African and addressed to a white audience."[12]

Equiano's long service as a slave and later as a sailor provided him with a unique narrative context. Slavery involved suffering; it was a living reminder of man's inhumanity to man. Seafaring entailed hazards and adventures, both of which put the traveler's physical and moral strength to the test. Each of these two narrative sources represented an important metaphor for the spiritual life with which eighteenth-century Evangelical readers were familiar. And nothing must have commended Equiano's autobiography more to them than his insistence on spiritualizing even the smallest incidents of his common life. As he writes, Equiano stresses the moral advantages of reflective narrative over the merely factual recording of secular experience. In choosing the reflective mode of autobiography, he identified himself with a revered tradition of converts, and thus the narrative was approved by the generality of Evangelical readers.

For all the mental torture that his enslavement caused him, Equiano still reasoned that such adversity was the will of God. He viewed his passing from the ownership of Mr. Campbell, the Virginian slaveholder, to the ownership of Captain Pascal as an act of providential deliverance, especially since Pascal proved to be the more humane master. He described it as the work of "the kind and unknown hand of the Creator who in very deed leads the blind in a way they know not."

That part of the *Life* which describes his activities as a small trader is very minutely recorded; every investment, sale, and profit is punctiliously itemized after this fashion:

> At one of our trips to St. Eustatia, a Dutch island, I bought a glass tumbler with my half bit, and when I came to Montserrat I sold it for a bit, or sixpence. Luckily we made several successive trips to St. Eustatia (which was a general mart for the West Indies, about twenty leagues from Montserrat); and in our next, finding my tumbler so profitable, with this one bit I bought two tumblers more; and when I came back I sold them for two bits, equal to a shilling sterling. When we went again, I bought with these two bits four more of these glasses, which I sold for

four bits on our return to Montserrat: and in our next voyage to St. Eustatia I bought two glasses with one bit, and with the other three I bought a jug of Geneva, nearly about three pints in measure. (*Life* 1:234)

Equiano takes great pride in computing the success of his petty commercial ventures, confident that it was made possible through providential favor. A consistent profit pattern of one hundred percent return on his trade in glasses and over one hundred and fifty percent return on the "Geneva" (gin) has increased his capital to a dollar, "well husbanded and acquired in the space of a month or six weeks," he announces with pious conceit. Such careful accounting of time and talents is undertaken not only as a form of material stock taking, but also with a sense of fulfilling a spiritual duty. The increase of riches is therefore seen as an outward visible sign of an inward spiritual growth.

In these examples, we see how the act of converting experience into narrative allows Equiano to invest his past activities with their proper spiritualized value and so to magnetize potentially the whole audience of Methodist and Calvinist Evangelicals who esteemed highly these spiritual qualities in literature. It is evident from these examples that Equiano had mastered an important skill related to the artifice of autobiography: he had derived from it a measure of his own material and spiritual prosperity. Starr calls this "autodidacticism." At the same time he had managed to underline for his readers a point that they already believed by faith and could now accept as fact: "that he (and therefore all black people) was susceptible to the same varieties of objective experience and internal emotions as whites and therefore was their human equal. In a description of the general functions of autobiography, Starr writes that it is instructive to the author and to the reader, just as "a ship's log is useful to him who keeps it and to others, should the voyage ever be repeated. Since every man is embarked on essentially the same spiritual journey, the record of one will be of use to all."[13]

In similarly minute detail, Equiano recounts his search for salvation that culminated in the powerful conversion event of volume 2. The story of his soul's progress towards salvation is told with passionate intensity; it describes the same broad stages as those prototypical memoirs of converts to Methodism contained in *The Lives of the Early Methodist Preachers* (1837).[14] First, he is struck by a sudden sense of sin and impelled to reflect on his spiritual state. Then comes a recognition of the need for salvation and, following this, a search for the means of redemption through acts of contrition, prayer, and Bible reading. Next, the soul sinks into an abyss of mental agony and helplessness, ultimately to be retrieved by an overpowering sense of purification and inward joy. Equiano describes the final stages thus: "I saw clearly with the eye of faith the crucified Saviour bleeding on the cross of Mount Calvary: 'the Scriptures became an unsealed book, I saw myself a condemned criminal under the law which came with its full force to my conscience, and when 'the commandment came sin revived, and I died.' I saw the Lord Jesus Christ in humiliation loaded and bearing my reproach, sin and shame. I then clearly perceived that by the deeds of the law no flesh living could be justified" (*Life* 2 : 146).

That he looked on his spiritual transformation as a key phase in the quest for full self-realization is obvious from the space he devotes to recollecting it in the *Life*. That he clearly saw his justification before God as a metaphor for justification in the world of racial prejudice is one of the unspoken rhetorical premises of the narrative. He celebrated that changed perception of his temporal and spiritual self in commemorative verses that speak a fervent message to those Evangelicals who were being won over to the cause of abolition:

> Thus light came in, and I believ'd;
> Myself forgot, and help receiv'd:
> My saviour then I know I found,
> For, eas'd from guilt, no more I groan'd.
>
> O happy hour, in which I ceas'd
> To mourn, for then I found a rest:
> My soul and Christ were now as one—
> Thy light, O Jesus in me shone!
>
> ("Miscellaneous Verses," *Life* 2 : 157)

Equiano's experience was so genuine and his faith so sincere that Wesley himself numbered the *Life* among his favorite books. It is recorded that on his deathbed he made a special request to have passages read to him from it.[15] What Wesley perceived, and indeed what the general audience of revivalist Christians must have found most inspiring, was that authentic image of their own standard of spirituality which Equiano had depicted so credibly because he had lived it so devoutly.

While it is true to say that Equiano-the-writer was a product of slavery, it is also remarkable that the autobiography does not devote greater attention to particularizing the horrors of slavery. Among abolitionist leaders, Equiano was certainly one of the best qualified to render a faithful account of the operations of the trade and of the conditions that existed in slave society. And yet, in spite of his special qualifications (personal experience and firsthand observation), the quantum of explicit antislavery statements is moderate by comparison with the emphases of Cugoano's *Thoughts* or Ramsay's *Essay*, for example. There are good reasons for this. Equiano seemed determined to win support for the cause of his enslaved fellows more by the subtler arts of self-revelation than by the hurly-burly tactics of polemical writing. Besides, he did not perceive his primary audience to be the confirmed enemies of the African (as Cugoano did): he was speaking more to the converted, both as to religious convictions and as to political awareness. Equiano's introductory statements to the *Life* show that while he had set his face firmly against romanticizing his life for the sake of popularity, he had also resolved to observe steadfastly the rules of decorum in imaginative art.

Although, as we shall see later in the chapter, Equiano made his most notable contribution to antislavery in his capacity as public agitator and political activist, his experiences as a slave and a Black sailor actually prepared him for these later roles. It is instructive to analyze his record of those experiences, to discover how time and maturity gave him a different perspective on them.

The recollection of how he felt on first entering the slave ship is a sharp illustration of how he transfigured the terror and confusion of the eleven-year-old boy into a persuasive appeal for reforming the slave trade. He used his perspective as a participant-witness to full advantage in recounting the acts of brutality the whites on board the ship used to assert their power over the captive Blacks. The intolerable stench that emanated from close, unsanitary quarters becomes a repugnant memory in the narrative; and the anguished cries of Africans in the pangs of torture and death strike a note of undisguised loathing for the political and economic system that thrived on the oppression of his people.

Equiano sets down these details without losing a sense of narrative propriety and without overwhelming the reader with their horrific nature. He is able to paint vivid and effective pictures without relentless vilification of his proslavery opponents or conscious wrenching at the emotions of antislavery sympathizers:

> The closeness of the place, and the heat of the climate, added to the number in the ship, which was so crowded that each had scarcely room to turn himself, almost suffocated us. This produced copious perspirations, so that the air soon became unfit for respiration, from a variety of loathsome smells, and brought on a sickness among the slaves, of which many died, thus falling victims to the improvident avarice, as I may call it, of their purchasers. (*Life* 1:179)

Of equal significance is that such passages, unencumbered as they are by heavy moralizing, are an accurate image of the narrator's naïve consciousness at the time of the events.

Five years later, however, he is much more conscious of the injustice of his status in the white world, and in similar fashion he makes the narrative mirror that consciousness. In December 1762, his master Pascal sold him to

Captain Doran. Pascal's decision was abrupt; his treatment of Equiano at that moment unprecedentedly severe. He accused Equiano of plotting to escape; but Equiano, confident of his innocence and no doubt discerning that Pascal was merely seeking an excuse to profit from his sale, put up a stubborn resistance:

> I was so struck with the unexpectedness of this proceeding that for some time I did not make a reply, only I made an offer to go for my books, and chest of clothes, but he swore I should not move out of his sight; and if I did he would cut my throat, at the same time taking his hanger. I began, however, to collect myself; and, plucking up courage, I told him I was free, and he could not by law serve me so. But this only enraged him the more; and he continued to swear and said he would soon let me know whether he would or not, and at that instant sprung himself into the barge from the ship, to the astonishment and sorrow of all on board. (*Life* 1:175)

Equiano injects considerably more emotional energy into his prose style here than he does in the slave ship scenes. He treats the event as marking a significant moment in the development of his conscious rebellion against slavery. He reevokes the seething passions of that charged confrontation with marked dramatic force. He had learned his lessons in human freedom from the edifying talks of Daniel Queen; he had apparently listened with a keen ear to the first rumblings of the legal battle to outlaw slavery within England itself. In an exchange with Captain Doran that followed the confrontation with Pascal, he stakes a confident claim to justice and human rights:

> When I came there [on board Doran's ship] Captain Doran asked me if I knew him; I answered that I did not; "Then," said he, "You are now my slave." I told him my master could not sell me to him, nor to anyone else. "Why," said he, "Did not your master buy you?" I confessed he did. "But I have served him," said I "many years, and he has taken all my wages and prize-money, for I only got one sixpence during the war; besides this I have been baptized; and by the laws of the land, no man has a right to sell me:" And I added, that I had heard a lawyer and others at different times tell my master so. (*Life* 1:176)

The ethos of the West Indian and American colonies was to elicit some of Equiano's bitterest antipathy. To him the West Indies seemed to be a moral wilderness, wherein white men had become debauched by the climate and calloused by their greed to extract the highest profits from the labor of the slaves. He saw the social order there as one supported on a precarious structure of repressive laws, tortures, and acts of depravity. He characterized the state of human relationships as unnatural, a shocking antithesis to the enlightened values on which European civilization prided itself, nurturing in its very repressiveness the seeds of its own destruction:

> When you make men slaves, you deprive them of half their virtue, you set them in your own conduct an example of fraud, rapine, and cruelty, and compel them to live with you in a state of war; and yet you complain that they are not honest or faithful. You stupify them with stripes, and think it necessary to keep them in a state of ignorance and yet you assert that they are incapable of learning. . . . And are ye not struck with pain and horror to see partakers of your nature reduced so low? But above all, are there no dangers attending this mode of treatment? Are you hourly in dread of an insurrection? (*Life* 1:224)

Equiano had little to complain about on his own account. His master in the West Indies, Robert King, was a mild-mannered Quaker who treated him with compassion and had a reputation as "a man of feeling" among the slaves of the island. But the disabilities that his fellow Blacks suffered were too glaring to escape his notice. His sense of the ultimate immorality of slave society was quickened by the low value placed on Black life in the West Indies. He criticized the practice of selling slaves like meat, at a price of three to six pence per pound. He denounced the exploitive practice of some owners who farmed out their slaves at a favorable rate of return to themselves but at a very low wage to the slaves. Equiano seemed particularly outraged that such depreciation of the slaves' human value should be sanctioned by a law of Barbados which prescribed no fine for a master who killed or dismembered a slave and only fifteen pounds sterling if the master did so "out of wantonness, or only bloodymindedness, or cruel intention" (*Life* 1:218).

Although Equiano devotes this stage of the narrative largely to describing slave life in those islands he had visited, he still manages to keep the autobiographical mode his dominant form of discourse by impressing on the reader his credibility as a participant-witness. Therefore, when he details the horrifying cruelties of masters who cut pieces from their slaves' flesh as they beat them or nailed them to the ground and poured sealing wax over their bodies, he presents such actions not merely as items from a familiar catalog but as the authentic reports of an eyewitness. The intention, stated or implied, is always to show that punishments were excessive and that the system which permitted them should be abolished.

The connection between the atrocities inflicted on the slaves and the very high mortality rate among them was not lost on Equiano. He named islands where an annual supply of twenty thousand new slaves was needed to replace those who died yearly. He estimated that the life expectancy of the average African slave in Barbados, for example, was a mere sixteen years.

While he used his intimate knowledge of actual conditions to condemn the system, he was also careful to preserve a sense of balance and fairness in order to present a complete picture of West Indian society. In the main, he attributed the high mortality to the problem of absentee owners. He depicted the resident overseers as a contemptible lot who had little capacity for efficient management and whose depraved moral characters were a scourge to the slaves:

> They pay no regard to the situation of pregnant women nor the least attention to the lodging of the field negroes. Their huts, which ought to be well covered, and the place dry where they take their little repose, are often open sheds, built in damp places; so that, when the poor creatures return tired from the toils of the field, they contract many disorders, from being exposed to the damp air in this uncomfortable state, while they are heated and their pores are open. This neglect conspires with many others to cause a decrease in the births as well as in the lives of the grown negroes. (*Life* 1:208)

But he showered high praise on those benevolent masters who, residing on their estates in the West Indies, took a personal interest in the management and well-being of the slaves. Among these, his own master Robert King earned exceptional credit. King followed an enlightened policy of treating his slaves well, because he recognized that their health and happiness were his personal gain. He valued Equiano highly, often expressing open appreciation for his faithful service. Then there was that "most worthy and humane gentleman [Sir Philip Gibbes] who is a native of Barbadoes," who allowed his slaves two hours' break at midday, made ample provision for their food, and extended many other indulgences and comforts, "so that by these attentions he saves the lives of his negroes, and keeps them healthy and as happy as the condition of slavery can admit" (*Life* 1:210).

Such examples of benevolence fortified Equiano's belief that the slave owners were not uniformly rapacious or naturally cruel; it seemed to him that the slave system exercised just as rigid a tyranny over them as they did over the slaves: "For I will not suppose that the dealers in slaves are born worse than other men—no; it is the fatality of this mistaken avarice, that it corrupts the milk of human kindness and turns it into gall" (*Life* 1:223).

Few things in the moral order of West Indian life drew more forceful condemnation from Equiano than the violation of female slaves. Sailors, clerks, and sundry white men habitually raped slave women in transit on King's ships. In the absence of any systematic legal deterrents to such behavior, the offenders were not averse to taking indecent liberties with girls as young as ten years of age. The high incidence of such acts was a bitter affront to Equiano's native pride in African womanhood; it wounded him all the more deeply because, as a Black man and a slave, he was powerless to defend the victims' honor. His attack against these practices was a stinging repudiation of the double standard of sexual morality that prevailed in the slave colonies: a black man had his ears cut off for cohabiting with a white prostitute, "as if it were no crime in the whites to rob an innocent girl of her virtue; but most heinous in a Black man only to gratify a passion of nature; where the temptation was offered by one of a different colour, though the most abandoned of her species" (*Life* 1 : 206–7).

In a society built on the ethics of racial inequality before the law, rape was just one of the numerous indignities that members of the dominant group used to assert their power over the masses. Equiano expressed similar intolerance for other manifestations of the double standard. He denounced a whole range of vexing incidents, which he had either witnessed or suffered himself. According to his accounts, a slave carrying anything from a bundle of grass to a bag of fruits to the marketplace was the potential victim of outright robbery by lawless whites. Equiano cited cases from his own experience as a small trader to illustrate the fradulent devices whites often used to swindle Blacks out of personal property.

But such hazards were by no means the exclusive lot of the slaves. The lives of free Blacks in the colonies were hedged about by similar injustices. Some of them were denied their freedom after they had earned it. Others were kidnapped once more into slavery after manumission. Equiano cited the case of Joseph Clipson, a free mulatto from Bermuda, who was unceremoniously captured by a ship's captain in Montserrat and recommitted to slavery, in spite of Clipson's personal entreaties and the protests of others who were familiar with his character and status (*Life* 1 : 247–48).

While slaves often escaped abusive treatment by casual persons, because they were the property of others, free Blacks, lacking the benefit of any such protection, were subject to harassment and beatings. As always, Equiano corroborates his reports of these violations of human rights with incidents from his own experience. On two separate occasions he was assaulted and placed under arbitrary arrest in Savannah, Georgia. Once, in 1764, he was brutalized and later thrown into jail by one Dr. Perkins, for merely socializing with Perkins' slaves. Then, in 1767, he was arrested and detained on some trumped up charge of infringing an absurd curfew regulation. Equiano chafed at the requirement that free Blacks still had to advertise themselves like slaves before they could leave one colony for another (*Life* 2 : 176). It outraged his sense of justice that no Black aggrieved in any of these ways could expect redress from the courts, since the laws did not accept the testimony of Blacks against whites. In reflecting on the precarious status of the free Black, Equiano wrote:

> Hitherto I had thought only slavery dreadful, but the state of a free negro appeared to me equally so at least, and in some respects even worse, for they live in constant alarm for their liberty; and even this is nominal; for they are universally insulted and plundered without the

possibility of redress; for such is the equity of West Indian laws, that no
free negro's evidence will be admitted in their courts of justice. (*Life*
1:249–50)

What direct addresses Equiano makes to proslavery partisans are sparse,
although none the less cogent. Apologists for the European slave trade
rationalized it by pointing to the existence of slavery in Africa. Equiano
candidly admits that the Ibos and their neighbors kept slaves, but he makes
some important distinctions. He insists that his people sold and enslaved
only those who were prisoners of war or such as were "convicted of kidnapping, or adultery, and some other crimes, which were esteemed heinous."
He affirms that slaves were treated as members of their masters' households,
sharing the work thereof with free members, rather than being relegated
exclusively to the performance of menial labor or bearing any stigma of
social disgrace as a mark of their status (*Life* 1:26–27). This description
agreed with the testimony of Cugoano and others, but stood in manifest
opposition to those commentaries that painted West Indian slavery as benign compared to African. Equiano also took to task those publicists who
depreciated the slaves' contribution to the colonial economy by depicting
them as unskilled drudges whose upkeep outstripped their productivity.
With remarkable virtuosity in logical argument, Equiano asked rhetorically
why it was that the purveyors of such opinions were also the most stubborn
opponents of abolition: "I suppose nine-tenths of the mechanics throughout
the West Indies are negro slaves; and I well know the coopers among them
earn two dollars a day; the carpenters the same, and oftentimes more; as
also the masons, smiths, and fishermem, &c. and I have known many slaves
whose masters would not take a thousand pounds current for them" (*Life*
1:203).

It was in statements of this kind that Equiano proved his inestimable
value to the abolitionists. Hitherto, the proslavery forces challenged antislavery spokesmen on the ground that they criticized the slave system out of
emotional sentiment springing mainly from inaccurate information—in
short, they tried to discredit them because, for the most part, they had not
witnessed slavery firsthand. Equiano had. He was able to make a special
contribution to the evidence already supplied by Benezet, Ramsay, and
Clarkson, throwing the full weight of his unimpeachable integrity behind
that evidence. Proslavery's last refuge was to raise a spurious allegation that
he was not born in Africa, as he claimed, but on the Dutch island of Santa
Cruz. Equiano was able to lay that charge to rest by invoking the testimony
of all those prominent persons who knew him as a slave boy traveling in and
out of England on navy ships.[16]

On the whole, these sequences of explicit antislavery discourse in the *Life*
stand out as examples of honest argument in the interest of noble humani-

tarian goals. Equiano displays great discipline of mind in keeping humanitarian purposes the single-minded motivation of his narrative. One of his chief impressions was that the slave trade was entirely "a war with the heart of man." With perceptive philosophic insight, he viewed its continuance as a threat to the survival of those liberal institutions on which the progress and prosperity of human civilization rested. In short, he took the position that the degradation of any single race of humans would ultimately touch the whole species, because slavery destroyed those natural affections that distinguish human beings from beasts (*Life* 1:220–26).

These were strong objections, evidently aimed at the humanitarian sentiments of a British public whose social consciousness had evolved beyond the purely sentimental effusions of Sancho's time to the practical concern for relieving poverty and distress wherever they existed. Always the man of action himself, Equiano found this shifting of emphasis in abolition strategy towards more active political agitation congenial to his temperament. His remarks to Captain Doran, cited above, indicate that he took an early interest in the words and deeds of abolitionist leaders. The evidence of his acquaintance and cooperation with prominent abolitionists is clear and impressive. While still in the West Indies, he had met Ramsay, and he kept up an association with him throughout his later time in England. Similarly, he had a close working relationship with Clarkson and his professor, Dr. Peckard.[17]

Equiano's first significant contribution to antislavery activism was his intervention in 1774 in the case of John Annis. The case has been detailed in chapter 1 of this study,[18] but it is important to note here that it gave Equiano his first contact with Granville Sharp, "that philanthropist who received me with utmost kindness, and gave me every instruction that was needful on the occasion," Equiano recalled.[19] Equiano was to keep up a steady correspondence with Sharp throughout the years of intense abolitionist activism. An entry in Sharp's diary for 19 March 1783 shows that it was Equiano who brought him reports of the scandalous Zong case, in which 132 African slaves were willfully drowned at sea. An epidemic had broken out aboard the ship and the slaves were gravely stricken. The ruling motive of the ship's captain, Luke Collingwood, was mercenary: he knew that if they had died of natural causes, the ship's owners would have had to absorb the loss, but that if he could report their deaths as accidents, then the ship's underwriters would honor the claim. Equiano was determined that this crass brutality should not go unpunished and that the owners' greed should not be rewarded at the expense of African life. The courts, however, ruled in favor of the owners, on the principle that slaves were property. But the efforts of Equiano and Sharp had impressed the public with a grim measure of the slave trade's inhumanity and won further sympathy for the abused Africans.[20]

Two years after the Zong case, Equiano made contact with the powerful Quaker Committee for Abolition. In October 1785 he led a delegation to the Quaker Church in Lombard Street and delivered an address in appreciation of the committee's work on behalf of his fellow Africans. The Quakers assured him that they would continue their agitation until their final object—complete abolition—was achieved. Equiano was impressed by the Quakers' reputation for treating their slaves mildly. He praised the fine example of leadership they set by manumitting their slaves long before abolition and without secular coercion. A visit to Philadelphia gave him the opportunity to observe their charitable and educational work among the Blacks of that city. He held them up as a model for other slaveholders to follow.

Next, Equiano brought the plight of his fellows to the attention of higher powers. On 21 March 1788 he presented a petition to Her Majesty, Queen Charlotte, appealing to her benevolence and compassion in the cause of abolition. This was a timely and imaginative strategy. The question of the slave trade had by this time reached Parliament, and the queen's record for private acts of liberality was a distinguished one. One clause in his petition reveals that Equiano's target was really the king, who if any one, had the influence that could alleviate the Africans' sufferings: "I presume, therefore, Gracious Queen, to implore your interposition with your royal consort, in favour of the wretched Africans; that by your Majesty's benevolent influence a period may now be put to their misery; and that they may be raised from the condition of brutes, to which they are at present degraded, to the rights and situation of freemen. . . ." (*Life* 2:245).

In the closing years of the 1780s, the activities of the Abolition Committee took on greater sophistication. Having decided to concentrate their pressure on Parliament, they coordinated strategies with the Clapham Sect and made their presence felt by regular attendance at Parliamentary sittings. They fairly inundated Parliament with petitions—by 1788 they had presented over one hundred to the House—and Equiano played his full part in the intense lobbying campaign that ensued. He became a regular visitor to Parliament, heading a delegation of other Black leaders and holding consultations with individual members of Parliament. On two separate occasions he was received by the prime minister and the Speaker of the House.[21] During 1788, Equiano also wrote several letters to the press about events and developments in the Black struggle. These letters were, until recently, unnoticed in secondary sources, but Shyllon has discussed them in a journal article and collected them in an appendix to his book.[22]

Perhaps no single aspect of his public career did more to test Equiano's loyalty to his people and his integrity as a leader than his involvement in the Sierra Leone Repatriation Scheme. In November 1786, he was appointed commissary of stores to the expedition, a post that he accepted, it seems, after much hesitancy and not a few suspicions about the bona fide reputations of the expedition's leaders: Joseph Irwin, the agent; Fraser, the parson; and one Dr. Currie. His suspicions soon proved well founded when he noticed that the agent was breaching official regulations by allowing certain white passengers aboard the transport ship who were not certified for passage by the government committee and who clearly intended to go as adventurers and opportunists. In a letter he wrote to Cugoano outlining the grounds for his dissatisfaction he called the white leaders "villains," intent on exploiting Blacks for their own self-interest.[23]

As commissary, he was well placed to expose other flagrant abuses: he complained that supplies were not being issued according to contract; that the prospective settlers were in need of adequate food, clothing, medicines, and beds. His impatience with these and other irregularities brought him into conflict with the unscrupulous agents. He accused them of misappropriating the finances of the scheme and of mistreating the Blacks. The agents wrote to the committee and to the Treasury accusing Equiano of arrogance and failure to cooperate. Equiano got word of the charges laid against him in a letter from Sir Charles Middleton, which also mentioned the more serious allegation of inciting the Blacks to mutiny.

The failure of the agents to cooperate with him left Equiano frustrated: "I do not know how this undertaking will end; I wish I had never been involved in it, but at times I think the Lord will make me very useful at last." Equiano's reports were substantiated by those of another Black leader, A. E. Griffith, also a member of the expedition. He wrote: "The people in general are very sickly, and die very fast indeed, for the doctors are very neglectful to the people, very much so."

Reviling Equiano as a troublemaker, the proslavery forces had him dismissed from his post in March 1787. Through his fearless agitation and his passionate desire to see his people treated fairly, he kept the matter current in the public press. The *Public Advertiser* carried both his letter to Cugoano and a subsequent sympathetic editorial ventilating the fears of the Black settlers; but later it took the side of the agents and of Equiano's critics, accusing him of making false statements and alleging that the true reason for his dismissal was "gross misbehaviour to the officers, the crew and his fellow Blacks." In the same paper, on 14 April 1787, Equiano was both roundly and wrongly traduced; the editorial was colored with racial overtones, depreciating Equiano's character, calling for an end to such "black reports," and threatening disclosure of "dark transactions" of a Black (presumably Equiano), if further public questioning of the organizers' motives was pursued.[24]

Another letter, written from Teneriffe thirteen days after the expedition had sailed from Plymouth, stirred up further public animosity against Equiano. The writer, "Fraser the parson," painted a glowing picture of racial harmony existing between the white crew and the Black emigrants: "Instead of the general misunderstanding under which we groaned through their means we now enjoy all the sweets of peace, lenity and almost uninterrupted harmony. The odious distinction of colours is no longer remembered and all seems to conspire to promote the general good."[25] But the reliability of these reports was highly questionable. The ship's captain had written earlier to the Navy Board stating that there had been sickness among the Blacks, occasioned by their poor diet of salt provisions, and that fourteen deaths had occurred since their departure.[26]

Notwithstanding these adversities, the *Advertiser*'s editorial fairly swelled with self-congratulation the day after the publication of Fraser's letter. The writer, heaping further censure on Equiano, gloated that Fraser's letter vindicated their confidence in the success of the expedition and justiffied their criticism of Equiano. The paper called Equiano "hypocritical and imposing in his behaviour to gentlemen of good faith and intentions."

As is evident from the course of the public debate so far, none of Equiano's detractors made any serious attempt to examine or disprove the allegations leveled against him; instead, they resorted to vilification and name-calling. The negative representations against him were persuasive enough to sway even so loyal a friend and collaborator as Granville Sharp.[27] Most likely, Sharp was influenced by exaggerated reports, like Fraser's, and by the not entirely disinterested opinions of Prince Hoare, who appears to have colluded with Irwin in the admittance of unauthorized passengers.[28]

Equiano remained defiant in the heat of all this controversy. In answer to the aspersions against his character and to the charges concerning his conduct, he wrote a letter to the *Public Advertiser* vindicating himself.[29] He maintained that the reason for his dismissal was a report he had made to the Navy Board accusing Irwin of peculation in the contracting and supplying of the expedition.

As if by some perverse form of poetic justice, the outcome of the Sierra Leone expedition truly vindicated Equiano's high-principled remonstrances. As a result of numerous delays in England, the settlers arrived in the colony at the start of the rainy season and so were unable to do any cultivation. Their accommodations were inadequate and tropical diseases ravaged their numbers—about a third, Irwin included, died from these afflictions and from inadequate diet.

It is important to stress that Equiano never doubted the honorable intentions of the government officials who administered the expedition in England. He lauded the humanitarian concern and judicious planning of both the Treasury and the Navy. The final blame he placed squarely on the shoulders of the middlemen—the managers and the agents. And despite the fact that the Lords Commissioners of the Treasury decided (in dismissing Equiano and appeasing his enemies) to err on the side of what they then perceived as politic and expedient, both the commissioners and the Navy Board retained high opinions of Equiano's reputation and conduct. The Navy Board wrote: "in all the Transactions the Commissary has had with the Board he has acted with great propriety and has been very regular with his information. . . ."[30] The Treasury, without any bureaucratic shuffling, reimbursed Equiano promptly for his expenses and paid him the salary due for his four months' service.[31]

Although this early attempt at realizing a philanthropic experiment in Sierra Leone almost foundered on the greed and folly of a few of its organizers, the new spirit of reform in which the project was conceived did not by any means die. And if proof were needed that Equiano fully identified himself with the experiment's most liberal objectives, one need look no further than the record of his activities and pronouncements during the years 1789 to 1792.

Abolitionists were dogged and persistent in their condemnation of the slave trade, but they possessed enough imagination and flexibility to harness the winds of intellectual change to suit the objectives of their cause. Equiano's campaigning through various parts of Great Britain coincided with the emergence of a new power bloc of capitalist industrialists. This group was beginning to agitate against the traditional mercantilist philosophy, which protected the West Indian sugar interests at the expense of other entrepreneurs and at considerable cost to the British consumer and taxpayer. The group supported a policy of free trade that would open up new markets and spread the benefits of progressive commerce more widely among the British people. In championing a reformed commerce, they naturally opposed the West Indian monopoly and unwittingly (at first) supported the abolitionists. The abolitionists quickly grasped this coincidence of interests and lost no time in courting their alliance. Equiano became one of the most intelligent interpreters of the new economic thinking in abolitionist circles.[32]

As early as 1788, Equiano had written a letter to Lord Hawkesbury, president of the Privy Council for Trade, outlining proposals for a new relationship between Britain and Africa, based on conventional trade, commerce, and industrialization.[33] Now, during his travels, he disseminated those same ideas in the industrial towns. It was no mere coincidence that his abolitionist sponsors arranged for him to visit Birmingham, Manchester, Nottingham, and Sheffield and addressed his letters of introduction to some of the leading citizens of these towns. Birmingham gave Equiano an enthusiastic welcome; Sheffield, center of the steel industry, had, by the time of his arrival, started a protest movement in favor of importing rum and sugar from the East Indies.[34] Together, these towns were the strongholds of the cotton manufacturers, the shipowners, and the sugar refiners—all interests that stood to benefit from an expansion of trade with Africa.

Thus, the abolitionists and the free trade forces were able to make common cause against the West Indian plantocracy and coalesce into a stronger force to break the power of the sugar barons. Equiano provided the "friends of humanity" with abundant proof about the undesirability of the slave trade, and the free trade interests awakened the British public to the costliness to them of the sugar monopoly and to its function as a disincentive to progressive enterprise.

The program for reformed trade that Equiano promoted during his campaign was the same one he outlined in the letter to Lord Hawkesbury and essentially that which he included in the closing pages of the *Life*. The advocates of commercial and industrial expansion would have found their ideas ably represented in Equiano's proposal, perhaps more persuasively so, since Equiano was an African and genuinely interested in Africa's progress and prosperity. Equiano called on the British to reshape their relations with Africa by substituting trade in human bodies for trade in raw materials and manufactured goods. He understood that the material interests of traders and manufacturers would be aroused to support this scheme, for it was calculated to extend their markets and increase their profits. Africa's rich natural resources would fulfill Britain's industrial needs, and Britain's manufactures would in turn find a lucrative market among Africa's teeming millions: "It is trading upon safe grounds," he coaxed. "A commercial intercourse with Africa opens up an inexhaustible source of wealth to the manufacturing interests of Great Britain, and to all which the slave trade is an objection" (*Life* 2:250–51).

It is indicative of Equiano's remarkable proficiency in abolitionist political and economic thought that he was able to enunciate this policy as eloquently as he did. But he did more than retail what must then have been an orthodox creed among most antislavery leaders. He invested the new ideology with his own patriotism and his firm vision of Africa's future greatness. He perceived that a new relationship, constructively pursued, could potentially give to Africa the best that European civilization had to offer. In concord with other philanthropists of the period, he cherished the optimism that if Europe could pursue peaceful relations with Africa as stubbornly as it prosecuted the slave trade and extend its love of freedom to the Black race, a new era of progress would embrace the whole world. He coupled this vision of secular progress with a vision of Christian messianism, drawing inspiration and expression from the Evangelical idiom describing the First Coming: "May Heaven make the British Senators the dispersers of light, liberty, and science, to the uttermost parts of teh earth: then will be Glory to God on the highest, on earth peace, and goodwill to men: Glory, honour, peace, &c. to every soul of man that worketh good, to the Britons first, (because to them the Gospel is preached) and also to the nations" (*Life* 2:248).[35]

One reservation may be expressed about Equiano's support for this policy of commercialization. He expressed more enthusiasm for Africans' adopting British manners, fashions, and customs—in effect, cultural imperialism—than might have been prudent. It may not have occurred to him that the "civilizing" benefits of broadened cultural and economic relations with Africa were not a fair exchange for the considerable material profits the Europeans would derive from full-scale colonization. Given the formidable resistance the abolitionists faced in their struggle to end slavery, they either thought that exploitation of material resources was a lesser evil than exploiting human bodies or, in their optimism for a new age of universal equality and harmony, they were not as mindful of consequences as they might have been.

Equiano's personal reputation and the public reception of the *Life* can be finally appraised by a sampling of contemporary judgments. Wherever he went during his years of antislavery campaigning (1789–93), he was attended by the good opinions of the "friends of humanity." The testimonial statements contained in the letters of introduction he took with him from town to town show that he had won the respect of prominent humanitarians around England.[36] Both Peter Peckard and Thomas Clarkson commended him highly. The leading philanthropists of the industrial towns in his circuit appeared notably impressed by the force of his personal presence and the integrity of his narrative. Thomas Digges of Belfast adjudged him "an enlightened African of good sense, agreeable manners, and of excellent character." Digges also attested to Equiano's association with Sir William Dolben (the sponsor of the parliamentary bill to limit the number of slaves carried on slave ships), Granville Sharp, and John Wilkes. Digges accorded Equiano the distinction of being a "principal instrument in bringing about the motion for the repeal of the Slave Act."[37] William Eddis of Durham praised Equiano in like terms, alluding appreciatively to his African proposal as "a plan truly conducive to the interests of Religion and Humanity."[38]

For the most part, the *Life* drew very favorable critical reviews from the press. Reviewers seem to have been impressed most by its unmistakable authenticity and by the genuine sincerity of its author. William Langworthy, who wrote a letter of credit on Equiano's behalf of William Hughes at Devizes, commented: "The simplicity that runs through his Narrative is singularly beautiful and that beauty is heightened by the idea that it is true. . . ."[39] The reviewer in the *General Magazine* called it "a round unvarnished tale . . . written with much truth and simplicity" and seemed deeply affected by its account of slavery's brutality. He expressed what must have been the common response of sensitive readers: "The reader, unless perchance he is either a West Indian planter or a Liverpool merchant, will find his humanity often severely wounded by the shameless barbarity practised towards the author's hapless countrymen in our colonies."[40]

Only the *Gentleman's Magazine* was niggling in its praise. Its reviewer found the narrative style "very unequal" and the work as a whole "an innocent contrivance to interest national humanity in favour of negro slaves." And, as though to detract from Equiano's achievement, the writer trotted out the well rehearsed "good-for-a-Black" qualifications that have persistently dogged the achievements of so many Black artists: "These memoirs," he insinuated, "place the writer on a par with the general mass of men in the subordinate stations of civilized society, and proves that there is no general rule without an exception."[41]

Equiano's career as a Black abolitionist is nothing short of illustrious. When he retired from seafaring, he had served many masters, had been an independent small trader for four years, and was thoroughly familiar with the operations of slavery. He therefore brought to abolitionist agitation the benefit of credibility born of personal experience. He contributed to antislavery a variegated background and an intense personal history not unlike those which Saint Paul brought to his work in the early Christian church. Equiano too had been shipwrecked several times, scourged, arrested, and imprisoned. Not surprisingly, he thought he perceived in all his mixed fortunes the constant hand of Providence preparing him for a great work.

Conclusion

One of the rewards of a pioneer study is that it repays industry by illuminating the dark corners of the understanding. Further, it opens up new ground for the venturesome to chart at some future time when tired tissue has been repaired by well-won respite. Several new directions have suggested themselves during the course of this research. A more detailed study of Sancho's literary and social relations with notable figures like David Garrick, John Hamilton Mortimer, Joseph Nollekens, and the duchess of Queensberry should establish more precisely the Black writer's connection with the intellectual life of his time. Deciphering the identity of those correspondents whom Sancho identifies only by their initials should also clarify several of the issues concerning his life and thought on which there can be now no final certainty. In Cugoano's case, a diligent search of the memoirs of his master, Richard Cosway the miniaturist, or of the remains of Scipione Piattoli (1749–1809), the Italian champion of Polish independence who is credited with a very appreciative encomium of Cugoano's character, should flesh out the spare biographical skeleton we have of him.[1] Still more remains to be said about the profound conversion experience Equiano relates in his *Life;* the antecedents of that work and its relation to the wider religious traditions of English Protestantism could be studied with much profit to the critical scholarship surrounding the *Life.* Moreover, we might tap an invaluable source of knowledge about all three men if we could trace the lives of their descendants and discover to what extent the eighteenth-century legacy has survived. Many other questions could be raised, and searching for the answers would no doubt be exhausting, though not by any means exhaustive. For the most part, the particular terms of this inquiry and the scarcity of documentary materials place these concerns beyond immediate realization. For the present, however, two main lines of reflection warrant expansion in the closing remarks that follow. These will serve, on the one hand, to render a final evaluation of the achievements of Blacks writing in the eighteenth century and, on the other, to suggest some possible uses that these authors' work represents within the larger framework of recent literature by Blacks and of critical writing about it.

In the historical context of the Western world in the eighteenth century, the emergence of a literature written by Blacks about themselves was a distinctly revolutionary event. The writings of Sancho, Cugoano, and Equiano were as much the reflexes of oppression and as profoundly informed by the animus of resistance as the conscious acts of subversion and sabotage that the slaves practiced in the colonies. As the Western mind searched for a myth to provide a moral and philosophical basis for slavery, it contrived the artifact of the "Negro," a creature of pure animal spirits, insensible and unimaginative. But that myth came gradully to be undermined and eventually refuted by some of the very persons whom it was intended to victimize. The writings examined in this study show how three Black men of uncommon ability translated the experience of their encounter with racial prejudice and slavery into literary form; they show that these writers became partners in fashioning a new myth through their art, as decisively as the architects of the Haitian Revolution made their contribution to that myth through the creation of an independent republic, run by intelligent Black leaders and regulated on liberal principles and civilized standards.[2]

The managers of slave society desired to control the minds of the slaves and to limit their capacity for improvement by permanently denying their human right to freedom and self-determination. They endeavored to relegate them to a faceless existence. And, accordingly (at least in their public manifestations), the slaves adopted a life of shadowy submissiveness. But, as far as they were permitted, they celebrated their authentic identity in the traditional forms of discourse, in rites of song, dance, and religion, thus preserving discrete facets of their cultural inheritance throughout long years of oppression. Where, as in the case of Sancho, Cugoano, and Equiano, the mind was exposed to the higher attainments of human culture and exercised by the stimuli of superior thought, the struggle to preserve the self in the face of repression and denial was dramatized on a different stage and in a different mode. These three figures, by virtue of their intellectual development, were compelled to articulate for the European public the dilemma the African suffered in his drive to reach full self-realization in a world hostile to his image and presumptuously confident about his subhuman identity.

Ironically, the very precariousness of their social status assisted them in shaping rhetorical positions that were at once persuasive to their audiences and faithful to the shared experiences of their brothers and sisters in bondage. Each writer demonstrated a level of technical sophistication and moral authority that challenged his readers to consider new ways of seeing the African.

Sancho expressed this self-awareness in apologetic, complaisant terms, concealing the trenchant possibilities of his style and clothing himself in a garb of meekness and self-mockery. Thus he won that immunity which a society will typically allow an outsider whom it perceives as unthreatening to its way of life. But having won his audience's approval, he consciously satirized their bigotry and their blindness. Cugoano, with his more combative temperament, challenged the prevailing assumptions about slavery and exposed the false morality of its proponents. He met the Africans' detractors on the hard ground of systematic inquiry and rational analysis, offering by these methods convincing proofs to counteract anti-African propaganda. He brought a victim's peculiar insights to expose the contradictions inherent in a culture that subscribed to philosophies of universal goodwill and widespread progress but yet excluded his race from that world view. By identifying the Africans' sufferings with those of the Israelites, he dignified the African problem and claimed for his people a special role in shaping the course of history. Equiano's choice of the autobiographical mode yielded the double advantage of aiding his personal quest for self-knowledge and of displaying to the skeptical the full human possibilities of a Black man touched by Evangelical religion and enlightened by Western thought. The example of his devout life and the record of his tireless leadership in the campaign for abolition are two of the little-sung achievements of Black people in the eighteenth century. He transcended the formidable barriers of bigotry and prejudice to leave a definitive index of the African mind's capacity when liberated from the stultification of common slavery.

Through their writing, these men discovered themselves anew and planted a more favorable image of their race in the public mind. They had, both wittingly and unwittingly, become makers of a new myth, key agents in facilitaitng the climate of reform that made abolition and emancipation possible. The following observations, written by Lord Brougham in 1803, show how effective the new image and the new myth were, even among the most intelligent part of the nation: ". . . however deficient in civilization, the negroes are evidently capable of acquiring those wants and desires which are the seeds of industry; they are endowed with powers, not only of body but of mind, sufficient to render their improvement and high refinement a matter of absolute certainty under a proper system of management. . . ."[3]

The triumvirate of Black literary expression in eighteenth-century England confronted a discriminatory social and political system and played their part in changing it. Their importance as precursors in the literary tradition that has addressed itself to ontological and existential issues definitive of subsequent Black authorship is this: they set an agenda of values for such authorship that has shaped permanently the meaning of literacy and the profession of letters in postcolonial and still-colonized Black societies. A study in both continuity and change, their legacy holds two main uses for the amelioration of contemporary popular and specialized attitudes to the African past.

In the first place, the legacy (and the vision) must be so carefully preserved as to ensure the survival of our vital traditions, and to be counted among the singular achievements of Black people. They should serve as faithful guides in our continuing quest to reconstruct the past and discover our place in it. They should deepen our sense of our history and establish the indefeasible right of African peoples to participate equally in shaping the human future.

The strict regime of slave societies had long encouraged the belief that the slaves lived only at that level of existence consonant with their degraded condition. It was widely assumed that they lived totally in the worlds their masters made, grasping only the most elemental notions of experience. Discerning scholarship and constant critical revaluation are demonstrating that the slaves drew from adversity an apprehension of life of which the hostile white world remained ignorant or skeptical for a long time. The ordinary slave was, at best, only half-conscious of it; but Sancho, Cugoano, and Equiano expressed it in their works as a special poetry that is forged in suffering and wrung out of chaos. It is in essence the individuated and inalienable consciousness that Blacks bring as their votive offering to the altar of life. Modern readers ought to find in these works an affirmative statement of the Black's existential reality as Sancho, Cugoano, and Equiano experienced it in a world fashioned for them by others and as they preserved it behind the veil of their own private universe.

The second area of utility has academic implications. Black literature of the eighteenth century affords the contemporary critic and scholar an important reference point from which to plot the overall history and development of formal expression among representatives of the African race. For the full story of the race's cultural acts cannot be told if the contribution to antislavery intellectual history of Sancho, Cugoano, and Equiano is not taken into account. Nor can true justice be done to the even longer tradition of African literacy and learning in Europe (which these three carried on), if their equally distinguished predecessors Juan Latino, Anthony William Amo, Jacobus Eliza Capitein, Francis Williams, and Job Ben Solomon are omitted from the record.

The three writers central to this study were the principal architects of a discourse identifying the problem of slavery as the ultimate criterion against which the moral integrity of Western civilization should be measured. In concert with others of kindred social and philosophical persuasion, Sancho, Cugoano, and Equiano exerted a unique power through their respective rhetorical voices that dramatically transfigured the image of the demoralized Black while simultaneously garnering for themselves authorial credibility. These authors and their texts participate in a process of expropriating the symbolic systems of language and its allied arts to reinvent themselves for themselves and to revise the discourse about Africa and Africans. Their authentic experiences and expressions make it possible for succeeding artists and thinkers to reconstruct the Black aesthetic.

Notes

CHAPTER 1. THE BLACK PRESENCE

1. *The Works of Tacitus,* The Oxford Translation, rev. ed., (London, 1884), 2:355.

2. J[oel] A. Rogers, *Sex and Race* (1944; reprint, New York: H. M. Rogers, 1967), 1:55.

3. See Kenneth Little, *Negroes in Britain* (London: Routledge & Kegan Paul, 1972), 187; and Paul Edwards and James Walvin, "Africans in Britain, 1500–1800," in the *The African Diaspora,* ed. Martin Kilson and Robert Rotberg (Cambridge: Harvard University Press, 1976). These sources do not consider the Roman evidence sufficient to support the African claim.

4. *Scriptores Historiae Augustae,* trans. David Magie (Cambridge: Harvard University Press, 1960–61), 1:424–27.

5. For a full analysis and description of the evidence, see Roger Warwick, "Skeletal Remains," in *The Romano-British Cemetery at Trentholme Drive, York,* ed. Leslie P. Wenham (London: Her Majesty's Stationery Office, 1968), 146–57.

6. Edward Scobie, *Black Britannia* (Chicago: Johnson Publishing Company, 1972), 5–11. Chapter 1 of this book gives a lively account of the social impact of Blacks in England.

7. Edwards and Walvin, "Africans in Britain," 177.

8. *Acts of the Privy Council of England, 1542–1568,* n. s. 1596–97, ed. John Roche Dasent (London: Eyre and Spottiswoode, 1902), 26:16–21.

9. James Walvin, *Black and White* (London: Allen Lane, 1973), 36–37.

10. *Diary of Samuel Pepys,* ed. Robert C. Latham, 11 vols. (Berkeley: University of California Press, 1970), 3:95, 9:510.

11. Folarin O. Shyllon, *Black Slaves in Britain* (London: Oxford University Press, 1974), 3–5.

12. James Sutherland, *Background for Queen Anne,* quoted in Wylie Sypher, *Guinea's Captive Kings* (Chapel Hill: University of North Carolina Press, 1942), 3.

13. Scobie, *Black Britannia,* 12–13.

14. Michael Craton, James Walvin, and David Wright, *Slavery, Abolition and Emancipation* (New York: Longmans, 1976), 72. Although slavery was illegal in England, the sale of Black slaves was carried on quite openly. A street in Liverpool was nicknamed "Negro Row" to announce this commerce.

15. In this classification, I am following the categories described by J. Jean Hecht in "Continental and Colonial Servants in Eighteenth-Century England," *Smith College Studies in History* 40(1954): 1–61. This is the most extensive account of Blacks in domestic service in England during the period. See also Hecht, *The Domestic Servant Class in Eighteenth-Century England* (London: Routledge & Kegan Paul, 1956), and Dorothy Marshall, "The Domestic Servants of the Eighteenth Century," *Economica* 9 (April 1929): 15–40.

16. J. J. Crooks, "Negroes in England in the Eighteenth Century," *Notes and Queries* 154(1928): 173–74.

17. Craton, Walvin, Wright, *Slavery,* 172. See also Hecht, "Continental and Colonial Servants," 37.

18. The records of the Royal African Company, the African Committee, and philanthropic bodies like the Society for the Propagation of the Gospel provide circumstantial details about these scholars and the arrangements made for their studies in England. J. J. Crooks ("Negroes in England") documents the expenses of two other native youths who visited England from 1753 to 1755.

19. M. Dorothy George, *London Life in the Eighteenth Century* (1925; reprint, London: Kegan Paul, 1951), 219–22.

20. Philip Curtin, ed., *Africa Remembered* (Madison: University of Wisconsin Press, 1967), 15.

21. James Boswell, *Life of Johnson,* 3rd ed. (New York: Oxford University Press, 1933), 160.

22. Scobie, *Black Britannia,* 24–25; Walvin, *Black and White,* 70–72.

23. Sir Jonah Barrington, *Personal Sketches and Recollections of His Own Times* (Glasgow and London: Cameron and Ferguson, 1876), 367.

24. In addition, Hogarth's pictures, like those of Zoffany, Sir Joshua Reynolds, and Gainsborough, reflect the ever widening spheres of Black involvement in English social life. Both Scobie (*Black Britannia*) and Walvin (*Black and White*) reproduce a good selection of representative prints.

25. Carl Bernhard Wadstrom, *An Essay on Colonization* (1794; reprint, New York: A. M. Kelley, 1986), 695. See also Walvin, *Black and White,* 59.

26. Walvin, *Black and White,* 52–53.

27. The most thorough treatment of the displaced Loyalists' problems can be found in Ellen Gibson Wilson, *The Loyal Blacks* (New York: G. P. Putnam's Sons, 1976), 138–39.

28. *The Gentleman's Magazine* 34(October 1764): 493.

29. Walvin, *Black and White,* 46–47.

30. Ignatius Sancho, *Letters of the Late Ignatius Sancho,* introd. Paul Edwards, 5th ed. (1830; reprint, London: Dawsons of Pall Mall, 1968). This is the most authoritative edition, from which all textual references in this study will be drawn. Sancho followed an invariable practice, perhaps out of his Shandean whimsy, of identifying his correspondents only by the initial letters of their surnames; but his first editor, Mrs. Crewe, has numbered the letters, and references throughout this study will follow her ordering.

31. See also Letters 13, 14, and 58.

32. Ottobah Cugoano, *Thoughts and Sentiments on the Evil of Slavery,* introd. Paul Edwards (1787; reprint, London: Dawsons of Pall Mall, 1969), hereafter cited as *Thoughts.*

33. Slaves, and even free Blacks, were commonly kidnapped by such agents for a price in England. The practice was a gainful one for whites who were themselves often poor and needy.

34. Equiano's efforts were unsuccessful. Such incidents tested the true import of the landmark Mansfield decision (1722) in the case of James Somerset (see chap. 5) and were to continue well into the nineteenth century.

35. Olaudah Equiano, *The Life of Olaudah Equiano or Gustavus Vassa, the African,* introd. Paul Edwards, 2 vols. (1789; reprint, London: Dawsons of Pall Mall, 1969), hereafter cited as *Life.*

36. Walvin, *Black and White,* 57.

37. For further discussion of mixed attitudes to Blacks, see Philip Curtin, *The Image of Africa: British Ideas and Action, 1780–1850* (Madison: University of Wisconsin Press, 1964), 35; and J. Jean Hecht, "Continental and Colonial Servants," 43, especially for her discussion of the popularity and unpopularity of Black servants.

38. Edwards and Walvin, "Africans in Britain," 183; Sir John Fielding, *Extracts from the Penal Laws*, quoted in Shyllon, *Black People in Britain, 1553–1833* (London: Oxford University Press, 1977), 97.

39. Little, *Negroes in Britain*, 219–20.

40. George Birkbeck Hill, *Johnsonian Miscellany* (Oxford, 1817), 1:291.

41. Notwithstanding a hostile public posture, intimate black-white liaisons existed on the upper rungs of society. Hogarth's paintings mirrored serveral such relationships; gossip circles rang with the scandal of the duchess of Queensberry's relationship with her Black protégé, the incomparable and dashing Soubise. For further details, see Scobie, *Black Britannia*, 89–95, and Walvin, *Black and White*, 52–55.

42. Shyllon, *Black People in Britain*, 93.

43. *The London Chronicle* 16(29 September–20 October 1764): 317.

44. Edward Long, *Candid Reflections*, quoted in Walvin, *Black and White*, 55.

45. "Spotted Negro Boy," *Notes and Queries*, n. s., 6(1900): 55–56.

46. James Tobin, *Cursory Remarks* (London, 1785), 117, 188n.

47. Cedric Dover, *Hell in the Sunshine* (London: Secker & Warburg, 1942), 159.

48. Both Hecht ("Continental and Colonial Servants," 46) and Curtin (*Image of Africa*, 35) propose that the popular English attitude was one of moderate xenophobia rather than of racism as we know it today.

49. Sir John Fielding, quoted in Shyllon, *Black People in Britain*, 97. Similarly, as Fielding mentions, baptism and church membership were thought to render slaves free. See also Walvin, *Black and White*, 64–67.

50. *The London Chronicle* 31(23 June 1772): 598c.

51. Shyllon, *Black People in Britain*, 81, 119.

52. Philip Thicknesse, quoted in Dover, *Hell in the Sunshine*, 159.

53. *The London Chronicle* 15(18 Feb. 1764): 166c.

54. Aleyn Lyell Reade, *Johnsonian Gleanings* (London: Arden Press, 1912), 2:15.

55. Hecht, "Continental and Colonial Servants," 49.

56. *St. James' Evening Post*, quoted in Shyllon, *Black Slaves in Britain* (London: Oxford University Press, 1974), 81.

57. Shyllon, *Black People*, 81.

58. Scobie *Black Britannia*, 31. The most complete account of Latino's life and literary work is Valuarez Spratlin's *Juan Latino, Slave and Humanist* (New York: Spinner Press, 1938), on which I have drawn extensively. Short biographical notes on Latino can also be found in Jahnheinz Jahn's *Neo-African Literature* (New York: Grove Press, 1968), 31–34.

59. The best account of Amo's life is given in William E. Abraham's *The Mind of Africa* (Chicago: University of Chicago Press, 1962), 128–30, which is my chief source here. For purposes of comparison I have used Henri Gregoire's *Moral and Intellectual Faculties of Negroes* (1808; reprint, College Park, Maryland: McGrath Publishing Company, 1967), 173–76, a generally valuable text, which must be used with care, because Gregoire is not always scrupulously accurate, and his text is often vitiated by errors factual and technical. Both Scobie, *Black Britannia*, and Curtin, *Africa Remembered*, make brief notice of Amo.

60. The full title of Amo's Latin treatise is "Dissertatio inauguralis philosophica de humanae mentis ΑΠΑΘΕΙΑsuae sensionis ac facultates sentiendi in mente humana absenta et carum in corpore nostro organico ac vivo praesentia." There is now also a full modern English translation entitled *The ΑΠΑΘΕΙΑ of the Human Mind or the Absence of Sensation* (Halle and Wittenberg: Martin Luther University, 1968).

61. Except as otherwise indicated, the substantive facts of Capitein's career have been drawn from F. L. Bartels' "Jacobus Eliza Capitein, 1717–1747," *Transactions of the Historical Society of Ghana* 4, no. 1(1959): 1–13.

62. Gregoire conjectures that Capitein may have been influenced by Dutch planters to take this proslavery position. See 204.

63. For the broad outlines of Williams's life, I have followed the memoir in Edward Long's *History of Jamaica* (London, 1774), 2:475–84. As Long's expressed intention was to prove the inferiority of Blacks and assert the superiority of whites, his work is naturally biased. For a fairer assessment, see Gregoire, *Moral and Intellectual Faculties of Negroes*, 207–12, and Scobie, *Black Britannia*, 27–31.

64. None of Williams's biographers is any more precise about the date of his return.

65. T. H. MacDermot, "From a Jamaican Portfolio," *Journal of Negro History* 2(1917): 147–59. This is an objective and refreshing critique of Williams.

66. MacDermot, "Jamaican Portfolio," 153.

67. All the sources cited above on Williams reprint this ode, as well as a selection of his other works.

68. Long, *History of Jamaica*, 484.

69. David Hume, "Essay on National Characters," in *Essays Moral Political and Literary* (1742; reprint, London: Longmans Green, 1875), 1:252n.

70. Quoted in Scobie, *Black Britannia*, 29.

71. James Ramsay, the author of *Essay on the Treatment and Coversion of Slaves in the British Sugar Colonies* (London, 1784), 238. Ramsay was an Anglican clergyman who lived in the West Indies for twenty years.

72. Ramsay, *Treatment and Conversion of Slaves*, 239.

73. Unless otherwise indicated, the biographical details on Phillis Wheatley have been taken from Vernon Loggins, *The Negro Author: His Development in America* (New York: Columbia University Press, 1931), and from William H. Robinson, *Phillis Wheatley in the Black American Beginnings* (Detroit: The Broadside Press, 1975), a brief but perceptive appreciation. A more comprehensive critical study is Merle A. Richmond's *Bid the Vassal Soar* (Washington, D.C.: Howard University Press, 1974).

74. The countess was patroness of two other eighteenth-century Blacks: James Albert Ukawsaw Gronniosaw, who dedicated his autobiography, *Narrative of the Most Remarkable Particulars. . .*, to her; and John Morrant, an ex-slave from America, whose *Narrative* (1785) and *Journal* (1789) seemed to have been published at the countess' encouragement. See Loggins, *Negro Author*, 31–33.

75. See Richmond, *Bid the Vassal Soar*, 33.

76. William Legge (1731–1801), earl of Dartmouth, became secretary of state for North America in 1772. He was also president of the British Board of Trade and a steadfast proslavery advocate. Phillis Wheatley dedicated a poem to him.

77. Gronniosaw's *Narrative* is often dated 1770, but this is dubious; 1774 is thought to be a more reliable date.

78. The elegy had seen over ten editions in Boston, Newport, and Philadelphia, and two editions in London. At least four poems from the 1773 volume had been printed previously. An early version of the poem "On Recollection" appeared in March 1772.

79. For a useful review of critical notices about Phillis Wheatley's poetry, see Julian D. Mason, ed., *The Poems of Phillis Wheatley* (Chapel Hill: University of North Carolina Press, 1966), xxxvi–xlviii.

80. See Letter 58.

81. Quoted in Shyllon, *Black People in Britain,* 197.

82. Thomas Clarkson, *An Essay on the Slavery and Commerce of the Human Species, particularly the African* (Philadelphia, 1786), 110–12.

83. Quoted in Mason, *Poems of Phillis Wheatley,* xxxix. According to Mason, the *Christian Examiner* was a critical journal of high caliber, perhaps the most important in America between 1830 and 1835.

84. Thomas Jefferson, *Notes on Virginia,* ed. William Peden (Chapel Hill: University of North Carolina Press, 1955), 140.

85. Quoted in Robinson, *Phillis Wheatley,* 28.

86. Robinson, *Phillis Wheatley,* 28.

87. Robinson adduces evidence based on Phillis' own revisions and changes made by editors and censors to show that she was not as benign as many critics believe. He finds a fairly clear racial consciousness covertly conveyed through biblical allusions and moral themes (see *Phillis Wheatley,* 57–62). He finds greater self-assertivemess in her London poems, especially the poem addressed to Lord Dartmouth. Finally, he recognizes realistically that if Phillis had been any more explicit, the colonial press would have rejected her work (see 30–38).

88. I base my descriptive details for this group on Shyllon, *Black People in Britain,* 45–66.

89. The first group of such students were twenty Congolese princes who arrived in Portugal in 1516.

90. Cf. Shyllon. *Black People,* 45–46. The most famous of these cases was that of the young Prince Annamaboe. He was entrusted to a slaving captain and sent to be educated in England; but the captain sold him. The captain's treachery reached official circles, and the British government ransomed the prince.

91. Biographical details of Quaque follow those in Bartels, "Philip Quaque 1741–1816," *Transactions of the Historical Society of Ghana* 1, part 5(1955): 153–77.

92. Those youths were sent to Liverpool whose fathers desired them to acquire a practical education in trade and business matters.

93. Shyllon, *Black People in Britain,* 58.

94. My account of Job's life derives mainly from the biographical sketch in Curtin, *Africa Remembered,* 17–59. Curtin's source, the earliest and most comprehensive record of Job's enslavement and travels, is Thomas Bluett's *Some Memoirs of the Life of Job, the Son of Solomon, the High Priest of Boonda in Africa* (London, 1734).

95. Oglethorpe was later to become the first governor of Georgia. He was a reformer and philanthropist and had initially refused to permit slavery in the colony.

96. Bluett, quoted in Douglas Grant, *The Fortunate Slave* (London: Oxford University Press, 1968), 90. This is the most complete modern biography of Job and a highly valuable source on other related matters.

97. Grant, *Fortunate Slave,* 94.

98. Grant, *Fortunate Slave,* 99–101.

99. Grant, *Fortunate Slave,* 94.

100. Grant, *Fortunate Slave,* 108.

CHAPTER 2. THE INTELLECTUAL MILIEU

1. Current histories trace the rise of antislavery to a radical shift in the "intellectual and religious assumptions of the West." For a cogent critique of this shift and

the relation of antislavery to the Enlightenment, see C. Duncan Rice, *The Rise and Fall of Black Slavery* (Baton Rouge: Louisiana State University Press, 1976), 153–85, to which my interpretation is indebted.

2. Lester G. Crocker, *The Age of Enlightenment* (New York: Walker and Company, 1969), 2–3. See also Peter Gay, *The Science of Freedom*, vol. 2 of *The Enlightenment: An Interpretation* (New York: Alfred Knopf, 1969), 407–23, for a review of the Enlightenment's contribution to abolition. These are the two principal sources of my facts on the Enlightenment.

3. Aristotle, *The Politics*, trans. H. Rackham, ed. J. E. C. Welldon (New York: Macmillan, 1897), 1 : v–vi.

4. Thomas Hobbes, *Leviathan* (London, 1651; New York: Scolar Press, 1969), 151–56; and the "De Corpore politico," in *The English Works*, ed. Sir William Molesworth (London, 1840), 4 : 150–53.

5. John Locke, *Two Treatises of Government* (London, 1689; New York: Hafner Publishing Company, 1947), 143.

6. Locke, *Two Treatises*, 132.

7. Craton, Walvin, Wright, *Slavery*, 196; see also Gay, *Science of Freedom*, 409–10.

8. Sypher, "Hutcheson and the Classical Theory of Slavery," *Journal of Negro History* 24(1939): 273.

9. Anthony Ashley Cooper, Lord Shaftesbury, *Characteristics* (London, 1711), book 2, part 1, sec. 3, p. 331.

10. Frances Hutcheson, *A System of Moral Philosophy* (London, 1734–38; reprint, 1755), 1 : 19–20.

11. Hutcheson, *Moral Philosophy*, 1 : 300.

12. Sypher's article, "Hutcheson and Theory of Slavery," illuminates the revolutionary impact of Hutcheson's humanitarian ethics on the course of antislavery in Europe as a whole.

13. See Jean Jacques Rousseau, *The Social Contract* (1762; reprint, New York: Hafner Publishing Company, 1947), 9–13; see also Mercer Cook's "Jean Jacques Rousseau and the Negro," *Journal of Negro History* 21(1936): 294–303, a concise critique of Rousseau's particular contribution to antislavery and his influence on French abolitionists.

14. The ensuing discussion of race and creation follows Curtin's critical study of the relevant eighteenth-century thinking thereon in *The Image of Africa: British Ideas in Action, 1780–1850* (Madison: University of Wisconsin Press, 1964), 42.

15. Curtin suggests a distinction between the Englishman's treatment of individual Africans (generally tolerant as the century proceeded, especially in domestic circles) and the Englishman's mental image of the "abstract and collective Negro" (*Image of Africa*, 42).

16. Long, *History of Jamaica* 2 : 336–84.

17. Adam Smith, *Theory of Moral Sentiments*, ed. Dugald Stewart (1759; reprint, London: Henry G. Bohn, 1853), 288.

18. Smith, *Theory*, 299–300.

19. Blumenbach (1752–1840) is considered one of the founding fathers of anthropology. His classification of the human race influenced all the subsequent major anthropologists. His dissertation, *On the Natural Varieties of Mankind* (1775; reprint, New York: Bergman Publishers, 1969), is the work cited here.

20. Blumenbach, *Natural Varieties of Mankind*, 308.

21. Blumenbach, *Natural Varieties of Mankind*, 312.

22. Samuel Stanhope Smith, *An Essay on the Causes of the Variety of Complex-*

ion and Figure in the Human Species, ed. Winthrop Jordan (Philadelphia, 1787; Cambridge: Harvard University Press, 1965), 23. Smith was a Presbyterian minister, professor of moral philosophy at Princeton University and later president of that institution. The *Essay* is a pivotal work in American intellectual history.

23. Smith, *Essay on Complexion*, 163.

24. Charles Louis Montesquieu, *Persian and Chinese Letters*, ed. Walter Dunne (Paris, 1721; London, 1901), 217–18.

25. Montesquieu, *The Spirit of the Laws*, trans. Thomas Nugent, ed. J. V. Prichard (1748; reprint, London: George Bell, 1906).

26. Montesquieu, *Spirit*, 253–55.

27. Montesquieu, *Spirit*, 257.

28. Montesquieu, *Spirit*, 259. This is perhaps one of the most celebrated and widely quoted passages in Montesquieu.

29. For a discussion on Blackstone and other British intellectual figures influenced by Montesquieu, see Frank Thomas H. Fletcher, "Montesquieu's Influence on Anti-slavery Opinion in England," *Journal of Negro History* 18(1933): 414–25; Shyllon's *Black Slaves in Britain* (55–124) examines the impact of Blackstone's *Commentaries* and the controversy caused by his later emendations.

30. James Beattie, *Elements of Moral Science* (Edinburgh, 1790), 2:155–56; see also 164, 196.

31. Beattie, *Essay on the Nature and Immutability of Truth*, 2nd ed. (Edinburgh, 1771), 508–11. Another prominent English moral philosopher of the time who attacked slavery on the ground of Christianity and natural rights was William Paley. His *Principles of Moral and Political Philosophy*, 2 vols. (London, 1785) questioned the utility and necessity of slavery and supported gradual emancipation. See also Thomas Paine, "Letter on African Slavery in America," (1775), and *Rights of Man* (1791).

32. This threefold connection is fully explained in Rice, *Rise and Fall of Black Slavery*, 161–67. An important major study, dedicated entirely to this subject, is Betty Fladeland's *Men and Brothers: Anglo-American Anti-Slavery Cooperation* (Urbana: University of Illinois Press, 1972).

33. Michel Adanson wrote *Voyage to Senegal*, trans. 1759; William Bosman, *New and Accurate Description of the Coast of Guinea*, trans. 1765; and William Smith, *New Voyage to Guinea*, 1744.

34. Anthony Benezet, *Some Historical Account of Guinea* (1771; reprint, London: Frank Cass, 1968), 107.

35. See Dallas D. Irvine, "The Abbé Raynal and British Humanitarianism," *Journal of Modern History* 3(1931): 564–77.

36. Guillaume Raynal, *Histoire de deux Indes*, trans. J. O. Justamond (London, 1776), 457.

37. Irvine, "Abbé Raynal", 567–69.

38. Raynal, *Histoire de deux Indes*, 466.

39. George Fox, "Letter to Friends Beyond the Sea, that have Blacks and Indian Slaves," in *The Works of George Fox*, 8 vols. (1675; reprint, New York: A M S Press, Inc., 1975).

40. Quoted in Evelyn Douglas Bebb, *Nonconformity and Social and Economic Life, 1660–1800* (London: The Epworth Press, 1935), 158.

41. Reverend Morgan Godwyn, quoted in Benjamin Rush, *A Vindication of the Address on the Slavery on Negroes* (1773; reprint, New York: Arno Press, 1969), 14–15.

42. Bebb, *Nonconformity*, 159. For a concise account of Quaker antislavery

agitation, see David Brion Davis, *The Problem of Slavery in the Age of Revolution, 1770–1823* (Ithaca: Cornell University Press, 1975), 213–54.

43. Eric Williams, *Capitalism and Slavery* (Chapel Hill: University of North Carolina Press, 1945), 43.

44. In 1710 Christopher Codrington bequeathed two estates and three hundred slaves in Barbados to the Society for the Propagation of the Gospel. He desired the society to nurture a model community where masters and slaves would live in Christian harmony and cooperation. But the society failed to carry out Codrington's wishes, fearing that to do so would undermine the estates' profits. See further, Davis, *The Problem of Slavery in Western Culture* (Ithaca: Cornell University Press, 1966), 219–22.

45. Whitefield, quoted in Winthrop Jordan, *White over Black: American Attitudes Toward the Negro 1550–1812* (Chapel Hill: University of North Carolina Press, 1968), 214.

46. See Whitefield's Letter to Wesley, 22 March 1751, in Luke Tyerman, *Life and Times of Wesley* (New York: Harper and Brothers, 1872), 2:132.

47. The Methodist conferences in Britain strictly enjoined their missionaries in the West Indies and America to refrain from active political agitation to change the established order of plantation society. Missionaries were supposed to concentrate their efforts on evangelism and conversion and on promoting such harmony between masters and slaves as would eventually produce an amelioration of the slaves' lot. For a useful discussion of this official policy, see William J. Shrewsbury, *British Methodism and Slavery* (Heywood, England, 1862), 7.

48. Sypher, *Guinea's Captive Kings*, 70.

49. John Wesley, *Works*, ed. John Emory (New York, 1831), 6:292. Despite Wesley's untiring championship of civil liberties and social justice for the lower classes, he was not a political revolutionary, nor a religious one, for that matter. In fact, he abhorred any thought of what we would call popular democracy.

50. Wesley, "Thoughts upon Slavery," in *Works* 6:288.

51. For further discussion of the Methodist participation in the politics of abolition, see Shrewsbury, *British Methodism and Slavery*, 43.

52. Wesley, "Letter to Wilberforce on Slavery," in *Works* 7:231.

53. Ramsay, *Treatment and Conversion of Slaves*, 125–26.

54. Ramsay, *Treatment and Conversion of Slaves*, 203.

55. Ramsay, *Treatment and Conversion of Slaves*, 245.

56. Rev. John Newton, "Thoughts upon the African Slave Trade" (London, 1788), 24.

57. Newton, "African Slave Trade," 104. According to Newton's estimate, one-quarter of the slaves died in a four to six week voyage, and at least one-fifth of the seamen never returned, an annual loss of eight thousand.

58. Newton, "African Slave Trade," 104.

59. Newton, *The Journal of a Slave Trader, 1750–54*, ed. Bernard Martin and Mark Spurrel (1788; reprint, London: The Epworth Press 1962), xiii.

60. Clarkson, *History of the Rise, Progress and Accomplishment of the Abolition of the African Slave Trade by the British Parliament*(London, 1808), 1:207. This is the first comprehensive document on the accomplishment of abolition and a monument to antislavery scholarship; it documents not only the process of abolition but also the process of Clarkson's research.

61. Sypher, *Guinea's Captive Kings*, 29.

62. Curtin, *Image of Africa*, p. 68; see also Clarkson, *History of Abolition* 2:13–16.

63. Sypher, *Guinea's Captive Kings*, 17; Davis, *Slavery in Age of Revolution*, 220.

64. De Quincey, quoted in Rice, *Rise and Fall of Black Slavery*, 217.

65. The ensuing description of Quaker abolitionist activity is largely indebted to the fine scholarship reflected in Davis' excellent work on slavery, *Slavery in the Age of Revolution*, 213–54.

66. Davis, *Slavery in the Age of Revolution*, 221.

67. Davis' critique treats the Quaker antislavery initiative in America and Britain as an important instrument in the religious revival of the eighteenth century. Davis discusses at length the Quakers' extraordinary communication methods and assesses the importance of those methods in furthering antislavery. See *Slavery in the Age of Revolution*, 224–32.

68. Shyllon, *Black People in Britain*, 229.

69. Davis, *Slavery in the Age of Revolution*, 221.

70. Although the terms *abolition* and *emancipation* are often loosely interchanged, a critical distinction makes for more precise historical reference and interpretation—abolition being the movement to abolish the slave trade that culminated with the Abolition Act of 1807, and emancipation, the struggle for gradual liberation of the slaves on the plantations which ended with the Emancipation Act, 7 August 1833.

71. The biographical details on Wilberforce and the description of the Clapham Sect follows E. M. Howse, *The Saints in Politics: The Clapham Sect and the Growth of Freedom* (1953; reprint, London: Allen and Unwin, 1971). Another brief but useful study on both subjects is Earle E. Cairns, *Saints and Society* (Chicago: Moody Press, 1960).

72. Howse, *Saints in Politics*, 12.

73. Howse, *Saints in Politics*, 179.

74. Reginald Coupland, *Life of Wilberforce*, quoted in Howse, *Saints in Politics*, 27.

75. Quoted in Howse, *Saints in Politics*, 35.

76. Howse, *Saints in Politics*, 35.

77. Historians of abolition and antislavery have traditionally been grouped into two schools—the traditionalists, who attributed the abolition and emancipation of slavery largely or wholly to the upsurge in humanitarian sentiment and religious enthusiasm; and the economic determinists, who minimize the role of the above causes and argue that the colonial plantocracy was actively undermined and displaced by the emerging industrial and commercial elite in England. The two chief spokesmen for the traditionalist view are Reginald Coupland, *The British Anti-Slavery Movement* (London, 1933); and G. R. Mellor, *British Imperial Trusteeship, 1783–1850* (London, 1951). The publication of Williams' *Capitalism and Slavery* launched the first significant challenge to the traditional view, although Williams's analysis of the activities and impact of the Clapham Sect is not as well considered as it might be. Roger Anstey's *The Atlantic Slave Trade and Abolition* (London: Macmillan, 1975) follows the economic argument, but with more noticeable moderation.

78. Howse, *Saints in Politics*, 179.

79. For a discussion of this ignorance and the consequences for literature, see Sypher, *Guinea's Captive Kings*, 29.

80. Sypher, *Guinea's Captive Kings*, 110.

81. *The Works of Samuel Johnson* (London, 1810), 10: 315, 356–59.

82. Johnson, *The World Display'd* (London, 1759), in *Works* 2: 276.

83. Johnson, *The World Display'd*, 274.

84. Boswell, *Life of Johnson* 2:154.

85. Boswell, *Life of Johnson* 2:156.

86. Sypher recognizes this inconsistency in eighteenth-century publicists: the posture they adopted in their literary opinions was often quite radically different from that of their practical and political life.

87. Curtin, *Image of Africa*, 49.

88. Perhaps the most balanced appraisal of Cowper's life and work in a humanitarian light is Lodwick Hartley's *William Cowper, Humanitarian* (Chapel Hill: The University of North Carolina Press, 1938).

89. James Montgomery and James Grahame, *Poems of the Abolition of the Slave Trade* (London, 1809), ii.

90. *The Bee* (Feburary 1793): 215–16.

91. *Gentleman's Magazine* 79(1809): 1149.

92. *Edinburgh Review* 6(1805): 326–50. The following is a selection of further periodical contributions to antislavery: Robert Burns, "The Slave's Lament" (1792); Samuel Rogers, "The Pleasures of Memory" (1792); Robert Southey, "To the Genius of Africa" (1795), "The Sailor in the Slave Trade" (1798); William Bowles, "The Dying Slave" (1798); Thomas Campbell, "The Pleasures of Hope" (1799); Leigh Hunt, "The Negro Boy" (1802); Amelia Opie, "The Negro Boy's Tale" (1802), "The Lucayan's Song" (1808). After Sypher's book, the single most scholarly attempt to relate abolition literature to the wider history of ideas is undoubtedly Richard Kain's article, "The Problem of Civilization in English Abolition Literature 1772–1808," *Philosophical Quarterly* 15(1936): 103–25. I am in Professor Kain's debt for some of the major insights and bibliographical resources that went into planning this chapter.

CHAPTER 3. IGNATIUS SANCHO

1. The biographical details on Sancho in this chapter follow Joseph Jekyll's preface to the first edition of Sancho's *Letters* (London, 1782).

2. John, the second duke (1688–1749), maintained a country residence at Blackheath, near Greenwich. He seems to have been a man of humorous turn, a bit of an eccentric, but highly individualistic and charitable. For a lively sketch, see Bernard Falk, *The Way of the Montagues* (London: Hutchinson & Co., 1948).

3. *Gentleman's Magazine* 52(September 1782): 437.

4. Paul Edwards includes a selection of Sancho's musical work in the Dawsons edition (1968). Sancho is also credited with the authorship of several unperformed theatrical pieces, which apparently have not survived.

5. Review of the *Letters of Ignatius Sancho* in the *European Magazine and London Review* 2(September 1782): 199.

6. I have retained Sancho's idiosyncratic spelling and punctuation, to preserve the distinctive character of his Shandean style. Sancho almost always uses the dash in place of the comma, and sometimes in place of the period.

7. A. R. Humphreys, *The Augustan Age: Society, Thought and Letters in the Eighteenth Century* (New York: Harper & Row, 1954), 3.

8. Peter Gay, *The Science of Freedom*, vol. 2 of *The Enlightenment: An Interpretation* (New York: Knopf, 1969), 31.

9. This paradox is discussed by Lloyd Brown in his review of the *Letters of Ignatius Sancho*, in *Eighteenth-Century Studies*, 3(Spring 1970): 415–19. Brown

describes Sancho as a "cultural archetype."

10. Edwards and Walvin, "Africans in Britain," 200; see also O. R. Dathorne, "African Writers of the Eighteenth Century," *The London Magazine* 5, no. 6(September 1965): 51–58.

11. Many antislavery advocates had no doubt that slave trading was immoral or that slavery was inhumane. They were, however, rather cautious about the immediate, wholesale liberation of West Indian slaves. The arguments still held strong that slaves were private property to be disposed of as their owners desired, and that emancipation would cause severe economic dislocation in Britain. Major abolitionists like Buxton proposed, instead, a formula for gradual emancipation whereby slaves could be trained to use their new-found freedom constructively.

12. See also Letter 130, wherein Sancho applies to Mr. W——E to push the printing of a friend's book.

13. See also Letter 66.

14. Letter 39 and Letter 120.

15. Some of the authors and books he mentions are Bossuet, Bishop of Meaux, *Universal History*; Edward Young, *Night Thoughts*; James Thomson, *The Seasons*; and Voltaire, *Semiramis*.

16. He seems to have made regular contributions to at least three newspapers: the *General Advertiser*, the *St. James Evening Papers*, and the *Morning Post*.

17. Both letters to the *General Advertiser* are signed "Africanus" and are included in Mrs. Crewe's collection unnumbered. Sancho is supposed to have written others under the same pseudonym to the same paper, but I have not been able to locate them.

18. Brown, review of *Letters*, 418–19; see also Roger Abrahams, *Positively Black* (Englewood Cliffs, N. J.: Prentice-Hall, 1970), 38–39. Although made in specific relation to oral performance among New World Blacks, Abrahams' observations that Black expressive culture has a complex function in shaping the man of words may be applicable to Sancho's "performance" here.

19. The cult of feeling, which saw its full flowering in the middle years of the eighteenth century, is never wholly appreciated in the contemptible terms of fanaticism. Its values were endorsed by the Methodist Revival and institutionalized by the new interest in primitivism. For further discussion of this relationship, see Frederick C. Gill, *The Romantic Movement and Methodism* (London: The Epworth Press, 1937), 94; Lois Whitney, *Primitivism and the Idea of Progress in English Popular Literature of the Eighteenth Century* (Baltimore: The Johns Hopkins Press, 1934), 84.

20. Smith, *Theory*, 345.

21. Dr. William Dodd (1729–77), tutor to the fifth Lord Chesterfield, was indicted for forging a bond in his pupil's name. Many prominent persons petitioned for his pardon, but he was eventually executed for his crime.

22. Robert Nicklaus, "The Age of Enlightenment," in *The Age of Enlightenment: Studies Presented to Theodore Besterman*, ed. W. H. Barber, et al. (Edinburgh: Scottish Academic Press, 1967; London: Oliver and Boyd, 1967), 412; see also Ralph Ellison, "Twentieth Century Fiction and the Black Mask of Humanity," in *Shadow and Act* (New York: Random House, 1964), 24. Ellison writes that the Age of Rationalism conferred a new respectability on Blacks by making them symbols of value.

23. See Letter 134, p. 273.

CHAPTER 4. OTTOBAH CUGOANO

1. Of the three writers, Cugoano is the one about whose life we know least. Biographical details usually follow the Abbé Gregoire's account, which, though not entirely reliable itself, is yet the most complete primary source. See also Cugoano, *Thoughts and Sentiments*, intod. Edwards, iv, v–xiii, and 6.

2. Cugoano, *Thoughts and Sentiments* 5 n.2.

3. Cugoano, *Thoughts and Sentiments*, xii. While the 1787 edition of Cugoano's book is the most accessible, there exists a shorter version, published as an abstract in 1791, that, according to Paul Edwards, appears to be the original from which the 1787 text was expanded.

4. See Letter to the Prince of Wales, 1787; in *Thoughts*, Appendix, xx.

5. *Thoughts*, Appendix, xix–xxiii.

6. Shyllon, *Black People in Britain*, 177.

7. Shyllon, *Black People in Britain*, 173.

8. *Thoughts*, Appendix, xxi–xxii.

9. Shyllon, *Black People in Britain*, 178 n. 16.

10. The question of authorship is discussed in greater detail in Edwards' introduction to *Thoughts and Sentiments*, vii–xi. The two principal theories outlined in this section of my chapter are summarized from that source.

11. See Williams, *Capitalism and Slavery*, 134–36.

12. Biblical scholars suggest that the mark might have been a tattoo, widely worn by nomadic peoples of the Near East. See *New American Bible* (New York: P. J. Kennedy, 1970), 8 n. 15.

13. This passage is almost identical with Wesley's description in "Thoughts on Slavery," in *Works* 16: 452. Since that work was published in 1774, Cugoano or his collaborator could have read it and borrowed the passage for its striking quality.

14. See also Cugoano, *Thoughts and Sentiments*, 58–62, 117.

15. Several writers of the period commented on the disproportion in British law between crime and punishment; see Blackstone, *Commentaries* 4: 13; Cowper, *The Task*, book 1, 11. 732–38; Goldsmith, *Vicar of Wakefield*, chapter 27; Johnson, *Rambler* 114 (1751). See also Fletcher, *Montesquieu and English Politics* (London: Edward Arnold, 1939), 188–89.

16. See Cugoano, *Thoughts and Sentiments*, 72–76.

17. Quoted with adaptation from Micah 7: 7–11.

18. William Cobbett, *Parliamentary History of Great Britain* (London, 1806–20), 30: 659, col. 1.

19. Robert Isaac and Samuel Wilberforce, *Life of Wilberforce* (London: John Murray, 1838), 3: 182.

20. For a full discussion of these and other historical records of conquest and colonization, Cugoano, see *Thoughts and Sentiments*, 78–82.

21. Shyllon, *Black People in Britain*, 126–27.

22. Shyllon sharply criticizes the scheme and its organizers; see *Black People in Britain*, 133–38.

23. For a well documented appraisal of the reasons for repatriation, see Shyllon, *Black People in Britain*, 138–47.

24. See Smith, *Wealth of Nations* 1: 85, 85n; 1: 390–91. Smith calculated that, compared to free labor, slave labor was more costly and less productive.

CHAPTER 5. OLAUDAH EQUIANO

1. Both his marriage announcement and his obituary notice appeared in the *Gentleman's Magazine*, the former in 62(April 1792): 384; the latter in 67(April 1797): 356.

2. Equiano's master, Lieutenant Pascal, was transferred on promotion to several ships in these early months. Sometime early in 1758, he left HMS *Preston* to take up a new commission aboard HMS *Royal George*. Baker stayed behind on the *Preston* and died in 1759.

3. See Equiano, *Life* 1:31. Equiano explains that the name "Olaudah" meant "one favoured, one having a loud voice and well spoken." In ironic consistency with his future fate, it also meant "vicissitude or fortune."

4. Equiano mentions having read the following books (parenthetical references are to volume and page numbers of the *Narrative*): *The Conversion of an Indian*, lent to him by a Methodist gentleman (2:134); Allen's *Alarm to the Unconverted*, given to him by a Mr. G. S., the governor of Tothillfields, Bridewell (2:143–44); Fox's *Martyrology* (2:174) and Benezet's *Caution and Warning* (2:227). See Paul Edwards' introduction to Equiano, *Life*, lii–liii, for further discussion.

5. Paul Edwards evaluates these features more extensively in his introduction to Equiano, *Life*, xiii–xviii.

6. These two sources of evidence will be more fully discussed later in this chapter. Shyllon has researched and collected the largest number of Equiano's letters so far. See his *Black People in Britain*, appendix 3, "Letters of a Black Abolitionist," 246–63; and Edwards includes the testimonial letters from abolitionist sympathizers in his edition of the *Life*, appendix B, vii–xv.

7. Scobie *Black Britannia*, 79.

8. These remarks are the gist of a more extended scholarly discussion on the rise of autobiography, in Wayne Shumaker, *English Autobiography: Its Emergence, Materials, and Form* (Berkeley: University of California Press, 1954), 75.

9. Mary Williams Burger, "Black Autobiography: A Literature of Celebration" (Ph. D. diss., Washington University, St. Louis, 1973), 32.

10. G. A. Starr, *Defoe and Spiritual Autobiography* (Princeton: Princeton University Press, 1965), 19.

11. Gregoire, *Moral and Intellectual Faculties of Negroes*, 225.

12. Edwards and Ian Duffield, "Equiano's Turks and Christians: An Eighteenth-Century African View of Islam," *Journal of African Studies* 2(1975–76): 433–44.

13. Starr, *Defoe and Spiritual Autobiography*, 29.

14. Devout Christians had long taken their models for pious life and spiritual autobiography from Saint Augustine's *Confessions* and John Bunyan's *Pilgrim's Progress*. In the seventeenth and eighteenth centuries they found new sources in the spiritual memoirs of Puritans, Quakers, and Methodists, the latter providing the most influential prototype for converts to Evangelicalism, in the *Lives of the Early Methodist Preachers*. For a further discussion of Equiano's relationship to this tradition, see Angelo Vincent Costanzo, "The Art and Tradition of Black Autobiography in the Eighteenth Century," Diss. SUNY (Binghamton) 1976, p. 116.

15. Wesley, *Journal*, Vol. viii, p. 128; also quoted in Shyllon, *Black People*, pp. 236–37.

16. See Edwards' Introduction, Appendix A, "To the Reader," pp. iii–v.

17. Shyllon, "Olaudah Equiano: Nigerian Abolitionist and First National Leader of Africans in Britain," *Journal of African Studies*, 4 (1977), 443.

18. See Chapter 1, pp. 12–13.

19. Shyllon makes an important gloss about inaccurate reporting in the press; see *Black People*, pp. 226–27.

20. Shyllon, *Black People*, p. 228.

21. Howse, *The Saints in Politics*, p. 81; see also Shyllon, "Olaudah Equiano: Nigerian Abolitionist," p. 444.

22. See Note 6, p. 228.

23. *Public Advertiser*, 4 April 1787, n. p.

24. Quoted in Paul Edwards, Introduction, p. xxvii.

25. *Public Advertiser*, 2 July 1787. The "their" refers to Equiano, Green and Rose (presumably two other Black leaders), who had been dismissed.

26. See Shyllon, *Black People*, p. 155.

27. Edwards discusses Sharp's disenchantment with Equiano in Introduction, p. xl.

28. See *Public Advertiser*, 14 July 1787. See also Edwards, introduction to Equiano, *Life*, xl.

29. *The Advertiser*, for reasons best known to its editors, chose to carry only a partial report rather than a verbatim reproduction of Equiano's letter, in its issue of 14 July 1787.

30. Quoted in Edwards, introduction to Equiano, *Life*, xliv.

31. See Equiano's memorial and petition, *Life* 2:239–43.

32. For a full discussion, see Williams's *Capitalism and Slavery*, 154–57.

33. Shyllon reproduces the full text in *Black People in Britain*, Letter 9, 254.

34. Williams, *Capitalism and Slavery*, 159.

35. For a fuller appreciation of the pervasiveness of this vision in eighteenth-century humanitarian thought, see Kain, "English Abolition Literature," 122.

36. These letters all postdate the first publication of the *Life*, but they appeared in later editions. Edwards collects them in his introduction, Equiano, *Life*, appendix B, viii–xv.

37. See Digges's letter, Equiano, *Life*, appendix B, xiii.

38. Equiano, *Life*, appendix B, xiii.

39. Equiano, *Life*, appendix B, xv.

40. *General Magazine and Impartial Review*, July 1789, 315.

41. *Gentleman's Magazine* 59(June 1789): 539. For other critical reviews, see the *Monthly Review* 80(June 1789): 551–52 and the editor's introduction to the Leeds (1814) edition of the *Life*, reprinted in Shyllon, *Black People in Britain*, 237–38.

CONCLUSION

1. See Edwards' introduction to Equiano's *Life*, v.

2. The success of the Haitian Revolution inspired much optimism in antislavery and general progressive circles for the future of African peoples. For a representative expression of this faith in the future of Blacks, see John Browne Russwurm, "The Condition and Prospects of Haiti," in Richard Barksdale and Keneth Kinnamon, *Black Writers of America* (New York: The Macmillan Company, 1972), 190–91.

3. Henry Brougham, *An Inquiry into the Colonial Policy of the European Powers* (Edinburgh, 1803), vol. 2, bk. 4, sec. 2, p. 445.

Bibliography

Abraham, William E. *The Mind of Africa*. Chicago: University of Chicago Press, 1962.

Abrahams, Roger. *Positively Black*. Englewood Cliffs, N. J.: Prentice-Hall, 1970.

"The African's Complaint on-Board A Slave Ship." *The Gentleman's Magazine* 63(1793): 749.

Amo, Anthony William. *The ΑΠΑΘΕΙΑ of the Human Mind or the Absence of Sensation and the Faculty of Sense in the Human Mind*. Halle and Wittenberg: Martin Luther University, 1968.

Aristotle. *The Politics*. Translated by H. Rackham. London: William Heinemann, 1932.

Barrington, Sir Jonah. *Personal Sketches and Recollections of His Own Times*. Glasgow and London: Cameron and Fergusson, 1876.

Bartels, F. L. "Jacobus Eliza Capitein, 1717–1747." *Transactions of the Historical Society of Ghana* 4, no. 1(1959): 1–13.

————. "Philip Quaque, 1741–1816." *Transactions of the Historical Society of Ghana* 1, part 5(1955): 153–77.

Beattie, James. *Essay on the Nature and Immutability of Truth*. 2nd ed. Edinburgh, 1771.

————. *Elements of Moral Science*. 2 vols. Edinburgh, 1790.

Bebb, Evelyn Douglas. *Nonconformity and Social and Economic Life, 1600–1800: Some Problems of the Present as they Appeared in the Past*. London: The Epworth Press, 1935.

Benezet, Anthony. *Some Historical Account of Guinea*. 1771. Reprint. London: Frank Cass and Company, 1968.

"Biography and Memoirs." *The Monthly Review* 80(1789): 551.

"Black Social Life in 18th Cent. England." *The London Chronicle* 15(1764): 166c.

Bluett, Thomas. *Some Memoirs of the Life of Job, the Son of Solomon, the High Priest of Boonda in Africa*. London, 1734.

Blumenbach, Johann Friedrich. *On the Natural Varieties of Mankind*. 1775. Reprint. New York: Bergman Publishers, 1969.

Boswell, James. *Life of Johnson*. 3rd ed., rev. 1799. Reprint. New York: Oxford University Press, 1933.

Brougham, Lord Henry. *An Inquiry into the Colonial Policy of the European Powers*. 2 vols. Edinburgh, 1803.

Brown, Lloyd W. Review of *Letters of Ignatius Sancho, An African to which are Prefixed Memoirs of His Life by Joseph Jekyll*, introduced by Paul Edwards. *Eighteenth Century Studies* 3, no. 3(1970): 414–19.

Burger, Mary M. Williams. "Black Autobiography; A Literature of Celebration." Ph. D. diss., Washington University, Saint Louis, 1973.

Cairns, Earle E. *Saints and Society.* Chicago: The Moody Press, 1960.

Clarkson, Thomas. *An Essay on the Slavery and Commerce of the Human Species Particularly the African.* Philadelphia, 1786.

———. *The History of the Rise, Progress and Accomplishment of the Abolition of the African Slave Trade by the British Parliament.* 2 vols. London, 1808.

Cobbett, William. *Parliamentary History of Great Britain from the Earliest Period to the Year 1803.* 36 vols. London, 1806–20.

Cook, Mercer. "Jean Jacques Rousseau and the Negro." *Journal of Negro History* 21(1936): 294–303.

Costanzo, Angelo Vincent. "The Art and Tradition of Black Autobiography in the Eighteenth Century." Ph. D. diss., State University of New York, Binghamton, 1976.

Craton, Michael, James Walvin, and David Wright. *Slavery, Abolition and Emancipation.* New York: Longmans, 1976.

Crocker, Lester G., ed. *The Age of Enlightenment.* New York: Walker and Company, 1969.

Crooks, J. J. "Negroes in England in the Eighteenth Century." *Notes and Queries* 154(1928): 173–74.

Cugoano, Ottobah. *Thoughts and Sentiments on the Evil of Slavery.* Introduced by Paul Edwards. 1787. Reprint. London: Dawsons of Pall Mall, 1969.

Curtin, Philip, ed. *Africa Remembered: Narratives of West Africans from the Era of the Slave Trade.* Madison: University of Wisconsin Press, 1967.

———. *The Image of Africa: British Ideas in Action 1780–1850.* Madison: University of Wisconsin Press, 1964.

Dasent, John Roche, ed. *Acts of the Privy Council of England*, N. S. 26, 1596–97. London, 1902.

Davis, David Brion. *The Problem of Slavery in the Age of Revolution.* Ithaca: Cornell University Press, 1975.

———. *The Problem of Slavery in Western Culture.* Ithaca: Cornell University Press, 1966.

Dover, Cedric. *Hell in the Sunshine.* London: Secker and Warburg, 1942.

"The Dying African." *The Gentleman's Magazine* 61(1791): 1046–47.

Editorial Critical of Equiano's conduct in the Sierra Leone Expedition. *Public Advertiser*, 14 July 1787.

Edwards, Paul, and James Walvin. "Africans in Britain, 1500–1800." In *The African Diaspora: Interpretive Essays*, edited by Martin L. Kilson and Robert I. Rotberg, 172–204. Cambridge: Harvard University Press, 1976.

Edwards, Paul, and Ian Duffield. "Equiano's Turks and Christians: An Eighteenth Century African View of Islam." *Journal of African Studies* 2(1975–76): 433–44.

Ellison, Ralph. "Twentieth Century Fiction and the Black Mask of Humanity." In *Shadow and Act.* New York: Random House, 1964.

Equiano, Olaudah. Letter to Ottobah Cugoano concerning his frustrations in the Sierra Leone Expedition. *Public Advertiser*, 4 April 1787.

————.*The Life of Olaudah Equiano, or Gustavus Vassa, the African*. Introduced by Paul Edwards. 2 vols. 1789. Reprint. London: Dawsons of Pall Mall, 1969.

Falk, Bernard. *The Way of the Montagues*. London: Hutchinson and Company, 1947.

Fladeland, Betty. *Anglo-American Anti-Slavery Cooperation*. Urbana: University of Illinois Press, 1972.

Fletcher, Frank Thomas H. "Montesquieu's Influence on Anti-Slavery Opinion in England." *Journal of Negro History* 18(1933): 414–25.

Fox, George. "Letter to Friends Beyond the Sea, that have Blacks and Indian Slaves." In *The Works of George Fox*. 8 vols. New York: A M S Press, Inc., 1975.

Fraser (The Parson). Letter from Sierra Leone Expedition at Teneriffe. *Public Advertiser*, 2 July 1787.

Gay, Peter. *The Science of Freedom*. Vol. 2 of *The Enlightenment: An Interpretation*. New York: Knopf, 1969.

George, Dorothy M. *London Life in the Eighteenth Century*. 1925. Reprint. London: Kegan Paul, 1951.

Gill, Frederick C. *The Romantic Movement and Methodism: A Study of English Romanticism and the Evangelical Revival*. London: The Epworth Press, 1937.

Grant, Douglas. *The Fortunate Slave*. London: Oxford University Press, 1968.

Gregoire, Henri. *An Enquiry Concerning the Moral and Intellectual Faculties of Negroes*. Paris, 1808. Reprint. New York: McGraw Hill Publishing Company, 1967.

Gronniosaw, James Albert Ukawsaw. *Narrative of the Most Remarkable Particulars in the Life of James Albert Ukawsaw. Narrative of the Most Remarkable Particulars in the Life of James Albert Ukawsaw Gronniosaw, an African Prince, as Related by Himself*. Bath, 1770.

Hecht, J. Jean. "Continental and Colonial Servants in Eighteenth-Century England." *Smith College Studies in History* 40(1954): 1–61.

————. *The Domestic Servant Class in Eighteenth Century England*. London: Routledge and Kegan Paul, 1956.

Hill, George Birkbeck. *Johnsonian Miscellany*. 2 vols. Oxford, 1897.

Hobbes, Thomas. "De Corpore Politico." In Hobbes' *Tripos in Three Discourses*, vol. 4 of *The English Works*, edited by Sir William Molesworth, 77–228. London: John Bohn, 1840.

————. *Leviathan or the Matter, Forme and Powere of a Commonwealth Ecclesiastical and Civill*. London, 1651. Reprint. New York: Scolar Press, 1969.

Howse, E. M. *The Saints in Politics: The Clapham Sect and the Growth of Freedom*. 1953. Reprint. London: Allen and Unwin, 1953.

Hume, David. *Essays Moral, Political and Literary*. Edited by T. H. Green and T. H. Grose. 2 vols. 1742. Reprint. London: Longmans and Green, 1875.

Humphreys, A. R. *The Augustan Age: Society, Thought and Letters in the Eighteenth Century*. New York: Harper and Row, 1954.

Hutcheson, Francis *A System of Moral Philosophy*. London, 1755.

"Importation of Negro Servants into England." *The Gentleman's Magazine* 34(1764): 493.

Irvine, Dallas D. "The Abbé Raynal and British Humanitarianism." *Journal of Modern History* 3(1931): 564–77.

Jahn, Janheinz. *Neo-African Literature: A History of Black Writing*. Translated by Oliver Coburn and Ursula Lehrburger. New York: Grove Press, 1969.

Jefferson, Thomas. *Notes on the State of Virginia*. Edited by William Peden. London, 1787. Reprint. Chapel Hill: University of North Carolina Press, 1955.

Johnson, Samuel. *The Works of Samuel Johnson*. 12 vols. London, 1810.

Jordan, Winthrop. *White over Black: American Attitudes toward the Negro 1550–1812*. Chapel Hill: University of North Carolina Press, 1968.

Kain, Richard Morgan. "The Problem of Civilization in English Abolition Literature 1772–1808." *Philological Quarterly* 15(1936): 103–25.

Kilson, Martin L., and Robert I. Rotberg. *The African Diaspora: Interpretive Essays*. Cambridge: Harvard University Press, 1976.

Little, Kenneth. *Negroes in Britain*. 1948. Reprint. London: Routledge and Kegan Paul, 1972.

Locke, John. *Two Treatises on Government*. Edited by Thomas I. Cooke. 1698. Reprint. New York: Hafner Publishing Company, 1947.

Loggins, Vernon. *The Negro Author: His Development in America*. New York: Columbia University Press, 1931.

Long, Edward. *History of Jamaica*. 3 vols. London, 1774.

MacDermot, T. H. "From a Jamaican Portfolio." *Journal of Negro History* 2(1917): 147–59.

Magie, David, trans. *The Scriptores Historiae Augustae*. 3 vols. London: William Heinemann, 1922–32. Reprint. Cambridge: Harvard University Press, 1960.

Montesquieu, Charles Louis. *Persian and Chinese Letters*. Translated by John Davidson. 1721. Reprint. London: Walter Dunne, 1901.

––––––. *The Spirit of the Laws*. Translated by Thomas Nugent. Revised by J. V. Prichard. 2 vols. 1748. Reprint. London: George Bell and Sons, 1906.

Montgomery, James, and James Grahame. *Poems on the Abolition of the Slave Trade*. London, 1809.

"Mungo's Address." *The Bee or Literary Weekly Intelligencer* 13(1793): 215–16.

The New American Bible. New York: P. J. Kennedy, 1970.

Newton, Rev. John. *The Journal of a Slave Trader 1750–54*. Edited by Bernard Martin and Mark Spurrell. 1788. Reprint. London: The Epworth Press, 1962.

––––––. "Thoughts upon the African Slave Trade." London, 1788.

Nicklaus, Robert. "The Age of Enlightenment." In *The Age of Enlightenment: Studies Presented to Theodore Besterman*, edited by W. H. Barber, et al., 395–412. Edinburgh: Scottish Academic Press, 1967; London: Oliver and Boyd, 1967.

Notice of Equiano's marriage. *Gentleman's Magazine* 62(1792): 392.

Notice of Equiano's death. *Gentleman's Magazine*, 67(1797): 356.

"On seeing a Negro Funeral." *Gentleman's Magazine*, n. s. 2(1809): 1149.

Paley, William. *Principles of Moral and Political Philosophy*. 2 vols. London, 1785.

Pepys, Samuel. *The Diary of Samuel Pepys*. Edited by Robert C. Latham and William Matthews. 11 vols. London, 1887. Reprint. Berkeley: University of California Press, 1970.

Ramsay, Rev. James. *Essay on the Treatment and Conversion of the African Slaves in the British Sugar Colonies*. London, 1784.

Raynal, Guillaume Thomas. *Histoire de deux Indes: A Philosophical and Political History of the Settlements and Trade of the Europeans in the East and West Indies*. Translated by J. O. Justamond. 2nd ed., rev. 5 vols. London, 1776.

Reaction to Mansfield decision of Blacks present in courtroom. *The London Chronicle* 31(1772): 598c.

Reade, Aleyn Lyell. *Johnsonian Gleanings*. 11 vols. London: Arden Press, 1912.

Review of *Letters of the late Ignatius Sancho, an African. The European Magazine and London Review* 2(1782): 199–202.

Review of *Letters of the late Ignatius Sancho, an African. The Gentleman's Magazine* 52(1782): 437.

Review of *The Life of Olaudah Equiano, or Gustavus Vassa, the African. General Magazine and Impartial Review*, July 1789, 315.

Review of *The Life of Olaudah Equiano, or Gustavus Vassa, the African. The Gentleman's Magazine* 59(1789): 539.

Rice, C. Duncan. *The Rise and Fall of Black Slavery*. Baton Rouge: Louisiana State University Press; 1976.

Richmond, Merle A. *Bid the Vassal Soar: Interpretive Essays on the Life and Poetry of Phillis Wheatley and George Moses Horton*. Washington, D.C.: Howard University Press, 1974.

Robinson, William H. *Phillis Wheatley in the Black American Beginnings*. Detroit: Broadside Press, 1975.

Rogers, J[oel] A[ugustus]. *Sex and Race: The Saga of Miscegenation from the Dawn of History to the Present*. New York: H. M. Rogers, 1944.

Rousseau, Jean Jacques. *The Social Contract*. 1762. Reprint. New York: Hafner Publishing Company, 1947.

Rush, Benjamin. *An Address on the Slavery of the Negroes in America*. 1773. Reprint. New York: Arno Press and *The New York Times*, 1969.

Russwurm, John Browne. "The Condition and Prospects of Haiti." In *Black Writers of America*, edited by Richard Barksdale and Keneth Kinnamon, 190–91. New York: The Macmillan Company, 1972.

Sancho, Ignatius. *Letters of the Late Ignatius Sancho*. Introduced by Paul Edwards. 5th ed. 1803. Reprint. London: Dawsons of Pall Mall, 1968.

Scobie, Edward. *Black Britannia: A History of Blacks in Britain*. Chicago: Johnson Publishing Company, 1972.

Shaftesbury, Anthony Ashley Cooper. *Characteristics of Men, Manners, Opinions Times*. London, 1711.

Shrewsbury, William J. *British Methodism and Slavery*. Heywood, England, 1862.

Shumaker, Wayne. *English Autobiography: Its Emergence, Materials, and Form*. University of California Publications in English Studies, no. 8. Berkeley: University of California Press, 1954.

Shyllon, Folarin O. *Black People in Britain 1553–1833*. London: Oxford University Press, 1977.

———. *Black Slaves in Britain*. London: Oxford University Press, 1974.

———. "Olaudah Equiano: Nigerian Abolitionist and First National Leader of Africans in Britain." *Journal of African Studies* 4(1977): 433–51.

Smith, Adam. *Theory of Moral Sentiments*. Edited by Dugald Stewart. 1759. Reprint. London: Henry G. Bohn, 1853.

Smith, Adam. *The Wealth of Nations*. Edited by James E. Therold Rogers. 3 vols. 2nd ed. Oxford: Clarendon Press, 1880.

Smith, Samuel Stanhope. *An Essay on the Causes of the Variety of Complexion and Figure in the Human Species*. Edited by Winthrop Jordan. Philadelphia, 1787. Reprint. Cambridge: The Belknap Press–Harvard University Press, 1965.

"Spotted Negro Boy." *Notes and Queries*, n. s. 6(1900): 55–56.

Spratlin, Valuarez B. *Juan Latino, Slave and Humanist*. New York: Spinner Press Inc., 1938.

Starr, G. A. *Defoe and Spiritual Autobiography*. Princeton: Princeton University Press, 1965

Sypher, Wylie. *Guinea's Captive Kings: British Anti-Slavery Literature of the XVIIth Century*. Chapel Hill: University of North Carolina Press, 1942.

———. "Hutcheson and the Classical Theory of Slavery." *Journal of Negro History* 25(1939): 263–80.

Tacitus. *The Works of Tacitus*. The Oxford Translation. 2 vols. Rev. ed. London, 1884.

Tobin, James. *Cursory Remarks*. London, 1785.

Tyerman, Luke. *Life and Times of John Wesley*. 3 vols. New York: Harper and Brothers, 1872.

Wadstrom, Carl Bernhard. *An Essay on Colonization, Particularly Applied to the Western Coast of Africa, with Some Free Thoughts on Cultivation and Commerce*. 1794. Reprint. New York: A. M. Kelley, 1968.

Walvin, James. *Black and White: The Negro and English Society 1555–1945*. London: Allen Lane, Penguin Press, 1973.

Warwick, Roger. "Skeletal Remains." In *The Romano-British Cemetery at Trentholme Drive, York*, edited by Leslie P. Wenham, 111–76. London: Her Majesty's Stationery Office, 1968.

Wesley, John. *The Journal of the Rev. John Wesley*, ed. Nehemiah Curnock. 8 vols. London: Charles H. Kelley, 1909–16.

———. "Letter to Wilberforce on Slavery," 26 Feb 1791. In *The Works of the Rev. John Wesley*, 7 vols, edited by John Emory, 237. New York, 1831.

Wheatley, Phillis. *The Poems of Phillis Wheatley*. Edited by Julian D. Mason, Jr.

Chapel Hill: University of North Carolina Press, 1966.

Whitney, Lois. *Primitivism and the Idea of Progress in English Popular Literature of the Eighteenth Century.* Baltimore: The Johns Hopkins Press, 1934.

Wilberforce, Robert Isaac, and Samuel Wilberforce. *The Life of William Wilberforce.* 5 vols. London: John Murray, 1838. Facsimile. Ann Arbor, Mich.: University Microfilms, 1969.

Williams, Eric. *Capitalism and Slavery.* Chapel Hill: University of North Carolina Press, 1945.

Wilson, Ellen Gibson. *The Loyal Blacks.* New York: G. P. Putnam's Sons, 1976.

Index